A STEP AWAY FROM DEATH

Sergeant Sanders, counting as each Viet Cong soldier walked past him, had reached 80 when a loud crack sounded right beside him—one of the patrol members in shifting his weight had snapped a twig. But the Viet Cong unit kept moving—except for one man. He, after warily examining the vegetation alongside the road, began walking directly towards the patrol. Ten steps later and he and Sanders were looking into each other's eyes...

Also in the series
from Jove

A DISTANT CHALLENGE
The US Infantryman in Vietnam: 1967-72

Edited by Infantry Magazine
With reflections by LTC Albert N. Garland, USA (Ret.)

INFANTRY IN VIETNAM

EDITED BY

LTC ALBERT N. GARLAND, USA (RET.)

JOVE BOOKS, NEW YORK

...TO THE UNITED STATES INFANTRYMAN

The publishers acknowledge with gratitude the kind assistance of the Military Book Club in providing a corrected text and illustrations for this Jove edition of *Infantry in Vietnam*.

INFANTRY IN VIETNAM

A Jove Book / published by arrangement with
The Battery Press, Inc.

PRINTING HISTORY
Infantry edition published 1967
The Battery Press edition published 1982
The Military Book Club edition published 1982
Jove edition / February 1985

ISBN: 0-515-08054-3

Jove Books are published by The Berkley Publishing Group,
200 Madison Avenue, New York, New York 10016.
The name "JOVE" and the "J" logo
are trademarks belonging to Jove Publications, Inc.

PRINTED IN THE UNITED STATES OF AMERICA

10   9   8   7   6

FOREWORD

From the pages of this book, infantry leaders of tomorrow will be able to share the combat experiences of soldiers in Vietnam. For infantrymen to take heed of the lessons to be learned from the successes and failures is to insure that our experiences are not wasted.

On the battlefield of Vietnam, I saw the fighting for more than four years. I can say without reservation that our infantrymen were as well trained as any our nation has ever sent into battle. There they fought under extreme conditions: in chest-deep water and mud; through mangrove swamps, bamboo thickets, and dense jungle; and over mountainous terrain.

The American infantryman adapted well to that different kind of fighting. There were no fixed battle lines. It was a war of ambushes, booby-traps, and terrorists. It was one of searching and waiting. This war tested the courage, endurance and competence of our infantryman, as well as the depth and value of his training.

This manual was based on a continuing review and evaluation of the enemy's habits and practices, and incorporated tactics designed to defeat him. In any future combat, we must close with the enemy and defeat him. To win we must study the strengths and weaknesses of the enemy and train our young infantry leaders to do a professional job.

W. C. WESTMORELAND
General, United States Army (Retired)

September 1982

CONTENTS

MAPS

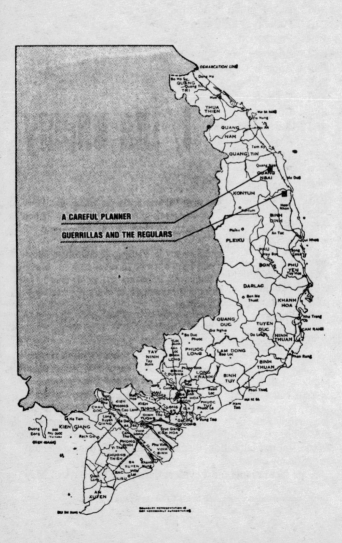

A CAREFUL PLANNER

GUERRILLAS AND THE REGULARS

I

The Enemy

MANY YEARS AGO Sun Tzu said: "If you know the enemy and know yourself, you need not fear the result of a hundred battles. If you know yourself, but not the enemy, for every victory gained, you will also suffer a defeat."

While not a phantom, the enemy in Vietnam is difficult to know. He fights when he wants and waits when he chooses—he is in his own country and his own environment; he makes the rules; quickly he spots weaknesses in security and capitalizes on every opportunity to incorporate surprise in his actions.

a careful planner

Captain Donald R. Robison, advisor to a South Vietnamese infantry battalion, had been told repeatedly that the enemy against whom his unit would be operating were poorly trained, poorly equipped, and unsophisticated.[1] In reality, Robison found the enemy soldiers to be dedicated, highly motivated individuals who, on occasion, and considering their general lack of formal military education, displayed an amazing degree of careful planning.

This fact became most evident during the last days of May

[1]Combat experience submitted by CPT Donald R. Robison, USA.

1965 in South Vietnam's Quang Ngai province when a South
Vietnamese infantry battalion was annihilated in less than 20
minutes by two separate but strategically placed enemy ambushes.

At the time the ambushes—despite their considerable success—did not appear to be more than the usual enemy tactic
of ambush and withdraw. But four days later, on 30 May, a
three-battalion South Vietnamese relief force, supported by an
armored personnel carrier troop, was decimated as it tried to
reach the original ambush site, even as the town of Quang
Ngai, the provincial capital, was attacked by terrorists and its
airfield brought under enemy mortar fire. *(Map 1)*

Military commanders in the area felt certain that the two
incidents were related, but just how closely related they did

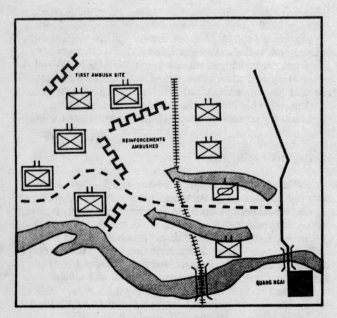

Map 1. A Careful Planner

not know until, on 31 May, a copy of Combat Order No. 1, ML/CD, 1st Regiment, Region V Liberation Army (a copy is at Appendix C) came into their possession. Then they knew that the enemy had most carefully prepared the operations which had seen the destruction of several good South Vietnamese units. The contents of the order not only indicated complete and detailed planning, they demonstrated quite graphically what no one has ever denied—the enemy possesses an excellent intelligence system, for his information on the free world forces and their movements proved to be amazingly accurate. Only those enemy units assigned to prevent reinforcements landing at Go Cao and for shelling that base's artillery positions did not fully accomplish their missions; these were secondary efforts, though, and did not have a material bearing on the overall operation.

the patient enemy

The men of Company C, 1st Battalion, 12th US Cavalry also found the enemy to be tough opponents.[2] In one operation, Company C was given the mission of sweeping the area which lay between two landing zones: LZ Milton, on which the company was initially located, and LZ Hereford, 3,000 meters to the south.

To provide continuous fire support for the company's overland sweep, Company C's commander had his weapons platoon lifted by four helicopters to LZ Hereford, where the platoon promptly took up firing positions. Running generally from north to south, LZ Hereford had all the outward appearances of being one of the safest places in the entire battle area. It was only a small clearing—about 100 meters long by 50 meters wide—and was situated on a long ridge, a seemingly unlikely target for an enemy attack.

Near noon, the main body of the company arrived in the clearing, its sweep from LZ Milton completed. None of the US troops knew that an irregular enemy unit since early morning had been watching their movements on and around the landing zone.

New orders soon arrived: Company C was to sweep from

[2]Combat experience submitted by CPT Donald F. Warren, USA.

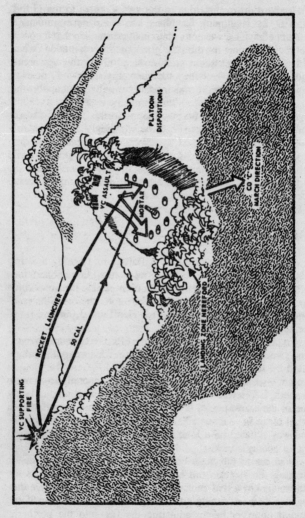

Map 2. The Patient Enemy

LZ Hereford down the ridge to the valley, there to rejoin the battalion. In developing his plans, the company commander decided to leave his weapons platoon in position so that it could furnish fire support for the rifle platoons as they moved down the steep, rocky, elephant grass-covered hill. After the company had completed the sweep, the weapons platoon—22 men—would be extracted from the landing zone by the supporting helicopters and would rejoin the company.

At 1400, after it had used its 81mm mortar to fire a number of requested reconnaissance by fire missions, the platoon received a radio message from the company commander that the supporting helicopters could be expected within 30 minutes. Immediately, those platoon members not actively engaged in the fire missions, began to collect the platoon's impedimenta in preparation for the flight to the valley.

Just before 1430, as the extraction helicopters were inbound, the completely unexpected happened. Two members of the platoon, seeing a number of enemy soldiers suddenly appear about five meters to their immediate front, opened fire with their M16s. As though this was a signal, other enemy located on a hill about 300 meters away and which overlooked the landing zone poured a hail of .50 caliber machineguns, 60mm mortar, and 40mm rocket launcher fire onto the weapons platoon positions. The 81mm mortar was knocked out almost immediately, and the platoon began to take heavy casualties. Forty or fifty of the enemy, under cover of the supporting fires, moved toward LZ Hereford, taking a few casualties but moving steadily forward. *(Map 2)*

The platoon's radio operator called the company commander; his message was brief: "Come back, we're being hit!" Immediately the company commander ordered his 1st Platoon, at the rear of the company column, to turn about and "Get back up the hill!" He then turned the remainder of the company around and scrambling, sliding, falling, the men made desperate efforts to run up the steep hill. But by now the company had been moving for almost two hours and it did not appear that they could arrive back at LZ Hereford in time to save the weapons platoon. Artillery fire was called for, and the artillery forward observer began adjusting the fire into the northern portion of the platoon's position. No thought was given to security, and it was not until much later that the company

•

commander realized his entire unit could have been destroyed in a classic ambush.

Up on LZ Hereford, the enemy swept over the weapons platoon positions and split into two groups, searching for the remaining Americans or looting the dead. Not knowing the platoon had been overrun, Company C's commander could not bring himself to give the order to have his supporting artillery fire into the heart of the platoon position.

Just 35 minutes after the first call for help, the enemy was gone. The weapons platoon had suffered grievously; 16 men killed, 6 wounded. The enemy had also stripped the dead of their personal effects, and had carried off 18 individual weapons, two AN/PRC-25 radios, and one 81mm mortar sight; they had left behind eight of their own dead and three weapons.

Because the enemy had not been seen, and because a rifle company had just conducted a sweep through the area, LZ Hereford had been considered safe and a weapons platoon had been left to provide its own security for a mere 90 minutes. But the enemy, who had been in the area the whole time and who had been observing the actions of Company C, had waited until the bulk of the company had moved a safe distance away, then, using surprise to the utmost, had moved in under heavy supporting fires to practically wipe out an American unit.

his many faces

In reality, the enemy forces in Vietnam consist of three distinct groups: the members of the regular army of North Vietnam (NVA), infiltrated into the Republic of Vietnam to assist the efforts of the National Liberation Front (NLF); main force Viet Cong, the military arm of the NLF; and local force Viet Cong, guerrillas organized in units from squads to battalions who are the military arm of the Viet Cong province and district establishments.[3]

The NVA soldier is well trained and equipped; an expert at camouflage, he uses anthills, tall grass, brush, trees, stumps, and trenches to conceal himself—some even wear green head masks to blend in better with the surrounding vegetation. He is usually armed with an automatic assault rifle, carries a pouch

[3]Combat experience submitted by CPT Myron Diduryk.

filled with Chinese stick (potato masher-type) hand grenades, and has a lot of ammunition. He wears a khaki uniform, and in a rucksack puts a clean uniform, a hammock, a nylon or light plastic poncho, a sack of rice, a ball of cooked rice, a small entrenching tool, sometimes a diary, pictures of his family or girlfriend, and more ammunition.

A number of the NVA soldiers carry first aid kits which contain some US manufactured drugs, while others carry metal boxes with mortar and rocket ammunition, or machineguns, or 40mm rocket launchers, or 81mm or 82mm mortars. He is an expert marksman, and his more apparent targets are radio operators and soldiers with chevrons on their sleeves. In small groups, he likes to probe US defensive perimeters at night, trying to locate weak spots and weapon emplacements. He tries to get as close as possible to US postions to apply his bearhug technique so as to prevent US units from using supporting indirect fires.

His assaults are made from an attack position that is as close to a defensive position as possible, and are usually preceded by rocket launcher and mortar fires. During and immediately following a battle he makes a fanatical effort to recover his dead, wounded, and discarded equipment, and grappling hooks and ropes tied around ankles are acceptable recovery means.

The local force Viet Cong is as different from the NVA soldier as red is from blue. These are the farmers by day and the guerrillas at night. They are spread far and wide and usually operate at squad and platoon level, although at times they will mass into company and battalion sized units for specific operations.

Generally speaking, the local Viet Cong is poorly trained and equipped when compared to the NVA soldier. He is sometimes referred to as "the bum." His training varies with districts, provinces, and units; he is a poor shot, although an occasional excellent sniper will be encountered.

The ability of a local force Viet Cong unit to accomplish its mission depends on the ability of its leader, whose leadership varies from poor to excellent. These units strike only when they are assured of a victory; they execute raids on US installations and ambush vehicular and foot columns; they are ingenious in the use of booby traps; and they can harass opposing forces at any time of the day or night under a multitude of circumstances. With the mission accomplished, the unit disappears; they do not want to stand and fight, only to harass.

Dressed in black pajamas, the local force Viet Cong is armed with any type of weapon he can procure. Usually it is of US manufacture—rifles, carbines, automatic rifles, and submachineguns. There is in his armory, too, a sprinkling of French and communist bolt action weapons. He also carries a couple of US fragmentation grenades, a US bayonet and, perhaps, a batch of punji stakes. He is good at concealing himself, and has a fantastic ability to perform his disappearing act and mix with the local populace.

The main force Viet Cong are different. Led by experienced and dedicated communists, who possess an excellent background in guerrilla warfare, the main forces are organized into regiments, battalions, and separate companies. They are well equipped and trained.

Like his NVA ally, the main force Viet Cong is an expert at camouflage and concealment; unlike his NVA ally, he does not stay and fight, although he does present himself as a formidable foe. Under heavy fire, though, he is liable to break, and once his forward elements collapse, his resistance collapses and he hastens from the battlefield. He is armed, predominantly, with automatic weapons of US and communist manufacture; carries either US or Chinese hand grenades; has plenty of ammunition; and uses 60mm and 81mm mortars extensively for fire support. He is also equipped with 40mm rocket launchers and heavy machineguns of 7.62mm and 12.7mm calibers. He is a good marksman and uses grazing fire to good advantage.

Where the NVA units make great efforts to evacuate their dead, wounded, and discarded equipment, so do the main force Viet Cong. In fact, the recovery techniques are similar, although not always successful. During one operation, for example, while a main force unit was attempting to disengage, a US platoon overran a main force battalion command post which, in addition to numerous documents, contained the lightly wounded battalion commander. Thirty-seven years of age, he had been fighting since 1949, first as a Viet Minh against the French and now, as a main force Viet Cong, against the US; he did not display any signs of defeat or anxiety—he insisted, in fact, that the Viet Cong would emerge victorious.

He spoke freely during the interrogation period, indicating that the morale of his troops was good—they had plenty to eat, sufficient ammunition, and were certain of winning. His favorite tactic was to surround the enemy and engage him in close-in fighting, and he liked to ambush helicopter landing zones. He liked to travel by day as well as by night; and, to cook their food, his men lit their fires in caves. If caves could not be found, the men ate cooked rice which they carried with them. After each battle, his battalion would assemble at a designated rally point; on the day of his capture, he had selected a US company command post as his rally point.

The main force Viet Cong, like his local force contemporary, is quite capable of performing the disappearing act. He has excellent knowledge of his area of operation and is a professional guerrilla fighter. He selects his time and place to engage an opposing force, but fights only when assured of a victory. He is adept in ambush techniques, a master of using booby traps, and follows closely the classic guerrilla warfare precepts: if the enemy is strong, avoid him; if the enemy is weak, attack him.

guerrillas and the regulars

Of course, the main force Viet Cong units depend to a great extent on the assistance they receive from the overall Viet Cong infrastructure and from the local force Viet Cong guerrillas. To illustrate the extent of this support, a six-day period of Viet Cong operations against the 1st Cavalry Division has been reconstructed from prisoner of war interrogations and from a careful and detailed analysis of captured documents. *(Map 3)*

On 19 September 1966, the 2d Viet Cong Regiment, 3d Division, had a good portion of its forces located in the Cay Giep mountains.[4] Major Khanh, the regimental commander, and elements of his reconnaissance company left the mountains on that date and moved to the village of Cat Tai, there to meet with members of the local village guerrilla unit to discuss the results of a reconnaissance which had been made of the US division's forward base at LZ Hammond. The reconnaissance had been conducted by the guerrillas for the 2d VC Regiment.

As a result of this discussion, Major Khanh felt that LZ Hammond presented a good target, so he, together with his

[4]Intelligence analysis submitted by COL Herbert E. Wolff and adapted by LTC William E. Panton.

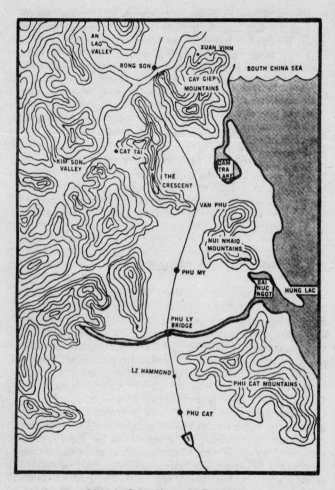

Map 3. Guerrillas and Regulars

reconnaissance elements, conducted a personal reconnaissance of the US base. Guerrillas served him as guides and assisted in disguising his soldiers as farmers, merchants, and cattle drivers. Major Khanh probably approached to within 1,000 meters of LZ Hammond during his personal reconnaissance.

Khanh was now convinced that he should attack the US base with both direct and indirect fire weapons and assault the US positions with his infantry. But the commanding general of the 3d Division, General Truc, disapproved of the infantry assault on the grounds that he could not provide the 18th Regiment, commanded by Lieutenant Colonel Xoan, or the 22d Regiment, commanded by Major Diep, to support the 2d Regiment. But he did give Major Khanh permission to proceed with the weapons attack.

Major Khanh returned to Cat Tai and began his arrangements. Local Viet Cong soldiers would provide his unit with guides to preselected mortar and recoilless rifle positions, and they would later assist in moving ammunition and arranging for care of his wounded. They would also maintain continuous surveillance of LZ Hammond and would inform him of any last minute changes in US troop disposition and strength. Other minor tasks were also assigned to the local forces, all of which fell under the North Vietnamese doctrine of "preparing the battlefield."

On the night of 23 September, Khanh's troops conducted an intense ten-minute attack of LZ Hammond with mortars and recoilless rifles and then withdrew over a booby-trapped route while guerrillas guided his companies through the safe lanes and posted snipers along the route of withdrawal to add to the delaying capabilities of the booby traps.

Khanh moved his units to Xuan Binh hamlet, and the troops went into hiding among the homes of the villagers. The soldiers were fed from pregathered rice stocks, and the local forces insured that no one left the village to tell of the unit's presence. An early warning net was also established by the guerrillas to insure that the regiment was not taken by surprise by either US or South Vietnamese troops. Reportedly Major Khanh posted no security of his own, apparently assured that the guerrillas would do a competent job.

Still undiscovered, and undisclosed, the regiment left Xien Binh hamlet on 25 September to return to the Cay Giep mountains. As a postscript to this action, an interesting incident took place on 19 October. On a fast light reconnaissance, the 1st Battalion, 9th US Cavalry, observed and killed three local guerrillas near LZ Hammond. A recovered document revealed that the guerrillas had previously conducted a damage assessment reconnaissance of LZ Hammond and that the commander of the 2d VC Regiment, not satisfied with that report, had directed that another be made. The guerrillas had been killed complying with that order. It was also noted that the original report of US losses had been exaggerated, but not as much as might be expected.

On 29 September, because of intelligence reports brought to him by various VC intelligence sources, Major Khanh felt that his Cay Giep positions were being jeopardized by the deployment of US forces, and that it was time for him to move his regiment back to the Kim Son valley, and area which afforded more running and hiding room.

The movement to Kim Son began at 2300 on 29 September. The companies maintained 500 meters distance between each other while, within the companies, the men maintained a one meter interval. Once again local guerrillas led the column through booby trapped, Viet Cong controlled hamlets. The preferred crossing point of Highway 1 was at the hamlet of Van Phu, but local intelligence agents informed Khanh that a South Vietnamese Regional Force (RF) company guarded the small bridge in the hamlet. Not wanting to chance discovery, Khanh changed the crossing point 1,500 meters to the north of the hamlet; as the local forces provided security 1,000 meters to the north and south and Khanh's own security went out 200 meters to either side of the crossing point, the 2d Regiment crossed Highway 1 in good fashion and continued an uneventful march through the Moi and Cay Sung passes into the Kim Son valley.

Each of the companies of the 2d Regiment was reportedly supported by 90 attached civilians who had been recruited by hamlet and village chiefs for service with the regiment for a six-month period to perform various services and labor; these civilians were also expected to accompany the 2d Regiment in combat.

The military support which the regiment had received had been made possible only because of the strong Viet Cong political organization entrenched at the province, district, and village levels. In addition, the political organization also pro-

vided other services to the regiment, including hospitals, re-
cuperation centers, mail carrier ferry service, porters, and
possibly even entertainment. All elements of the 3d Division
were heavily dependent upon the guerrilla support for the conduct of their operations. It was quite apparent from this operation that if the main enemy forces could be cut adrift from
the guerrilla units and services, especially food and intelligence, they would be much less effective and would become
easier targets for the free world forces in South Vietnam.

the viet cong soldier

A haze of myth and legend has swirled around the Viet
Cong regular soldier.[5] It is often forgotten that he is a human
being, and that as such he has his strengths and weaknesses,
his virtues and his vices, his hopes and fears. At times in battle
the Viet Cong soldier has shown extreme bravery, especially
when cornered, which causes some to credit him with the fa-
talistic courage of the Japanese fighting men in World War II.
This rather overpraises him, particularly if he is an average
soldier who has been imbued with the habit of guerrilla-like
evasion.

The so-called martial traditions of the Vietnamese have only
been resurrected by the battle of Dien Bien Phu, before which
they were inclined to be ancient and rusty. The lack of fighting
spirit and determination to get into the kill once the fight warms
up may be partly due to his Buddhist background and the
Buddhist precepts against violence and taking life. Despite
communist efforts to obliterate these drawbacks, the Viet Cong
still has strong traces of them in his makeup.

Endurance, coupled with fortitude and patience, are qualities
the Viet Cong soldier has in good measure. He was born close
to the earth in rural poverty, has always had a hard life, and
has had to manage without many elementary comforts. But
though he performs seemingly incredible feats of endurance
with his slight and ready frame, his life span is not all that
long. He easily succumbs to diseases, such as malaria, and one

[5]This material on the Viet Cong soldier has been drawn from the article by Major
Edgar O'Ballance, "The Viet-Cong Soldier" which appeared in INFANTRY,
November-December 1966, pp. 4–7.

suspects that the death toll in Viet Cong formations must be fairly high.

His morale fluctuates, dependent upon success, failure, heavy casualties, fatigue, and desertion. At times it is high, at others it is low, and occasionally it is very low. He has much to contend with—boring routine, jungle melancholia, home sickness, lack of news of his family, and disillusionment with communism. He fears being badly wounded in battle, in ambush, or by a booby trap and left behind to die alone in the jungle like a wild animal. He fears being taken prisoner, and he fears what will happen to his family if he deserts or defects. He fears the United States fighting man, US firepower, and US aerial might, which his masters have underrated so badly. He has as many fears as he has hopes.

The communists play on his hopes and his fears, and the cadres try to harness them to the communist cause. From all of these efforts comes the result that the Viet Cong soldier, although laboring under certain disadvantages, is a formidable jungle fighter. The task of the free world forces is to find and confront him in his own environment, to force him to stay and fight so that he can be destroyed.

II
Intelligence

ONE OF THE most difficult problems in Vietnam is to find the enemy, because there the war is being fought on a battlefield that has neither a front nor a rear. The enemy himself is the only valid point of reference, and it is he who dictates the limits and the dimensions of the battlefield.

Timely intelligence, therefore, is a major ingredient in frustrating a cunning adversary in an environment which provides, at best, a meager supply of intelligence information. At the same time, a good counterintelligence effort is required to complement the acquisition of reliable intelligence. For good intelligence can provide the basis for planning and executing operations only if the counterintelligence effort can be made strong enough to prevent the compromise of any plan or action.

The enemy, admittedly, is hard to find. But finding him is not an impossible task. The enemy's habitats and habits constitute definite fingerprints, and often provide the clues which lead to his undoing.

where's charlie?

The small, separate units which make up the local force Viet Cong military strength normally consist of men, women,

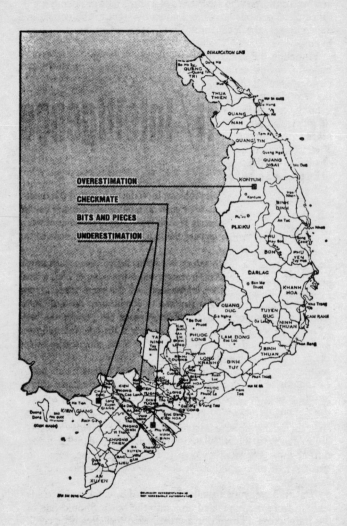

and even children who are natives of a unit's area of operations.[1] Since these persons are often known by sight to the people in their villages, the local force Viet Cong soldiers must go into hiding.

Although the selected hiding places may be somewhat removed from the villages where the soldiers are known, their basic needs will often give their presence away. For example, the Viet Cong soldiers require water for drinking, cooking, bathing, just as do most other human beings. A good source of water, then, must be readily available, even during the dry season, to a clandestine base area. Too, since the local force Viet Cong units cannot depend on well-developed logistical channels—particularly in areas under the control of free world forces—they must grow much of their own foodstuffs. Because rice constitutes the bulk of the diet, it is only natural that the local forces should plant numerous, small rice beds in areas of calm water, usually part of or adjacent to small streams. The rice diet is supplemented with bananas and the juicy, apple-tasting root of the manioc plant.

Exacting aerial reconnaissance can locate the local Viet Cong forces by finding and pinpointing their water supplies and their planting areas: rice paddies, banana trees, or the four- to eight-foot stalks of the manioc with their leafy tops. The reconnaissance might also pick up another sign of local Viet Cong habitation: animals. Pigs and chickens are allowed to run loose and, on occasion, the Viet Cong will trap small, wild animals with traps and snares—usually nothing more than leather thongs or ropes—attached to stakes concealed in a known animal feeding place.

More conclusive evidence of Viet Cong habitation is the spotting of huts and trails beneath the dense jungle canopy. Since the local Viet Cong forces operate in or near a populated area, their camp or base area must be within a half-day's walking distance of the populated area; they cannot locate much further away, or their purpose for existing in the area—to terrorize, to propagandize, to harass, to tax—would be defeated.

The trail network usually consists of several major trails leading from the populated area into the bush. Should one of the trails cross a stream or a creek, then the stream or creek should also be considered as a trail. The Viet Cong are past masters at deception, and hidden underwater trails can easily lead to a clandestine base.

Main force Viet Cong units are more difficult to locate for they establish their bases in more remote and distant areas. But those units do not spend much time in their base areas because they are constantly on the move, traveling to other areas to carry out assigned missions. They return only to rest, retrain, and reequip.

Too, the main force units occupy some of the villages in South Vietnam which are not under free world force control. In these villages, where food and water stocks are abundant, the main force Viet Cong live with their families and enjoy a change of pace from the rigors of active combat operations. They literally live in a sanctuary from air strikes and harassing and interdiction artillery fires; in their safe havens, their morale is high.

The villages themselves are protected by a close network of supporting bunkers and trenches, and every hut has an air raid shelter beneath its floor. Yet the presence of women and children in the villages is designed to afford additional protection from the artillery and aircraft of their enemies.

A lack of life and activity in a village, therefore, may well indicate that the main force unit is off on a mission, for the permanent inhabitants are afraid and go into hiding when their protectors are away. As with any other people, numbers give comfort to the Viet Cong, and the absence of numbers creates fear and apprehension among those who stay behind.

This psychology also works in reverse. The presence of the main force soldiers with their sophisticated weapons creates an air of confidence which permits the residents to move about freely. Rather than remain in hiding, the soldiers and civilians alike will work their fields and pause to look up at the aircraft flying overhead.

Around the isolated villages of thirty or forty huts can be seen hundreds of acres of rice paddies and farms, thick banana groves, and other indications of a larger population disproportionate to the relatively small number of huts. Surprise must be achieved and the entire area encircled before a search is initiated if any degree of success is anticipated. Even then extreme caution must be exercised to prevent the enemy from escaping through the numerous escape tunnels which interlace the ground beneath the village.

Each item of information that is gathered, therefore, must be evaluated for pertinence, reliability, and accuracy; it must be minutely examined as a possible key which will unlock the door to the enemy's plan of action.

checkmate

In late 1965, a South Vietnamese task force, making excellent use of intelligence acquired from various sources, was able to surprise and decisively defeat a Viet Cong force of 500 men on the latter's home ground. Fixed by fires from aircraft and supporting artillery, the Viet Cong force, because it had been surprised, was forced to stay and fight.[2]

On 10 December 1965, Vietnamese intelligence sources reported that a Viet Cong battalion was assembled in a sparsely populated area located in the Cau Ke district of Vinh Binh province, a district which had been long controlled by the Viet Cong and seldom penetrated by ARVN forces.

Quickly, then, Task Force 14 was organized at Can Tho, the headquarters of the IV ARVN Corps: the 1st and 2d Battalions, 14th Infantry; the 3d Battalion, 13th Infantry; and the 2d Troop, 2d Armored Cavalry Squadron, all under the commander of the 14th Regiment. Task force support was to be provided by the 27th River Assault Group (RAG), two armed helicopter platoons from the 13th US Aviation Battalion, one 105mm battery and one 155mm battery of artillery, and the 43d Ranger Battalion, a unit which could be used as either a reaction or a strike force; additional air support was to be furnished by both Republic of Vietnam Air Force (VNAF) and United States Air Force aircraft. *(Map 4)* As a counterintelligence measure, the location of the operations area and the operation order and overlay were not given to the participating battalion and troop commanders until two hours before the units were to be loaded on the RAG's landing craft for the 40 kilometer movement down the Bassac River to the line of departure (LD).

By 0100, 12 December, all units were loaded, including the M113 armored personnel carriers of the armored cavalry

[2]Combat experience submitted by CPT Donald E. Carlile, USA.

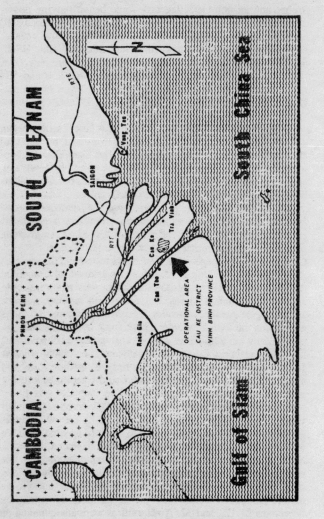

Map 4. Cau Ke Operational District

troop, and an hour later the task force began moving downstream, for the operation order called for the LD to be crossed at 0730.

Four hours after the task force had left Can Tho, USAF F100s and VNAF A1-E Skyraiders blasted the five objectives with 20mm cannon fire, napalm canisters, and 250 and 500 pound bombs. At 0650, the two artillery batteries began preparatory fires, and were soon joined by the .50 caliber machineguns and 20mm cannons of the RAG boats.

At high tide—0700—the armored personnel carriers began to disembark; they were immediately followed by the lead elements of each maneuver battalion. The landing was unopposed and a beachhead 1,000 meters long and 100 meters deep was soon established; on time, the forward units of all battalions crossed the LD. The terrain was typical of this region of South Vietnam—delta country, with inundated rice paddies sectioned by numerous small tidal canals which emptied into larger canals at various points; many mangrove and coconut trees growing along the canal banks; and with a sparse population.

The task force, with three battalions abreast and the armored cavalry troop screening the left flank, continued its unopposed advance until 0810 when the armored cavalry troop began to receive sporadic small arms fire. The enemy fire was returned immediately and the task force commander ordered his units to advance rapidly to seize the objectives. But the enemy reaction grew more intense and heavy mortar and automatic weapons fire began falling on the exposed ARVN soldiers moving across the rice paddies; the fire was coming from well concealed and apparently fortified woodline positions near objectives 21, 31, and 32.

Quickly sizing up the situation, the task force commander requested and received permission to airlift the 43d Ranger Battalion to landing zone 4 (LZ 4), one of several possible landing zones selected the previous evening. *(Map 5)* From LZ 4 the Rangers could deny the Viet Cong an exit from the operational area, and the battalion would be in a good position from which to attack objective 32. Additional air strikes were also requested, to include heavy concentrations of napalm on objectives 21, 31, and 32. Artillery fires were also planned on the three objectives to assist the forward movement of the infantry while the armed helicopters would furnish close support fires.

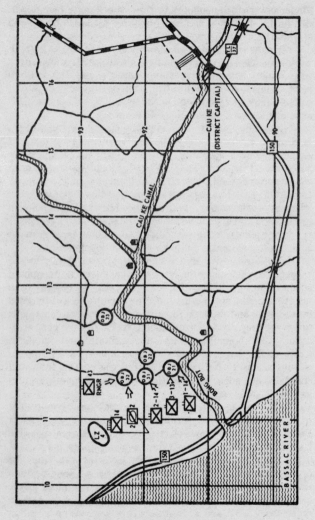

Map 5. Attack at Cau Ke

Under cover of the supporting fires, the Ranger battalion landed on LZ 4 at 0840 and began moving towards objective 32. *(Map 6)* Meanwhile, following several napalm strikes, artillery barrages, and aerial gunship rocket runs, the ARVN infantry maneuvered to within 300 meters of the three forward objectives—21, 31, and 32. The armored cavalry troopers, receiving some anti-tank fire, had dismounted from their carriers and were now placing fires on objectives 31 and 32 in support of the attacking infantry and Rangers.

The fighting continued hot and heavy for the remainder of the morning. Alternating on station, the two armed helicopter platoons provided continuous close supporting fires while the infantry, using their mortars and recoilless rifles against the fortified Viet Cong positions, increased the intensity of the fight in their effort to break through the enemy defenses.

Shortly after noon, the airborne command post and an airborne artillery forward observer both reported seeing unarmed individuals, both male and female, moving northeast out of the objective area. An assault was launched almost immediately; objectives 21, 31, and 32 fell at once, objectives 22 and 23 a little later. More than 130 Viet Cong soldiers died in this action, while 15 more were made prisoner. In addition, a number of enemy small arms and machineguns were seized. The ARVN task force suffered only light casualties: 15 dead, 43 wounded.

bits and pieces

Timely intelligence, too, is also a major ingredient in frustrating an expected enemy attack, for prior knowledge of an enemy's plan of action will always permit the development of adequate countermeasures. If the intelligence specialist has the experience and ability to reach a logical and accurate interpretation from the accumulated intelligence items, and if the completed intelligence estimate can be disseminated promptly to those friendly forces affected by the information contained in the estimate, an enemy's plan of action can be foiled and defeated. And so it happened in Kien Tuong province in April 1966.[3]

[3]Combat experience submitted by LT Thomas E. Patterson, USA, and adapted by CPT James L. Shepard.

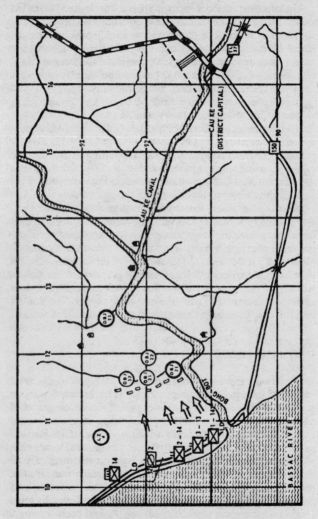

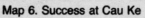

Map 6. Success at Cau Ke

In late 1964, the US Army's Special Forces had moved into Kien Tuong province and established five base camps. In each of the four districts of the province, an A Team had been set up to advise the Luc-Loung Dac-Biet (LLDB) Vietnamese Special Forces and the Civilian Irregular Defense Group (CIDG). At Moc Hoa, the provincial capital, a Special Forces B Team had been established to exercise command and to provide logistical support to the A Teams. *(Map 7)*

Kein Tuong was one of Vietnam's poorest and least populated provinces, and had been a guerrilla stronghold for many years. Located forty miles west of Saigon, sharing over 60 miles of international boundary with Cambodia, the province was a rural area dotted with rice paddies. Tall elephant grass prohibited even a standing man from seeing more than a few yards, and the province's lack of roadways made it an almost inaccessible region to reach along the ground.

During the next two years, the Viet Cong effort in the province collapsed almost completely. In the first four months of 1966 alone, over 700 Viet Cong had been killed, massive Viet Cong supply and munition caches destroyed, and Viet Cong control over the villages greatly diminished. In fighting back, the Viet Cong had had to resort to terrorist activities, increased taxation of local villages and conscription of teenage youths. Faced with fading popular support, the Viet Cong desperately needed a decisive victory over the South Vietnamese forces and the US Special Forces advisors.

They chose the night of 9 April 1966, the eve of Easter Sunday, for their attempt. The attacking unit was to be the main force 261st Dong Thap Battalion, reputed to be one of the best of its kind in Vietnam, supported by the heavy weapons company of the 267th Battalion and elements of the 269th Battalion.

At noon on 9 April, Sergeant First Class Charles Richard, an intelligence specialist assigned to the Special Forces camp A-415 in the Tuyen Nhon district, received a report from a local villager that the Viet Cong were preparing to attack somewhere within the district. "Should I believe this information?" was the first thought that ran through Sergeant Richard's mind; during the previous weeks similar reports had been coming in from other excited villagers, most of which had turned out to be false. The Special Forces men in the camp had been con-

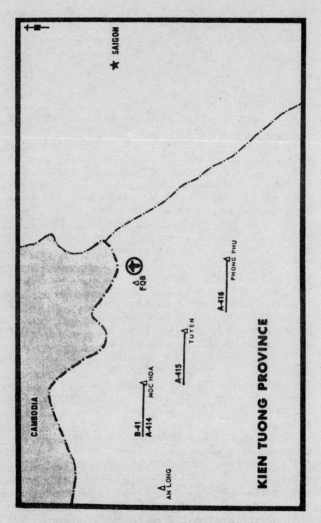

Map 7. Defense of Kien Tuong Province

stantly on edge, some for almost a year, and a natural tendency was to disregard this report, too.

But Sergeant Richard sensed that this report might be true, and after dovetailing the report into the other intelligence information he had on the Viet Cong in the area, concluded that the villager's report was valid. Earlier reports had indicated that the enemy had been massing troops along the Cambodian border, and the last two major Viet Cong attacks had taken place on major holidays—Christmas and Tet, the Vietnamese celebration of the lunar new year.

Sergeant Richard's next consideration was where the attack might take place. The three most likely targets were the district headquarters, the Special Forces camp A-415, and the forward operational base (FOB) of the Special Forces camp, an isolated 100-man outpost which was used as a forward staging area for mounting attacks against the Viet Cong. Situated six miles from the border, the outpost had been attacked twice in the preceding four months. Sergeant Richard selected the FOB as the most likely place that the Viet Cong would hit, but he did not discard the possibility that the Viet Cong would hit one of the other possible and likely targets.

Accordingly, then, all Vietnamese units were alerted and told to make necessary preparations for defending against the Viet Cong. The A-415 team called the B Team at Moc Hoa and laid on air strikes on all likely Viet Cong targets. Tactical plans to repel an attack were reviewed and rehearsed; and then the units sat back and waited for an attack that might not materialize.

But at 2307, 9 April, the attack did materialize, as sporadic small arms fire from a concealed position north of the operational base began to fall on the FOB. Staff Sergeants Robert J. Flemings and Rodney K. Flack, the two Special Forces men at the base, relayed the word to the B Team operations center that the attack had begun.

The operations center personnel immediately called the nearest US Air Force support element, and within a few minutes the Air Force's Captain Howard Davis was airborne and over the battle area in an 0-1 Bird Dog, a light observation aircraft. Captain Davis would serve as the Forward Air Controller (FAC) for the fighter bombers and the FC-47 Puff aircraft, the latter armed with gatling guns capable of firing over 6,000 rounds per minute, which could be expected over the base within another few minutes. In reality, just twenty-four minutes after the first enemy round had been fired, F100 fighter bombers and Puff were over the base ready to strike back at the Viet Cong.

Meanwhile, on the ground, the Viet Cong had followed their sporadic small arms fire with fire from light and heavy mortars, recoilless rifles, and light and heavy machineguns. The base's defenders estimated they were under attack by at least a reinforced Viet Cong battalion. Sergeant Flack moved from position to position inside the camp trying to locate the enemy's heavy weapons; as he found one, he would relay the location to Sergeant Flemings, who would then relay the location to Captain Davis. Captain Davis, then, would bring in his available aircraft on the Viet Cong, and tracer bullets from Puff hurled like a fiery rainbow over an area approximately the size of a football field. Time after time the rain of missiles from the sky broke up determined Viet Cong charges.

At 2340, a 15-man Viet Cong suicide squad charged the wall. The CIDG defenders killed three, wounded several, and halted the charge. The base's main defensive weapon—a 60mm mortar—was being fired as fast as possible by the other CIDG troops, driving back Viet Cong soldiers who were trying to overrun the north wall.

But, not to be denied, and under cover of the other fighting, another Viet Cong suicide squad slipped undetected into the camp. One of the enemy reached the LLDB command post and killed the noncommissioned officer in charge and the latter's radio operator. Fortunately, the napalm dropped by the F100s and the heavy volume of fire poured down by Puff kept the Viet Cong from exploiting this success, and gave the defenders time to direct a concerted counterattack against the enemy suicide squad, which had already set up a machinegun inside the camp. Rifle fire knocked out the enemy machinegun crew, and a quick drive as a follow-up ejected the remaining enemy from the camp. Shortly after, a Viet Cong flamethrower team scored a minor success by setting fire to a building within the camp from which CIDG troops were fighting. But after evacuating the building, the CIDG troops counterattacked and destroyed the enemy flamethrower team.

Following these failures to dislodge the Vietnamese from the base, the Viet Cong began firing white phosphorous mortar rounds into the besieged camp. One of the first rounds ignited the command post occupied by Sergeants Flack and Flemings and forced them to take their radio and medical supplies to a new position. Unfortunately, the radio was damaged during the move and would no longer operate.

Lacking communications with the ground, Puff began suppressing the fire from the enemy's weapons by using the enemy's tracers as a guide. Puff swept the enemy's guns with a deadly blanket of fire and soon all of the enemy machineguns which had been firing into the east side of the camp had been silenced. Since enemy fire continued from the north, however, the Special Forces operations center asked for, and received, additional air support: another flight of F100s to cover the enemy positions with napalm. As the F100s carried out their assigned mission, the defenders took a welcome break from the rigors of fighting and reorganized and regrouped.

The outpost was without communications until 0210, when radio contact was finally re-established through Vietnamese channels. For the next two hours the fierce battle continued; although heavily outnumbered, the camp's defenders, supported by the USAF aircraft, blunted all Viet Cong attacks. By this time, the Viet Cong had suffered numerous casualties, both dead and wounded.

A platoon of armed helicopters arrived at Moc Hoa at 0340, sent to help the defenders. The light section—two armed helicopters—was dispatched immediately to the battle area; the heavy section—three helicopters—was loaded with supplies and two Special Forces officers—Captains Ronald T. Shelton and William K. Hudson.

As the supply helicopters arrived at the FOB, the Viet Cong soldiers increased their fire trying to prevent the helicopters from landing. But the two escorting gunships returned the fire, suppressing it enough so that the three supply craft could land in the very center of the base. The vital supplies were quickly unloaded and the helicopters lifted off to join the fight.

This apparently convinced the Viet Cong force to break off the fight and to withdraw; by 0500, the badly mauled enemy force had broken all contact with the FOB. It was just as well. In the camp, on the north wall only four defenders remained alive. Two of these were wounded and had set up positions in a ditch outside the wall. Another had bluffed the Viet Cong by popping up at various places along the wall to deceive the attackers as to the actual number of defenders still alive. Four members of the Viet Cong suicide squad that had managed to get into the camp lay dead inside the perimeter. Sixteen of the defenders were dead, fourteen more badly wounded, and three were missing. Inoperative and discarded weapons were scattered among the smoldering buildings inside the wall.

Outside the wall, 40 enemy soldiers lay dead, and there were numerous signs that many wounded had been dragged away. Three machineguns, three assault rifles, a rocket launcher, several claymore mines, and a flamethrower had been left behind by the Viet Cong units. For a third time the Viet Cong had been unsuccessful in overrunning the forward observation base.

overestimation

While the intelligence gathered by Sergeant Richard was used promptly and effectively, and was evaluated for pertinency, reliability, and accuracy, there have been other cases in South Vietnam where intelligence was not so used, where, for example, the strength and combat power of an enemy force were either grossly overestimated or underestimated. While underestimating the size of an enemy force can be a costly error in combat, overestimating usually allows the enemy to go free.

During late October 1966, Company C, 2d Battalion, 8th US Infantry was involved in the first major operation—Operation PAUL REVERE IV—conducted by the 4th US Infantry Division since the latter's arrival in Vietnam a few weeks earlier.[4]

In the early afternoon hours of 28 October 1966, the soldiers of Company C were searching for the enemy north and west of the Se San River in Kontum province, an area that had not been penetrated by US troops in more than a year. Intelligence information indicated that there had been a considerable buildup of enemy assembly areas in the province during that time resulting mainly from the infiltration of large numbers of North Vietnamese Army (NVA) troops into South Vietnam.

Company C's movement through the dense vegetation was slow and tedious. The forward two platoons moved in a V-

[4]Special after action report adapted by CPT Terry H. Reilly.

formation; at the point of each V, two men, one with a compass, the other with a machete, guided and cut the way. At the rear, pace men kept track of the distances traveled.

Eventually the company came upon a trail about two meters wide which ran in a general north-south direction, with numerous branch trails leading off to either side. Vine guidelines for night traveling as well as animal traps were everywhere in evidence. The company also discovered a communications wire which had been laid along the western side of an adjacent ridgeline.

A squad sent forward to reconnoiter ahead of the point moved about 200 meters up the trail when the squad members heard voices and saw two NVA soldiers. The squad felt that the NVA soldiers might have come from an enemy base camp up on the ridgeline, so he turned his squad back and returned to the company to report the information.

Company C's commander, not wanting to use the trail to approach the suspected enemy camp, chose a finger of the ridgeline as his axis of advance. The ridgeline itself became wider near its top, leveling off at a hilltop and saddle complex which joined a slightly higher hill.

As the company moved cautiously up the finger, it came upon several huts; the trees around them were marked with black crayon markings on flat places that had been chopped in the trunks. As the men of the company clustered about to study the markings and to search the huts, a sniper opened fire; the men of the company sought cover and began returning the fire as best they could. As the firing died away, the company resumed its movements and soon entered a small village.

It was apparent that an enemy force had abandoned the village just a short time before the company's arrival, and off to the northwest, some 300 to 400 meters away, sounds of movement could be easily discerned.

The village huts were fairly new, and the bunker and tunnel fortifications were also new or still under construction. One elderly woman, apparently unable to move, and a few chickens and pigs wandering aimlessly about were the only signs of life in the village. The huts did contain tiny sandals and other articles of apparel to indicate that women and children had been among the village's inhabitants; an assortment of rice, dried fruits, and dried meats; NVA uniforms; French and Cambodian money; and a variety of small arms ammunition.

After a short break near noon, the company commander sent his 1st and 2d Platoons north across the saddle of the ridge while the 3d Platoon secured the west side of the village and the company headquarters and weapons platoon, the latter organized as a fourth rifle platoon, remained in the center of the village. *(Map 8)* As the two leading platoons reached the downward slope of the hill 200 meters to the north, a shot rang out in the 3d Platoon's area and a soldier dropped to the ground, wounded. Within minutes the enemy's fire grew heavier, and Company C's commander decided to leave the village to establish a perimeter defense of the hill then occupied by his two lead platoons. By 1500 the company was in a perimeter defense around the hill, preparing positions from which it could ward off an enemy attack.

Work was begun on hacking out a small landing zone on the northwest slope of the hill, while fields of fire out to 50 meters were being cleared in the three-inch bamboo thickets in front of each platoon. Foxholes were hard to dig in the rocky, root-laced soil, and most of the men ended up with shallow prone shelters built up with log and earth supplements.

A resupply helicopter arrived with rations, but could not land because the landing zone had not yet been cleared; the rations were kicked out of the door of the helicopter and recovered later by Company C's soldiers from the trees on the other side of a gully which ran in front of the perimeter.

By 2000 a sizeable portion of the LZ had been cleared, as well as the fields of fire around the perimeter; claymore mines had been set up in each platoon sector, and a four-man listening post set up forward of the 3d Platoon only about 20 meters from the edge of the village.

An hour later sounds of human movement came from the village, as the villagers apparently were taking advantage of the darkness to return to their huts; but artillery concentrations being registered by the accompanying forward observer from the 4th Battalion, 42d US Artillery, scared the people back out of the village. That night the company was on 50 percent alert around the perimeter.

At about 0250 the next morning, the sound of chickens squawking and logs being moved in the village alerted the men at the listening post and around the company perimeter. Apparently the NVA soldiers were unaware that Company C was

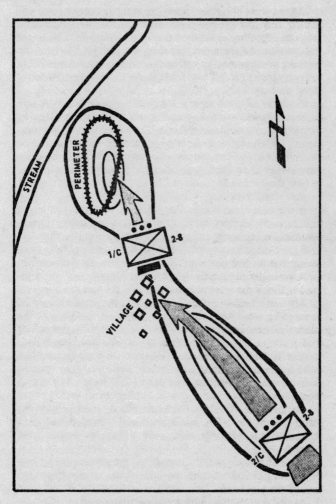

Map 8. Overestimation

still in the area. But, then, someone on the perimeter coughed. Immediately the NVA soldiers opened fire with automatic weapons, shooting in the direction of the cough with all tracer ammunition. As the enemy opened fire, the four men at the listening post jumped up and began running back towards the company perimeter; all four made it, but three suffered wounds along the way.

Moments later the enemy attacked in force, the NVA soldiers yelling and screaming as they moved forward. *(Map 9)* Heavy enemy automatic weapons fire concentrated on Company C's machineguns as the NVA soldiers advanced and crossed the gully. At this, the company commander ordered the claymore mines to be fired; together with a heavy volume of fire by both the 1st and 3d Platoons, the firing of the mines stopped the enemy advance.

In the meantime, the artillery forward observer was trying to walk in his artillery support, but he was encountering communications problems and could not make himself understood to his fire direction center. But though the artillery fires were too far out to give much aid in the close combat then raging, they were placed effectively on the enemy's routes of withdrawal, thus making it costly for the NVA soldiers to maneuver.

After 20 minutes of intensive fighting, the firing diminished to sporadic small arms fire, and by 0445 all contact with the enemy had been broken. At daylight, Company C's commander took stock of his situation. Two of his men had been killed, another 10 had been wounded. Because the landing zone had to be secured and improved to accept helicopters, he ordered each platoon to sweep an area out to 200 meters in front of their positions to clear out any remaining enemy and to count the enemy dead. Although numerous bloody trails pointed out places where the NVA unit's dead and wounded had been dragged from the battle area, only six enemy bodies were counted.

Sniper fire had caused Company C prematurely to go into a perimeter defense before the size of the enemy force had been determined. Had the company delayed, it might have developed the situation further and gained a decisive victory— it could have attacked an enemy squad, maneuvered against a platoon, or called for reinforcements and blocked a company.

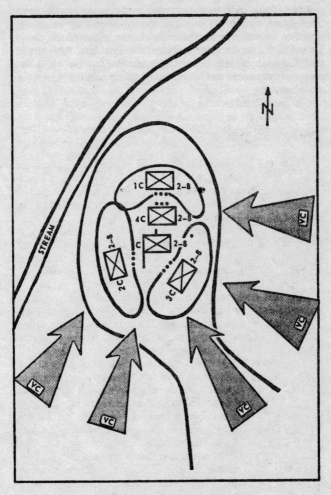

Map 9. The Enemy Attacks

Instead, the company was stopped in the accomplishment of its mission and forced into a defensive posture by an enemy force of an undetermined size. It lost the initiative and sat in its perimeter until the enemy called the next tune. As it turned out, Company C left its perimeter after being resupplied and evacuating its dead and wounded to go on with its search for an enemy force which had decided that then was not the time for decisive combat.

underestimation

While this particular US unit allowed an enemy force to go free, a few months earlier in Chao Duc province, a South Vietnamese infantry battalion had suffered heavy losses because its actions had been based on an underestimation of the capabilities of an enemy force.[5]

In South Vietnam, small outposts are often established to guard critical terrain features, bridges, and waterways. Some of these small outposts are merely extensions of district or province security, and consist of triangular dirt berms manned by Popular Force (PF) troops and their families.

One such support, at Xon Thay Cai in Chao Duc province, was overrun early one morning in May 1966. The occupants, 16 men, 12 women and children, were listed as either killed or missing. Since there were no survivors, the size of the attacking unit was never determined.

The hamlet chief of Ap Ngoc An, four kilometers to the south, notified the province chief in Chao Duc of the tragedy. By 1600 on the day following the attack, the South Vietnamese Army (ARVN) had decided to send troops back into the area to rebuild the outpost, and a battalion from the 9th ARVN Infantry Division was given the mission of rebuilding the outpost within three days. The battalion commander was told that the enemy had left the area, and that it was not thought that the enemy could react within the 72 hours allotted the battalion to rebuild the outpost. Unfortunately, this underestimation of the enemy's capabilities was allowed to dominate the planning for the battalion's mission.

The battalion selected for the outpost mission consisted of three rifle companies and one weapons company; it had a total

[5]Combat experience submitted by CPT James P. Hales, III.

strength of 322 soldiers, about average for an ARVN battalion but considerably smaller than a US infantry battalion. Each rifle company fielded 90 soldiers; the remainder of the battalion strength was in the headquarters section and the small weapons company.

On the second day following the incident which had triggered this ARVN reaction, the battalion arrived in the village of Ap Ngoc An; it carried its 81mm mortar, the rifle companies' three 60mm mortars, and two 57mm recoilless rifles, and a basic load of 40 rounds for each of the mortars. Since the enemy were thought to have left the area after the attack on the outpost, no supporting artillery had been allocated to the battalion.

At Ap Ngoc An, the battalion commander was met by the province chief who augmented the battalion with a Popular Force platoon of 26 men. It was expected that the PF platoon would man the outpost after it had been rebuilt. The province chief also briefed the battalion commander on the local situation and reaffirmed that there were no known enemy forces in the vicinity. The battalion then marched to the area and began work on reconstructing the outpost, halting work at 1600 to establish a defensive perimeter for the night. The hours of darkness passed without incident.

The following morning the regimental commander visited the battalion. The latter's commander presented his construction and security plan to the regimental commander who pointed out some possible weaknesses in the security plan and advised that the battalion be moved from the outpost to positions farther south by nightfall; he also suggested that the battalion should plan fires for the mortars, maintain a 50 percent alert, and employ platoon patrols on each flank of the battalion and squad outposts to the north and south. While a USAF AC-47 aircraft, a Puff, would be provided on call throughout the night, there would be no supporting artillery or tactical air support.

At 1500, after a full day's work, the battalion commander moved his units two kilometers to the south of the outpost and prepared for the night. *(Map 10)* In the new area, the companies sent out their patrols and began preparing defensive positions. The battalion area was bisected by a canal running generally north and south, and undergrowth extended to a width of 50 meters on each side of the canal; this afforded some concealment and excellent fields of fire over the dry rice paddies. None

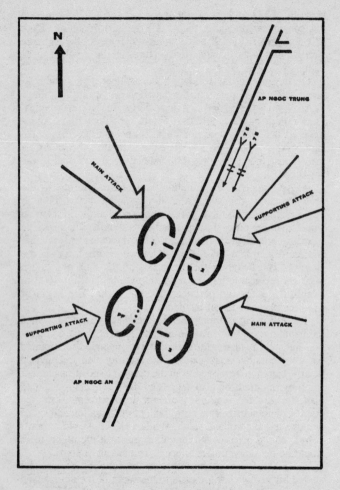

Map 10. Underestimation

of the positions extended beyond the undergrowth.

Just after 2000, the battalion commander received a radio message which told of two Viet Cong battalions being reported that afternoon in the vicinity of Luc Soc, three kilometers southeast of the battalion's position.

The early hours of the night passed quietly enough, but at 0200 a burst of machinegun fire awakened the sleeping soldiers, a burst fired by one of the battalion's soldiers who thought he had heard noises between his position and the outposts. His action undoubtedly saved many lives, for two minutes later the rice paddies on both flanks of the battalion's position came alive with waves of attacking Viet Cong.

The two Viet Cong battalions which had been reported to be in the area, reinforced by local guerrillas, had slipped through the battalion's patrols and had moved within 400 meters of the battalion's perimeter where they had dug assault positions completely undetected by the company outposts. Simultaneously with their assault, the Viet Cong units began placing 81mm mortar fire on the battalion command post and firing two 75mm recoilless rifles from north to south down the canal into the defenders' midst.

As soon as the firing began, a message had gone out for Puff; the aircraft arrived about 25 minutes later and started dropping flares. But after one burst from a gatling gun, the firing system jammed and Puff was unable to provide the desperately needed fire support. It did, however, continue to drop flares as it circled overhead. A second Puff was requested and it arrived 20 minutes later; but by now the Viet Cong assault troops were within 50 meters of the battalion's positions and Puff could not fire its guns for fear of hitting the defenders. Both ships continued to drop flares as the ARVN units vainly tried to repel the attacking Viet Cong.

Less than an hour after launching their attack, the Viet Cong units reached the tree line and penetrated into the northwest portion of the battalion's positions. All contact was lost with the 1st Company, and the PF platoon—also on the west side of the canal—was wiped out to a man. The 2d and 3d Companies and the battalion commander post personnel withdrew to the south, wading down the canal. The Viet Cong did not pursue. During the next day the regimental commander airlifted two additional battalions into the area; but the Viet Cong had gone.

the intelligence officer

Any campaign against guerrilla forces must take into consideration the entire operational environment; it must consider the cause for which the guerrillas claim to be fighting, the reasons why they are receiving support, and the basic conditions which justify or seem to justify the guerrilla movement.[6] These considerations often outweigh the classical considerations of weather, terrain, and enemy capabilities, for they determine the real capabilities of the enemy.

In conventional operations, for example, the commander's essential elements of information (EEI) frequently may deal with broad enemy capabilities and general enemy courses of action, or with the overall effects of the weather and terrain on both friendly and enemy capabilities. In counterguerrilla operations, on the other hand, EEI will often be more numerous, individually more restrictive in scope, and concern specific details of the area of operations or of the enemy.

Because guerrilla warfare is frequently conducted in relatively underdeveloped areas of the world, source information on the weather and terrain may be initially limited or difficult to acquire. But mobility is essential to conducting offensive operations against the guerrilla, so a knowledge of the effects of the weather on the terrain can have great bearing on the timing and nature of all operations. Although the weather may seriously restrict the mobility of the free world forces, it may also restrict the foot movement of the guerrillas and be helpful in fixing them in a position from which they must fight.

Using the time tested military considerations of terrain is still the most logical method for analyzing an area of operation. The major difference is that such definitions as key terrain and avenues of approach take on new meaning. For example, if a guerrilla force is known to be critically short of medical supplies, and a civilian hospital is located within a brigade's area of responsibility, then the hospital may be considered key ter-

---

[6]The material in this section has been taken from "The S2 in Counterguerrilla Operations" by Major Bill Bricker, USA, which appeared in the July-August 1966 issue of INFANTRY.

rain to the brigade. A town or village which has no tactical significance may also be considered key terrain if it has important psychological or political importance, as do most of Vietnam's provincial or district seats of government.

While the guerrilla may not look like a soldier, he fights like one, and intelligence personnel must become thoroughly familiar with the concept, tactics, and doctrines the guerrilla uses and believes in. Continual study, plus personal observation and experience, are essential. Order of battle information takes on great importance, although the computation of guerrilla strength does require some departure from usual procedures. Probably the most effective method is to account for guerrilla strength in total numbers rather than by units, although care must be taken to prevent gross overestimates of guerrilla strength. A realistic computation should also include time and distance computations to insure that the whereabouts of one force is not confused with another.

In the fighting in Vietnam, the importance of timely and accurate intelligence has assumed increased importance, and the small unit leader must understand and appreciate the need for reporting as well as the requirement for developing his own intelligence and reacting accordingly. The enemy must be located and fixed before he can be destroyed; units that understand the principles of surprise and simplicity and that make the greatest use of available intelligence are the successful ones.

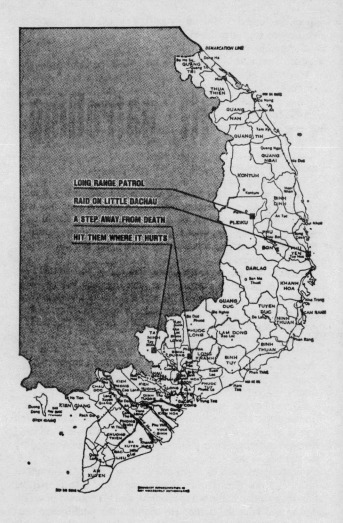

LONG RANGE PATROL

RAID ON LITTLE DACHAU

A STEP AWAY FROM DEATH

HIT THEM WHERE IT HURTS

III

Patrolling

BECAUSE THE ACQUISITION of accurate and timely intelligence is of the greatest importance in Vietnam, patrolling has again come into its own. Often an overlooked art, not always practiced as it should be, patrolling is an important asset to the infantry commander, particularly when his patrols are conducted by trained, well led, and enthusiastic soldiers.

Patrolling is one of those arts of war that should be mastered by all units and individuals engaged in an armed conflict. For patrols, when well conducted, can extend the eyes and ears of a commander to remarkable distances, and often enable a commander to locate and destroy an enemy force before the enemy force can locate and destroy him.

The enemy in Vietnam, both Viet Cong and NVA, is a master of the art of patrolling and rarely conducts an operation unless he has first made extensive preparations and conducted detailed reconnaissance patrolling. This was demonstrated by the actions of the Viet Cong unit which attacked the 1st U.S. Cavalry Division's Landing Zone HAMMOND. As a result of his efforts, the enemy often determines where a battle will be fought, how that battle will be fought, and his courses of action during and after the battle. He acquires the intelligence necessary to insure that his units will be as well prepared as possible before they move from a secure sanctuary; he acquires the needed intelligence by aggressive reconnaissance patrolling.

For US units, patrols are usually classified according to the mission they will perform. The two general classifications are combat and reconnaissance patrols, and patrol organization varies according to what the patrol is expected to accomplish. Reconnaissance patrols are sent out primarily to gather information; combat patrols, on the other hand, go out to destroy or capture enemy personnel, equipment, and installations, or to provide security. Similar to the combat patrol, with only slightly differing characteristics, the raid is a surprise attack on an enemy force or installation with the raiding force withdrawing after accomplishing its mission.

One of the most effective means for acquiring intelligence in Vietnam had been through the use of the long range patrol, which has again come into its own to probe, observe, and report from deep within enemy controlled areas. It has been proved again—as it had been proved during World War II and the Korean War—that a small group of well trained soldiers can survive in the enemy's environment, can penetrate deeply to locate the enemy's safe havens, and can either gather intelligence for future operations or, from concealed positions, direct aircraft or long range artillery fires onto unsuspecting enemy units.

a step away from death

Just how effective a long range patrol can be was clearly demonstrated in late 1966 by the 1st US Infantry Division's Long Range Reconnaissance Patrol (LRRP). Commanded by First Lieutenant Robert G. Pasour, the LRRP at the time consisted of 2 officers and 24 enlisted men; it had been used extensively in the past and now awaited another call for its services.[1]   .

On 26 November 1966 that call came: five men from the LRRP were to be infiltrated by helicopter into the southern section of War Zone D, just south of the Song Be River and about 50 miles east of Saigon, to sweep south to Song Be to report any enemy activity and storage areas and to plot any unreported roads or trails. The patrol would be out for five days. Although the 1st Division was then involved in Operation

[1]Combat experience related by 1LT Robert G. Pasour to CPT Anthony E. Hartle.

BISMARCK, Colonel Sidney B. Berry, Jr., the division's 1st Brigade commander, foresaw a later operation in War Zone D and had requested the sweep for the sole purpose of acquiring as much information about the area as possible.

The next evening, 27 November, found Sergeant Cleetus Sanders, the patrol leader, sitting tensely in a UH-1B helicopter flying to his patrol's drop site; the other four members of the patrol were in the same helicopter—the point man, radio operator, flank security, and rear security. The patrol would go in, as always, just as the dark of the tropical night descended to cover the landing.

From his seat near the helicopter's door, Sergeant Sanders could see at some distance to the rear Lieutenant Pasour's command control helicopter. And although Sanders could not see any other helicopters, he knew that the rest of the standard infiltration team was somewhere even further behind. The helicopter in which he was riding was the drop ship, the one that landed the patrol. A recovery ship would be only a few minutes away when the drop ship touched down, ready to come in for a pickup should something go wrong. Two armed helicopters were with the recovery ship and would provide suppressive fires if that proved necessary. The command and control helicopter would be in radio communication with the drop site and could direct activities if anything unexpected occurred after the patrol had landed.

Sanders checked his M16 rifle once again, and watched his men do the same as the helicopter flew steadily towards the drop site. He also reviewed the equipment he was carrying: a .357 magnum pistol; dehydrated long range patrol rations with a rice supplement; two canteens; maps; a hunting knife; and three fragmentation grenades. In addition, he had a lightweight radio set of the same type the radio operator carried—the AN/PRT-4 and AN/PRR-9.

At a signal from the pilot indicating they were going down to land, the members of the patrol completed their final checks and as the helicopter skids touched ground the five men left the ship and dashed for the tree line. The drop had been completed. *(Map 11)* In a few minutes, Sergeant Sanders had led the patrol to a heavy tangle of thorns, brush, and bamboo, and after crawling into the center of the thicket the men went to sleep knowing that the approach of an enemy force would awaken them.

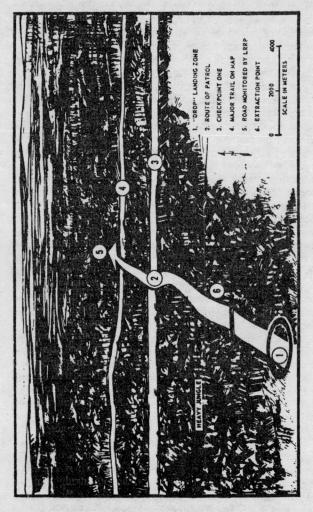

1. "DROP" LANDING ZONE
2. ROUTE OF PATROL
3. CHECKPOINT ONE
4. MAJOR TRAIL ON MAP
5. ROAD MONITORED BY LRRP
6. EXTRACTION POINT

SCALE IN METERS

0   2000   4000

HEAVY JUNGLE

Map 11. A Step Away From Death

At first light the next morning, the patrol moved out—their objective a large bomb crater on a road 1,200 meters to the north designated as Checkpoint One. The tracks of considerable traffic bypassing the crater had been seen from the air and Lieutenant Pasour wanted the patrol to observe the area during its second night out.

The patrol's movement through the heavy jungle was uneventful throughout the day and by 1800 it had reached the crater. A patrol report of this fact was relayed to Pasour through a small Army airplane, an O-1A Bird Dog, which had remained airborne throughout the day to serve as the relay station. Whenever the small plane had had to leave the air for refueling purposes, the pilot had given the patrol a 30-minute warning so that the patrol could set up a defensive position, for the patrol did not move unless it was in communication with its headquarters. During the night the radio relay duties would be taken over by a larger Army airplane, a U-1A Otter, which could remain airborne for a longer period of time.

Lieutenant Pasour told Sanders to wait on the south side of the road until dark, keeping the road under observation at all times, and then to move under the cover of darkness to take up an overnight position on the north side of the road.

Shortly after, Sergeant Sanders, only a few meters from the edge of the road, heard men approaching along the road from the east; a few minutes later, a column of enemy troops came into sight. The enemy soldiers were dressed in fatigue uniforms and wore steel helmets; they were well armed; and Sanders could identify one .30 caliber machinegun, several AK-47 assault rifles, and an assortment of carbines and rifles. Just as the column came abreast of the patrol's position, it stopped and the enemy soldiers moved off into the jungle on the north side of the road, stopping only a few meters from an open area.

The members of the patrol were painfully alert, for they could hear the enemy moving about and talking less than 50 meters away. At 2100 the tension broke as the enemy force moved back onto the road and continued moving west. Three hours later the patrol crossed the road, found a dense thicket, and slept until daylight.

In the meantime, Lieutenant Pasour had determined from an aerial reconnaissance that a trail some 400 meters to the north paralleled the road, and he directed Sergeant Sanders to move north to this trail and to check the area. By 1100 that morning, 29 November, Sanders' patrol had reached the trail and reported that it was in fact a heavily traveled road which carried both foot and vehicle traffic. Lieutenant Pasour then directed the patrol to set up on the north side of the road and observe the area for the remainder of the day. *(Map 12)*

Just after 1330, the patrol members heard the sounds of movement both to the east and west of their position. A few minutes later, two Viet Cong soldiers in black pajamas passed within 20 meters, and Sanders realized that in its present location within sight of the road, his patrol was directly in the path of the flank security elements of any large force which might move on the road. So he pulled his men back about 30 meters, stopping where the men could still hear, if not see, any road movement. The sound of movement did increase, and now the patrol could even pick up sounds of movement to its rear. At 1400 Sanders reported there were Viet Cong all around the patrol. Lieutenant Pasour told Sanders to move carefully to a position from which he could observe the road, for this information could prove of great importance.

An hour later, having reached a well concealed position only a few meters from the road, Sergeant Sanders and his men relaxed somewhat, for the sounds of movement were decreasing. About 1900 three oxcarts passed, moving from west to east. But, then, at 1930, a surprising sound echoed through the brush: a truck motor coughed into life some 200 meters east of the patrol and a few minutes later an old truck lumbered past the patrol's position. From the same direction came sounds of a large group of people moving about and chattering in Vietnamese. And though the patrol saw no more movement, voices and sounds of movement continued throughout the night. Analyzing the patrol's reports, Pasour felt that a considerable buildup was taking place in the patrol's vicinity.

The next day, 30 November, dawned cloudy and the sky was heavily overcast; because of the low ceiling the radio relay airplane was grounded. Accordingly, Lieutenant Pasour went up in his command and control helicopter. At 0730, Sergeant Sanders asked that his patrol be extracted, feeling that his position was becoming completely untenable. Viet Cong movement was increasing throughout the area, and he felt it was only a matter of time before the patrol was discovered.

Lieutenant Pasour agreed—the patrol had obtained the information needed and had located the enemy. From his aerial

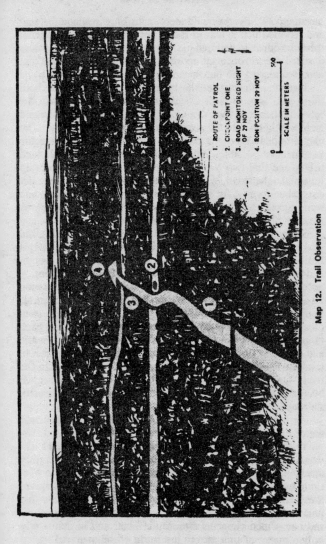

Map 12. Trail Observation

vantage point, Pasour could see that the only available landing zone from which to extract the patrol was at Checkpoint One, the large crater in the road to the south of the patrol's location. Pasour directed Sanders to move to that position to await pickup, and then alerted the pickup team of helicopters to stand by.

Twenty minutes later the patrol had reached the northern trail on its way towards Checkpoint One; glancing down the road, Sanders saw two Viet Cong soldiers come into view and he promptly ordered the patrol members to hit the ground. The men dropped to the ground and lay silently, trying to breathe as quietly as possible. What appeared to be a squad followed behind the first two Viet Cong soldiers; a still larger column followed. The small, wiry Vietnamese in the column were not dressed uniformly, for some wore fatigues, some khakis, some were dressed in black shirts and trousers. But each man was armed with a weapon of some type. *(Map 13)*

Sergeant Sanders, counting as each Viet Cong soldier walked past him, had reached 80 when a loud crack sounded right beside him—one of the patrol members in shifting his weight had snapped a twig. But the Viet Cong column kept moving— except for one man. He, after warily examining the vegetation alongside the road, began walking directly towards the patrol. Ten steps later and he and Sanders were looking into each other's eyes and were only a few feet apart. As if on cue, each of the five men in the patrol opened fire, shooting full automatic and emptying one magazine before moving on the dead run in a northerly direction, away from the Viet Cong unit. On the road, Viet Cong soldiers had fallen as though knocked down by a huge shock wave, and the enemy unit appeared completely surprised and confused.

For a few minutes at least the patrol was safe, but it would not be long before the Viet Cong force would recover and start out in pursuit. Sergeant Sanders realized this and radioed Lieutenant Pasour. The latter knew that the patrol could not possibly make Checkpoint One, for it lay on the other side of the Viet Cong unit; after telling Sanders to continue a northward movement, he began searching for another extraction site. By this time the Viet Cong unit on the road had somewhat recovered, and had started elements after the US patrol. The main body of the enemy column moved just north of the road and waited in the concealment of the jungle foliage for further orders.

As he continued to search for another landing zone, Pasour

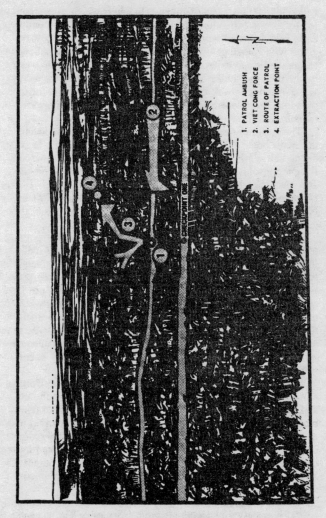

Map 13. Extraction

called for the two teams of armed helicopters which were standing by for the extraction attempt. The four ships arrived within eight minutes, and Pasour had Sanders mark the patrol's position with smoke before moving on. He then had the helicopters make firing passes on the smoke, flying from east to west; by the time the smoke had filtered through the trees, the patrol was far enough away to be clear of the fire. But some of the pursuing enemy were caught, and the rest became more cautious in their pursuit.

The gunships then worked their way to the south and located the main body of the Viet Cong, still bunched in the heavy vegetation north of the road. The helicopters roared down on the enemy soldiers, ripping the jungle apart with their rockets and machinegun fire. They were soon joined by USAF F4C Phantom jets which had been asked for by Lieutenant Pasour. Napalm and 500-pound bombs supplemented the efforts of the gunships.

In the meantime, Pasour continued his search for an extraction site, realizing the enemy could not be held off indefinitely. Finally he spotted an old bomb crater about 700 meters from the point of enemy contact and he directed Sanders to head for that spot. Although the recovery ship would not be able to land in the small opening, it carried a rope ladder which could be lowered to the men on the ground. The patrol finally reached the new extraction point, and the helicopter roared in and dropped the rope ladder. As the patrol members began to scramble up the ladder, they were taken under heavy enemy fire.

Sanders, the last man, was exhausted by his previous efforts, and had climbed only halfway up the ladder when he felt himself losing consciousness. Fortunately, before going out completely, he was able to attach a snap link which he carried on his web gear to the ladder. The pilot, knowing that he was low on fuel, under intense enemy fire, pulled pitch and roared into the air heading for an airstrip 15 kilometers away. Sergeant Sanders made the trip dangling from the rope ladder, unconscious.

The 1st Division's LRRP had gathered valuable information about enemy activity and the enemy's area of operation, and, though this had not been planned, inflicted heavy casualties on a large enemy force. Although the initiation and subsequent requirements of Operation ATTLEBORO, which developed into one of the largest operations of the war in Vietnam up to that time, prevented any immediate exploitation of the information that had been acquired, the patrol's efforts demonstrated the effectiveness of the long range reconnaissance patrol in a guerrilla environment.

long range patrol

Just one month before, the 5th US Special Forces Group had performed a similar—although with a much larger force—reconnaissance task as one of its units penetrated almost 50 kilometers into enemy controlled country to locate a major Viet Cong and North Vietnamese Army (NVA) infiltration route.[2]

In the late summer of 1966, while War Zone D was assuming increasing importance for the 1st US Division, intelligence reports were indicating that a buildup of enemy forces was taking place northeast of Duc Co in western Pleiku province. An increasing number of agent reports were mentioning the movement of main force Viet Cong and NVA units from the west and north into the Duc Co area, and while the presence of the infiltration route from the west had been known for some time, that from the north had not been. To confirm or deny the route was most important, particularly to the 3d Brigade, 25th US Infantry Division, which was moved to the Duc Co area to counter the enemy buildup. And so the Special Forces team at Polei Kleng—the closest friendly installation to the target area—was directed to send out a long range patrol to infiltrate into the suspected area and to initiate interdiction operations against any enemy lines of communication that might be uncovered.

On 11 October 1966 the patrol, on foot, left Polei Kleng. Made up of 14 US Special Forces soldiers and four platoons of Montagnard tribesmen who were members of the local Civilian Irregular Defense Group (CIDG), its objective lay some 40 kilometers to the northwest where the borders of three countries—Laos, Cambodia, South Vietnam—came together. Each man carried five days rations, two basic loads of ammunition, and numerous grenades, claymore mines, and demolitions.

Three days later, after a demanding forced march through

---

[2]Combat experience submitted by CPT James A. Fenlon.

dense jungle and avoiding all trails and open areas, the patrol reached the crest of the chain of mountains that shielded the suspected enemy infiltration route. This was the furthest into enemy territory that any friendly patrol had ever penetrated.

After two more days of painfully negotiating mountain streams, ravines, and steep ridges, the patrol reached the site which had been selected for the first resupply drop. Two A-1E fighter bombers, each carrying seven napalm containers to deceive the enemy that a resupply mission was taking place, made the drop at 0615, 16 October, from an altitude of 250 feet. The napalm containers held five days of rations, plus boots, uniforms, and radio batteries; after distribution, the patrol pushed on.

Progress was now limited to only four or five kilometers a day because to escape detection a route had been chosen through the mountains that crossed the ridgelines perpendicular to their long axes. Despite the difficult route, the patrol expected to reach its objective area by 25 October.

Bad weather, meanwhile, had forced the postponement of the second supply drop, and the stamina of the members of the patrol began to diminish. Fortunately, the weather did clear up long enough for a second aerial resupply mission to take place later in the afternoon of 23 October.

During the next morning, a platoon moved into the valley in which the infiltration route was believed to be located. The lead squad moved about 500 meters, encountered a swift mountain stream, but crossed the waist deep channel. On the far side, a trail paralleled the stream and led into the steep mountains south of the valley. The squad immediately deployed into a hasty ambush formation, concealed along the side of the trail. In a short time, a single Viet Cong soldier carrying a US carbine, moved down the trail from the direction of the high ground. When he reached the killing zone, he was taken under fire and fatally wounded. The enemy soldier carried no identification papers or documents.

Hearing the firing, Captain James A. Fenlon, the patrol leader, moved to the scene of the ambush, and deciding that the noise of the firing could have compromised the patrol's location, called the main body forward. Quickly establishing security to both flanks, the main body crossed the stream and trail and moved deep into the jungle along the base of the mountains; by 1630 it was in a clandestine assembly area, organized into a tight perimeter, prepared for the night. By this time the patrol had been moving for 14 days through very difficult terrain, and although a straight line distance of only 35 kilometers separated the patrol from its starting point at Polei Kleng, a map study of the route would indicate at least twice that distance had been covered. *(Map 14)*

Captain Fenlon now had to decide how he should deploy his forces, since the infiltration phase of his mission had been completed. The Plei Trop valley had been reached and the objective, if there actually was an infiltration route, lay not more than two days away. Fenlon called on his reconnaissance platoon and sent it out on an area reconnaissance while he kept the main body concealed in its present position; he wanted the reconnaissance platoon, if possible, to locate the trail the patrol was seeking before he again moved the main body.

The second squad of the reconnaissance platoon moved directly west for the entire day, crossing a series of small fingers jutting out from the mountains to the south. Finding nothing but old, apparently unused foot trails, the squad spent the night of 26 October on a small knoll about eight kilometers from the patrol base. Early the next morning, the squad began to descend the hill, but just before it reached the bottom it came upon a well concealed hut next to a rice field. The squad kept the hut under observation for about 30 minutes before surrounding it and searching the immediate area.

Inside the building, squad members found 500 pounds of unhusked rice, assorted housewares, but no occupants; outside the building, a footpath led into the valley. The squad leader, keeping the hut under observation, established a two-man security team down the path a distance of some 50 meters. A Viet Cong soldier came down that trail about an hour later, and was killed immediately by the security team. The information was relayed to the patrol base.

The other squads from the reconnaissance platoon had not discovered any signs of human habitation to the north and northeast, so Captain Fenlon moved the entire patrol to join with the squad at the hut. Although the hut was kept under observation for the remainder of the day, no further enemy sightings were made. That evening, the patrol moved further to the west and occupied a new patrol base on the final ridge

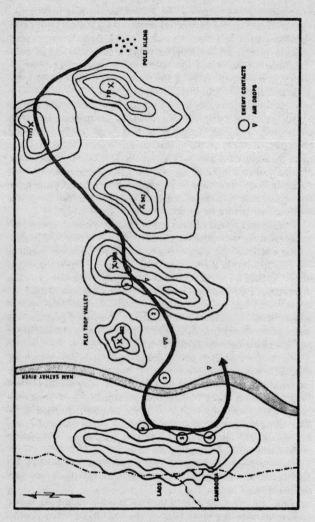

Map 14. Long Range Patrol

line before reaching the Nam Sathay river, which runs in a southerly direction and which parallels the Laotian-Cambodian border.

Once again the reconnaissance platoon went out to scout the area, and the next morning located a wide, well used trail on the patrol's side of the river. Concealing themselves in the bush, the members of the platoon waited. After about an hour, several voices were heard about 30 meters to the north, but no enemy was seen. An hour passed, then two. Still no sign of the enemy. Nothing could be heard but the sound of rushing water to the front, the Nam Sathay River.

Cautiously one scout moved to the edge of the trail and listened; still no voices or sound of movement could be heard above the usual jungle noises and the rushing water. But the imprint of boots could be seen on the trail, and this was significant. The previous patrol contacts had been with Viet Cong soldiers who wore the usual black pajamas and so-called "Ho Chi Minh sandals." Boots were a trademark of main force Viet Cong soldiers or North Vietnamese Army troops. Thus far, all the signs indicated that the enemy infiltration route lay somewhere between the river and the Cambodian border.

Captain Fenlon, with this information in hand, moved the main body of the patrol forward to join with the reconnaissance platoon. On the next day, 30 October, another resupply drop was taken, and all 14 napalm containers were recovered. Fenlon established his patrol in a tight perimeter again, well hidden in the jungle, and decided to send a small patrol across the river the next morning to scout the area on the other side.

Four men left the perimeter at 0200 the next morning, crossed the river, and cautiously began to reconnoiter the area in question. They had moved about 200 meters past the river when they encountered a wide, well used trail running north and south; the trail at this point was about three or four meters wide. Concealing themselves in the heavy undergrowth off the trail, the four patrol members began to observe, waiting for enemy movement they were certain would take place on a trail of this type.

At 1530 two men moved down the trail toward the south; each wore khakis, a black fatigue hat, and had on canvas boots; each carried an AK-47 assault rifle. The patrol knew immediately that they were NVA soldiers. The two were permitted to pass on, while the patrol continued its surveillance for the

rest of the day and night, but with no further results. Early
the next morning the four men retraced their path, recrossed
the river, and rejoined the main patrol.

Captain Fenlon felt that the trail the four men had discovered
was, in actuality, the infiltration route for which his patrol had
been searching. Sending a squad to maintain surveillance at
the river crossing site, he sent a radio message to C Detachment
headquarters in Pleiku describing the trail and its location. It
was obvious to Fenlon that heavy contact could be expected if
NVA soldiers were in the area in strength.

Fenlon moved the patrol across the river early on 2 November, and established an ambush along the trail with claymore
mines emplaced along the entire length of the killing zone. At
0800 a squad of NVA soldiers, with each man pushing a bicycle
and his weapon slung across his back, moved into the ambush,
were taken under fire, and dispatched. Straddling the rear wheel
of each bicycle was a saddlebag arrangement of metal boxes
containing 50 new potato masher type hand grenades. After
photographing the hand grenades and the dead soldiers, the
bicycles were booby trapped with flashlight batteries and claymore mines, and the patrol, minus one squad, moved to the
south to set up another ambush.

Shortly after noon, a lone NVA soldier moving north was
killed by the main body; but since nothing further had developed
at the site of the first ambush, the stay-behind squad was called
in to rejoin the main body. The squad had moved about 1,000
meters, following the trail left by the main body, when a heavy
volume of fire erupted from its front and the first two men in
the column went down under the hail of enemy bullets. An
NVA platoon, investigating the earlier firing, had discovered
the trail left by the main body and had established an L-shaped
ambush between the squad and Captain Fenlon's unit.

Eventually, after some harrowing moments, the squad managed to break contact and escape through the jungle back to
the river. Moving south, it rejoined the main body. Now that
the NVA forces in the area were apparently probing in some
strength, Fenlon decided to recross the Nam Sathay and break
all contact with the NVA forces on the trail side of the river.

Two of the four platoons made it across the river without
incident, but then NVA soldiers tried to flank the patrol by
crossing the river to the north about 150 meters from the crossing site. They were taken under heavy fire, though, and after

three of the party had been killed the remainder withdrew; there were no further attempts by NVA soldiers to cross the river.

Successfully across the river, Fenlon moved the patrol back to the base camp which had been established on 30 October. Two days later, he and his men were exfiltrated by helicopter, their mission successfully completed. The patrol's base camp was taken over by a two-company force of South Vietnamese Army troops who were acting as a blocking force for the 4th US Infantry Division. The NVA buildup had triggered Operation PAUL REVERE IV.

By avoiding trails and selecting difficult terrain for its route, the patrol had been able to move for a distance of 50 kilometers into enemy territory without being compromised. The judicious use of reconnaissance and security elements permitted the patrol to continually surprise the enemy. Though outnumbered by the enemy, the patrol had been able to fight at times and places of its own choosing, maintaining superior firepower over the Viet Cong and NVA soldiers which had been encountered.

Reconnaissance patrols of the type conducted by the 1st Division's LRRP and the 5th Special Forces Group are but one of the many different kinds of patrols conducted deep within enemy controlled territory in Vietnam.

hit them where it hurts

Two other successful tactical measures against the enemy in Vietnam have been combat patrols and raids. Combat patrols, for instance, have immense value in jungle operations, particularly when they can use the great mobility provided by the helicopter. Small combat patrols, carefully rehearsed and following meticulous and detailed planning, possess the inherent advantage of surprise because it is impossible for the enemy to develop adequate countermeasures over the entire battle area without paying too high a price in manpower, materiel, and time.

In April 1966, six helicopters lifted off the airstrip at Soui Da, a pentagon-shaped Special Forces A camp located about 17 kilometers northeast of Tay Ninh city and about 80 miles northwest of Saigon.[3] Aboard the helicopters were eight Special

---

[3]Combat experience submitted by CPT Jose M. Flores.

Forces soldiers and a platoon of 37 soldiers from the local Civilian Irregular Defense Group (CIDG). The mission: a combat patrol deep into War Zone C to destroy the Bo Tuc bridge near the large Viet Cong city of Katum. Intelligence reports and aerial spottings had shown that the enemy was using trucks and oxcarts on the main unimproved roads in the objective area to move large quantities of supplies and personnel. The Bo Tuc bridge was a key feature, and its destruction would materially hamper the enemy's logistical efforts.

Captain Jose M. Flores, the patrol leader, had earlier conducted a visual reconnaissance of the bridge site from a small observation aircraft. He had found that the terrain near the bridge consisted of thick brush and scattered clumps of trees, and that it was possible to land six helicopters 200 meters south of the bridge. On his return from his aerial observation flight, Flores had developed his plan of action: he would take a group of CIDG and Special Forces soldiers in by helicopter to the vicinity of the bridge, land, secure four of the avenues of approach to the bridge, destroy the bridge within 15 minutes after landing, and then have his group extracted immediately by helicopter to foil any enemy reaction.

One of the most important men on the mission, as Captain Flores realized, would be the team's demolitionist, whose biggest problem was to determine the number and type of charges he would need and where he would have to place them to get the desired results. The demolitionist had felt that instead of blowing the whole bridge, it would be better to blow just parts, so as to let the other parts twist under their own weight; this would make it harder for the enemy to repair or to put in a new bridge on the same site. With this in mind, he had decided that he would need 11 one-pound, composition four (C-4) charges.

Now he had to solve the problem of fixing the charges to the steel members of the bridge and of blowing those charges within the short time allotted by Captain Flores' plan. He remembered that if he mixed the C-4 with engine oil he could get a highly sticky charge, one that once slapped against an object would remain in place without additional tying or taping. This simple technique, finally perfected after some experimentation, made the demolition portion of the plan dovetail nicely into the allotted time frame.

In his other preparations, Captain Flores had found an area close to Soui Da that closely resembled the objective area, except for the bridge. The best that Captian Flores had been able to do about the latter problem had been to arrange for the use of a hastily erected foot bridge.

Two days before the actual operation, Flores had held his first rehearsal on the ground that he had picked out near the camp. The patrol element practiced loading and unloading from helicopters, actions they were to take at the objective, and the signals that would be used during the operation. A second rehearsal had been conducted the next day; in both, the platoon of CIDG soldiers had shown a great deal of enthusiasm and a willingness to do well. They had not yet been told of their destination or been filled in on all of the details of the forth-coming patrol.

Early on the day picked for the operation, the CIDG patrol had been brought inside the camp's perimeter and had been briefed and then isolated—now they knew where they were going and what they were supposed to accomplish. The matter of greatest concern to all, including Captain Flores, was the lack of specific information about the enemy's strength and dispositions near the bridge.

As the helicopters neared the landing zone and began to lose altitude, the troops on board prepared for the landing. Two armed helicopters, sent ahead, had marked the landing zone with green smoke and stood by to give close fire support if such support should be needed.

Hardly had the troop helicopters touched down than the soldiers were out of them, moving rapidly to their prearranged positions. The demolition team and Team Alpha, the team's security element, pushed onto and over the bridge; the other security elements deployed quickly and systematically. *(Map 15)*

As the demolition team began its work of emplacing the charges, heavy shouting erupted across the bridge in Team Alpha's area. Seconds later the two teams positioned along the stream also started to fire. Just as Team Alpha reported over the radio that there were many Viet Cong to its front, several grenades fell on the western bank of the stream close to the bridge.

The helicopter fire team leader pressed Captain Flores for

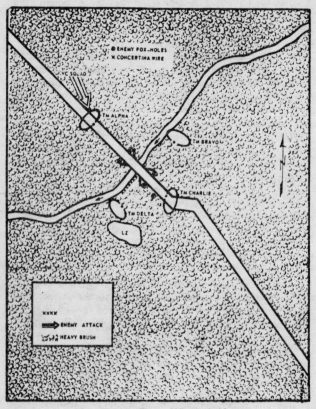

Map 15. Hit Them Where It Hurts

a target; but the latter, knowing that the two armed helicopters represented his only quick, close fire support, held off, preferring to have that support available if the situation should take a more definite turn for the worse.

Just as suddenly as it had begun, the enemy firing ceased. There were no casualties in any of the teams, although one Viet Cong soldier had been killed. Apparently the Viet Cong force had consisted of a squad of about seven to ten men.

At the bridge the demolition team finished its work and announced it was ready to detonate the charges. Captian Flores pulled Team Alpha back across the bridge, alerted the helicopters of the impending explosion, and had everyone on the ground take cover.

The charges went off with a tremendous explosion, and pieces of steel and wood were thrown high into the air in a cloud of black smoke. Most of the bridge had been blown to pieces; but the remaining parts of the bridge had been dropped and twisted as planned.

The helicopters to pick up the troops came in then, landed, and within seconds had the troops aboard. The two armed helicopters buzzed around, firing their rockets into the jungle around the landing zone to protect the other helicopters while they were on the ground. Lifting off and flying first at tree top level, the transport helicopters quickly rose to 2,500 feet and headed for home. Captain Flores looked at his watch—he and his patrol had been on the ground for just about 15 minutes. He sat on the floor of the helicopter and relaxed, watching the soldiers in the other helicopters wave at him as big, proud smiles lit up their faces. The CIDG had performed well.

But Captain Flores also knew that the key to the success of the operation had been careful, detailed planning followed by the two methodical rehearsals. Conducted on terrain similar to that found at the objective, the rehearsals had accomplished two things: they had insured that each man learned and executed his assigned job quickly and without mistake, and they had created a high state of morale and enthusiasm among all the men who were going on the patrol. Looking back, he knew that he could not have asked for a better performance.

raid on little dachau

The raid, too, had been a most effective tactic. Numerous examples can be drawn to illustrate the successes obtained by free world forces that have penetrated into the enemy's jungle or mountain strongholds to rescue prisoners or to conduct surprise attacks on enemy forces or installations. One of the better examples of this type of operation was the raid conducted in September 1966 by the Tiger Force (an all volunteer reconnaissance unit) of the 1st Battalion, 327th US Infantry, then a part of the 1st Battalion, 101st US Airborne Division.[4]

The 1st Brigade had just completed Operation HAW-THORNE and had begun to relieve the Republic of Korea (ROK) Marine Brigade which had been securing the rice harvest in the rich Tuy Hoa valley along the coast of South Vietnam midway between Nha Trang and Qui Nhon. The 95th NVA Regiment was known to be in the steep, rocky, jungle covered mountains to the south that formed the wall of the valley where the 1st Battalion, 327th US Infantry, commanded by Lieutenant Colonel Walter E. Meinzen, patrolled day and night from widely separated company perimeters dug into the valley floor. The Tiger Force, led by Captain Tom Agerton, was positioned on Hill 51, a critical rise of ground that broke the monotonously level valley floor and dominated the immediate surrounding area. Five hundred meters of rice paddies separated the small hill from the ominous looking mountains. *(Map 16)*

At 1000 hours on a typically hot and humid September morning, members of Tiger Force spotted movement in the woodline at the base of the mountains. As they watched, two men dressed in black pajamas emerged from the woods, running madly towards Hill 51. Captain Agerton ordered his men to hold their fire.

As it turned out, the two men were unarmed and willingly surrendered to the first Tiger Force outpost they encountered. During the interrogation period which followed, the men told an almost incredible story of a Dachau-type prison camp from which they had escaped the previous night. The camp, according to the story, was hidden away deep in the mountains and had, at one time, contained 90 prisoners, including one ROK Marine. Now, the men said, ony 40 prisoners survived, all in poor health and near starvation; the other prisoners either had been tortured or starved to death.

Colonel Meinzen had heard rumors during earlier operations in this area of the existence of just such a prison camp. The question that he had to answer now was had the two informers in fact escaped from the camp, or had they been sent to lure a US unit into the formidable mountains which hid the 95th NVA Regiment?

After further interrogation, verification, and analysis, cou-

[4]Combat experience submitted by LTC Walter E. Meinzen.

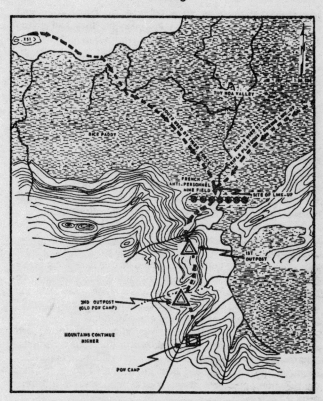

Map 16. Raid on Little Dachau

pled with the willingness of one of the escapees to lead a US force to the camp, Meinzen alerted Tiger Force for a raid—a quick dash in, and quick dash out, hopefully with the 40 survivors.

The escaped prisoners provided a detailed diagram of the entire prison compound, to include the location of the camp, and a description of all camp buildings, guard posts, and defensive positions. They even provided information on the early morning routine followed by the nine guards and the prisoners. But the escapees also said that the prison camp reportedly had been moved after any internee had made good an escape, and probably this would happen again now that they had gotten away successfully from the enemy's grasp.

Skeptical that all of this might lead only to an ambush, Colonel Meinzen alerted two rifle platoons to go with Tiger Force, and plotted supporting artillery fires all along the route the raiding party would take. Helicopter gunships were placed on strip alert, additional medical personnel attached to Tiger Force, and a squad of South Vietnamese Popular Force (PF) soldiers detailed to go along to help in talking with the prisoners once the camp had been reached. Agerton's force would also carry two RC-292 antennae to improve its communications capabilities, while an additional helicopter was placed on a standby basis should radio contact fail. An airplane equipped with a loud speaker and carrying an interpreter was also requested to assist the raiding party in the objective area.

Meinzen and Agerton selected the route Tiger Force would follow, basing their decision mainly on the ability of the guide to maintain his bearings. The two rifle platoons, starting from their own defensive perimeters, would link up with Tiger Force in the open valley before the entire raiding party moved into the mountains. Unfortunately, an old French mine field lay across the selected route, but both officers felt the field could be negotiated safely and without complications.

Just after dark, Tiger Force was relieved on Hill 51 and started moving into the valley to link up with the rifle platoons. Shortly afterwards, those units also reported their departure. Meinzen and his command post group settled down to wait; the question uppermost in everyone's mind was "Is it a trap, or is it for real?"

The link up of Tiger Force with the rifle platoons should have taken place by 2300, despite the rain which had begun to fall. But that time came and went, and no link up was reported. By midnight it was obvious that something had gone wrong: although Tiger Force and the rifle platoons were reporting that they were at the rendezvous point, neither group could see the other.

Since visibility was almost zero, and because one rice paddy or stream looked just like another, Colonel Meinzen told each group to hold where they were and to send out patrols to try to make contact. To help his units orient themselves, he had harassing and interdiction (H and I) artillery fires placed on known points in the near vicinity and a flare fired over Hill 51. He knew that his units could be within 50 meters of each other and still not know it.

By 0220 the two parties still had not come together; Meinzen was on the verge of ordering Tiger Force to break its light discipline when word came in that a patrol from one of the rifle platoons had made contact with Tiger Force. Ten minutes later, all of the raiding party were assembled and moving towards the mine field. Fortunately, a safe passage through the field was made, thanks in large measure to two engineers, each equipped with a portable mine sweeper.

In spite of the darkness and rain, the guide was positive that he knew where he was and appeared confident in his ability to lead the raiding party to the prison camp. But he had to go by the only way he knew—by the trails. Captain Agerton pondered the consequences of this, but then motioned to the guide to lead the way. Agerton fell in right behind the guide, making certain that the guide knew that the US captain had taken the safety off his M16 rifle. The guide would be the first target if an ambush were encountered.

Progress along the trail the party was following was swift and quiet. Behind the well dispersed Tiger Force, the rifle platoon moved by bounds. Everyone was keenly alert. But then, suddenly, the guide raised his hand and stopped. Through a translator he told Agerton that the first of two Viet Cong outposts lay just ahead, located in a cave at the next bend in the trail.

Three Tiger Force men stripped down and armed only with knives moved off the trail and disappeared in the direction of the cave. In minutes they were back—the cave had been unoccupied.

Darkness was just turning to light when the second outpost was encountered, and the delay in achieving link up at the start of the raid was now beginning to exert an ominous influence on the success of the mission. If everything had gone according to plan, the rifle platoons at this very moment should have been moving into preselected positions around the prison compound and the Tiger Force should have been ready to dash into the camp. But, now, the protective darkness was giving way, and the raiding party might encounter considerably more difficulty than it had originally bargained for.

In the interest of speed, Agerton abandoned the former cautious approach his force had been using to dash directly upon the camp which lay only 300 meters beyond the second enemy outpost. He directed one of the rifle platoons to leave the trail, bypass the outpost, and as quietly but as quickly as possible, to move into position around the compound. In the meantime, the Tiger Force would dispose of the outpost and, followed by the second rifle platoon, doubletime up the trail to the prison camp.

The rifle platoon sent to bypass the outpost was quickly swallowed up in the thick jungle, and though its progress was slow and difficult at first, movement quickened as the light improved. The three men forming the point soon signalled that they had found the trail leading from the outpost to the camp, but that five members of a wood cutting detail, guarded by two Viet Cong soldiers, were on it. That also meant that the prison camp was awake, something the raiding party had wanted to avoid if at all possible. The platoon could hardly afford to wait any longer, yet firing at the guards would alert the other Viet Cong soldiers at the camp.

The platoon's dilemma was solved when firing suddenly broke out from the vicinity of the second outpost. Tiger Force had been fired on as it had approached the outpost by a Viet Cong soldier who had been returning to his post after relieving himself in the nearby woods. He and his two comrades were quickly disposed of, but the enemy at the prison camp would certainly have heard the shots. It was certain that the two guards with the wood cutting detail heard them, for they immediately fled into the jungle, but not before one had been wounded.

As Tiger Force doubletimed up the trail and the first rifle platoon deployed around the camp, the second rifle platoon set up a perimeter near the outpost which had just been overrun. No other shots were fired; the remaining Viet Cong guards had fled by the time the security and assault elements of Tiger Force reached the compound. All that remained behind were the prisoners and their prison.

Standing in the center of the compound, the men of Tiger Force were stunned by what they could see. Here in the middle of the Vietnamese jungle they had found a prison camp as revolting as the one that had existed at Dachau during World War II. The prisoners looked like scarecrows; they were sick and near starvation; every bone in their bodies protruded. They could only stare in dumb amazement at the American soldiers who had suddenly descended upon them. One prisoner, small, emaciated, lay curled up in a ball on the ground—he had died during the night. Almost sickened by the sight, Tiger Force moved quickly to evacuate the area.

The loud speaker equipped aircraft was called in to broadcast an appeal to any prisoners scattered by the Viet Cong guards to return to the compound. While this was going on, the camp was thoroughly searched and prepared for destruction, and the most able prisoners were taken off to the side for questioning. After a big pot of rice prepared by Tiger Force had been happily consumed by the newly liberated prisoners, the little Dachau was burned to the ground and the long trek home begun.

A total of 35 prisoners were finally collected by the raiding party; 11 of the men were in such bad physical condition that they had to be carried. The last group that had come in were the five wood cutters, and this only after the voice coming from the airborne loud speaker had convinced them that the Americans were there to help them, not to harm them.

When the raiding party reached the valley floor again, it halted long enough for the prisoners to be picked up by helicopter and taken to Colonel Meinzen's command post where they were again fed, clothed, and given much needed medical attention. General Westmoreland, viewing the hollow but happy faces of the liberated Vietnamese, summed up the feelings of all those present when he said, "Seeing these pathetic little people certainly revives memories of the horror camps at Dachau and Buchenwald. It's hard to believe that the Viet Cong are treating other Vietnamese like this, but I am delighted that the 'Screaming Eagles' were successful in freeing them."

The decision to conduct the raid had been a difficult one to make, not so much because of the military factors involved, but because of the human factors. Militarily, 100 US soldiers were being employed to destroy, at best, 10 of the enemy's soldiers. No one could have criticized a decision to turn down the raid. A raid had little to gain but 100 troops to lose. But from a human point of view, the raid had to be conducted, and every soldier who participated knew it.

Time, as always, played a critical role. The long delay in achieving the link up of forces could well have been fatal. It did later cause caution to be almost completely abandoned to beat the fast approaching dawn, and this caused the prison guards to be prematurely alerted to the approach of the raiding party. Under other circumstances, all of the prisoners could have been found dead.

The balance of boldness with caution during the raid had been highly commendable, and the raid's success had lasting and far-reaching effects not only upon the liberated prisoners and other Vietnamese in the region, but also upon the determination, dedication, and morale of the participating US troops. The Viet Cong had been given credit for being able to rigidly control all areas not physically held by free world forces. Yet the carefully prepared, well conducted, and boldly executed raid deep into jungled mountains known to contain an NVA force had been successfully accomplished without a single friendly casualty. An enemy sanctuary had been opened to friendly view, the rigid control proved a myth. It was shown beyond doubt that the enemy could be struck hard, over and over again, regardless of where he set up camp.

IV
Ambushes

ONE OF THE most successful tactics employed by the enemy in Vietnam has been the ambush, the most common form of enemy offensive operation that free world forces can expect to encounter. One of Captain Fenlon's squads had been ambushed as it withdrew from a stay-behind ambush position, fortunately without heavy losses.

Usually, though, the enemy's ambushes are based on much more thorough intelligence and detailed planning and executed with surprise, shrewdness, and determination. Certainly not all of them are successful, for in many cases counterambushes have proven to be most effective deterrents, while well-trained friendly forces have been able to overcome the devastating initial effects of an ambush to inflict severe casualties on the ambushing force.

The jungle ambush is not new to US units. But in South Vietnam variations exist which are debilitating to the unprepared. Because of the density of the jungle undergrowth, ambushes are conducted at close quarters—often at less than 15 meters—and within seconds a unit can be under intense, accurate, automatic and small arms fire. To survive, a unit must be able to react quickly and violently, even though it may lose as much as 50 percent of its strength right at the very start of the fight.

In moving to an ambush position, an enemy unit uses ex-

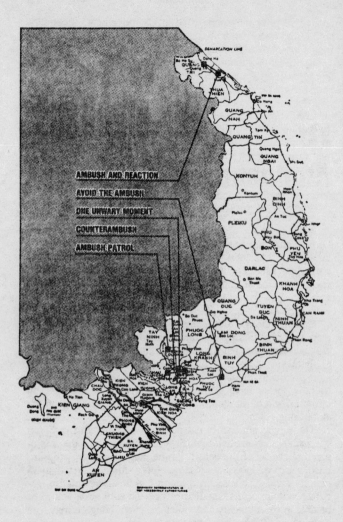

AMBUSH AND REACTION

AVOID THE AMBUSH

ONE UNWARY MOMENT

COUNTERAMBUSH

AMBUSH PATROL

tensive security measures to cover its movement; secondary ambushes, away from the site of the principal ambush, are frequently used to destroy or delay a relief force.

The enemy scrupulously observes silence and immobility in the ambush area and does not begin firing until the attack is heralded by prearranged signal, usually given by the element charged with halting the head of the column that is being ambushed. The action is usually violent and short-lived, and if the ambushed force has been overwhelmed and there is no apparent threat of local reinforcements moving into the area, then the enemy soldiers quickly collect what usable supplies and equipment they can, destroy the rest, and withdraw. Speed is essential to their success, although they will be particularly certain to salvage any ammunition.

When the ambushing force is not strong enough to destroy an ambushed force completely, then the actions of the ambushing force are terminated by prearranged signal when a counteraction begins to take shape. A planned withdrawal, covered by security detachments, is ordered, often by several different routes to frustrate the pursuers, while small detachments are used to maintain visual contact with and to report on the pursuing units.

Security and alertness are the key words which govern combat actions in Vietnam, for the war being waged there is not governed by conventional rules. Each unit, for example, regardless of its size, must be able to provide some type of security for early warning purposes, and must possess sufficient firepower, or have adequate fire support available, to ward off an enemy ambush force until help arrives.

Complacency, an attitude which sometimes overcomes even the best unit, must be guarded against day and night; it has no place in the combat zone. At the moment a unit drops its guard, or relaxes its vigilance, it becomes vulnerable to an enemy who recognizes surprise as a principle of war and who will attack at the most unexpected moment. A US infantry rifle platoon learned the lesson the hard way.

one unwary moment

In October 1965, the 173d US Airborne Brigade invaded a formidable Viet Cong military bastion—the so-called Iron Triangle.[1] This relatively small area, about 30 miles northwest of Saigon, had long been considered invincible by the Viet Cong forces and North Vietnamese Army (NVA) soldiers.

On 8 October, the brigade, moving by air and along the ground, entered the enemy dominated area. And although the initial assaults met only light resistance, the days which followed were filled with small brush contacts punctuated by the explosion of enemy mines which had been set out in large numbers to catch the unwary and unsuspecting.

Two days of punishing movement through the dense undergrowth had netted the 1st Platoon, Company B, 2d Battalion, 503d US Infantry, exactly nothing. The most dramatic feature of their sweep had been seeing the awesome destruction caused the jungle and the huge craters dug out of the ground by the strikes of the US B-52 bombers which had immediately preceded the initial assault.

On the morning of 10 October, the 1st Platoon left Company B's overnight perimeter to take the lead in the company's wedge formation. The hot sunlight which filtered through the jungle canopy revealed no signs of the enemy. At 0930 one of the squads of the platoon broke out into an open rice paddy, and the platoon leader moved forward to take a look at the open area. It was covered by large, four-foot-high, pointed stakes firmly implanted in the ground; only a quick look was needed to see that the stakes had been put in recently.

Feeling that an enemy force must be nearby, the platoon leader led his men cautiously across the paddy; one squad covered while the men in the other two squads crouched low and dashed to the far side. When the far side of the paddy had been secured, the third squad was brought over and the entire platoon again pushed into the jungle.

Near noon, as the company approached an intermediate objective—a point on the ground in a large rubber plantation—shots rang out to the front. The 1st Platoon leader dashed forward, but decided, after a quick look around, that the shots represented only sporadic sniper fire. Company B's commander, Captain Elwood P. Sutton, though, halted his 2d and 3d Platoons and told the 1st Platoon leader to check the area

[1]Combat experience related by CPT William K. S. Olds to CPT Anthony E. Hartle.

to the front; he wanted no part of an enemy ambush and was going to take all the necessary precautions to insure that his unit was not engulfed by a hail of surprise enemy fire.

The 1st Platoon found no enemy soldiers, but it did uncover two hastily prepared booby traps: 81mm mortar rounds concealed on the ground rigged to be detonated from a concealed position some distance away. If the platoon had charged the sniper positions when it had first come under fire, it would have walked right into the booby traps. The platoon leader knew now that the enemy was keeping close track of the company's activities.

A few minutes later, after the company's forward movement had been resumed, the 1st Platoon linked up with the battalion's reconnaissance platoon, the commander of which told the 1st Platoon leader that enemy activity had been reported to the south. After briefing his squad leaders on this new intelligence information, the platoon leader moved his men toward their last objective—a road some 600 meters to their front, and reached it with no other incident. Expecting to receive instructions from Captain Sutton to form a defensive perimeter, the 1st Platoon leader deployed his men and set out local security elements.

Moments later Captain Sutton arrived and issued new instructions: the company had been told to move south along the road and to round up all of the civilians in the area; the latter would be turned over to the brigade's civic action teams which would be moving up the road from the south. The 1st Platoon would again act as the lead platoon.

Knowing that Australian Army units in conjunction with other US units had ripped through the southern section of the Iron Triangle, and having itself driven over almost the entire northern sector of the Triangle with little enemy contact, and now assigned a mission that was essentially a civic action task, the men who made up Company B's 1st Platoon began to feel somewhat complacent. They felt that the operation was about over, that the enemy had again evaded a powerful sweep of free world forces.

As it formed the point of the company's column, feeling that the pressure of finding the enemy was off, the men of the 1st Platoon moved out on the road, the 1st Squad leading with one fire team just off each side of the road. Because the vegetation along the sides of the road was quite thick, the platoon formation soon turned into an elongated wedge with the 1st Squad in the lead.

The platoon had moved only about 200 meters when the 1st Squad leader, Staff Sergeant Richard Banks, sent word back that his men had come upon enemy bunkers, tank traps, and foxholes along the road and were checking them out. Knowing that Captain Sutton would want to know what had happened, the 1st Platoon leader, with his radio operator following close behind, raced forward to see for himself what his 1st Squad had uncovered. *(Map 17)*

He had no sooner arrived at the squad's position than numerous claymore mines, set off by the enemy, detonated simultaneously and raked the open area with flying metal. Booby trapped 81mm mortar rounds exploded and heavy small arms fire poured into the platoon from the jungle wall. The first enemy blast killed five men, including the platoon sergeant and the platoon's aid man; eleven others were wounded, including the platoon leader. The bodies of the wounded and dead lay completely isolated in the killing zone, making it virtual suicide for anyone to attempt to help those still alive.

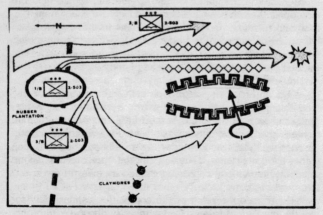

Map 17. One Unwary Moment

The enemy continued to fire at the bodies in the road while the remaining men from the 1st Squad—in a heroic gesture—stood up, opened fire and assaulted the enemy positions. But less than 30 meters from the road enemy soldiers in bunkers and trenches returned the fire, supported by compatriots in the numerous trees which bordered the road. The 1st Squad went to the ground, but kept up its fire; the 3d Squad, under Staff Sergeant Russell Howell, moved up and began firing into the enemy's flank. Now, too, Staff Sergeant Wallace Baker's 2d Squad and Staff Sergeant Willie Boyd's Weapons Platoon had moved up to set up a base of fire to support the 1st and 3d Squads. The fighting was at extremely close quarters and even though friendly armed helicopters were in the air overhead and the platoon was within range of friendly artillery, the close distances prohibited the calling in of the available supporting fires.

When the Weapons Platoon's machineguns opened fire and the 2d Squad reached a position from which it, too, could support by fire, the tide of battle began turning. Within 10 minutes the platoon had established an effective base of fire and had achieved fire superiority.

Meanwhile, Captain Sutton had sent his 2d Platoon to the east and his 3d Platoon to the west to flank the enemy's positions, and these movements caused the entrenched enemy—estimated as a Viet Cong company—to break off the fight and withdraw deeper into the Iron Triangle. While the enemy left the bodies of 17 men in the ambush positions, Company B paid for the battle with 8 dead and 25 wounded. The battle could be considered a draw.

And, so, for one unwary moment, for falling victim to complacency, the 1st Platoon had walked into an enemy ambush and suffered significant casualties. Although the platoon routed the ambush through extraordinary individual efforts and through the quick reaction of those units not caught in the killing zone, the 1st Platoon learned again that complacency has no place in the battle area. Stringent security measures—in this case, proper flank security—has to be observed at all times, and leaders at all levels have to accept the responsibility for seeing that their men do not relax their vigilance. With proper flank security, the 1st Platoon would have detected the enemy ambush, and the key the enemy needed to be successful—

surprise—would have been taken from him. With surprise gone, the enemy could have been fixed in place and would have become easy prey for friendly artillery and air strikes.

ambush and reaction

A few months later, the 2d Battalion, South Vietnamese Marine Corps, began a seemingly routine motor march along National Route #1 from Hue to Dong Ha, roughly 70 kilometers to the northwest.[2] From Dong Ha, the battalion would conduct a series of offensive operations against the enemy forces which had been operating in the area.

The route from Hue was considered clear since no major contact with the enemy had been made along the route for the last 10 months. The battalion was tactically entrucked with the 1st Company leading, followed by the 3d Company, the battalion command group, the Headquarters and Service Company, the 2d Company, and, last, the 4th Company. The battalion commander's ambush instructions in his companies had been perfunctory, even for a situation in which contact was considered to be remote. The instructions:

• Dismount when hit.
• Group by companies.
• Stand and fight as directed by battalion.

Artillery fires had been preplanned along the route out to the range limits of the supporting artillery units, and an artillery forward observer (FO) team moved with the battalion; one battery of 105mm howitzers and one battery of 155mm howitzers would furnish the support so long as the column was within range. For reconnaissance, air spotting, and communications assistance, a South Vietnamese Air Force (VNAF) light airplane would circle over the march column.

After an hour on the road, the battalion was about 14 kilometers from Hue and just outside the range of its supporting artillery batteries. The column was moving over low and rolling hill country, with the open terrain interrupted here and there with rows of short shrubs and thin strands of tall trees. The vegetation was heaviest northeast of the road, with a dense tree line about 300 meters away. Observation and fields of fire in

²Combat experience submitted by LTC P. X. Kelly, USMC.

this direction ended about 75 meters from the head of the column where a slight rise masked all but the tall trees beyond. To the southwest, observation was generally unobstructed, ranging out to 500 meters; fields of fire in this direction were good, but the ground beyond 500 meters was in defilade from the road. The sky was clear, and the day was hot as the temperature hovered between 85 and 90 degrees.

This was the exact place the enemy had selected for an ambush, and it was executed by a reinforced main force Viet Cong battalion at about 0830. The observer in the light airplane had not spotted the enemy, whose camouflage could not have been better, and so the column was taken completely by surprise. At first, an accurate and intense volume of small arms, recoilless rifle, and mortar fire struck the column from its left flank; three trucks were hit within the first few seconds, the column halted and the troops dismounted and deployed along the southwest side of the road, facing in the direction of the enemy fire. But since they had little cover or concealment, casualties began to mount. The back blast from the enemy's recoilless rifles could be seen along the low hills to the front, and small groups of Viet Cong soldiers could be observed maneuvering toward the road. (*Map 18*)

Immediately the battalion commander ordered all of his units to move to the relative sanctuary of a railroad cut some 60 to 75 meters up the road. Since all of the enemy fire had come from the southwest, if the battalion could reach the cut, it would be in a better position to react to the enemy's fires.

But as the units closed on the railroad, the battalion met a blast of fire from an enemy force, estimated to consist of at least two companies, which was in well camouflaged positions near the cut. The battalion commander was mortally wounded, and every man in the command group fell to the enemy's fire. A few South Vietnamese marines managed to reach the cut but they were soon cut down by enemy machinegun fire directed down the railroad tracks from the northwest and by a vicious enemy company-sized attack.

Further down the railroad, the remainder of the Headquarters and Service Company joined up with the 2nd and 4th Companies to set up a defensive perimeter; up the railroad, the 1st and 3d Companies formed a solid perimeter defense in a position that afforded them excellent fields of fire in all directions.

Only six minutes had passed since the ambush had been

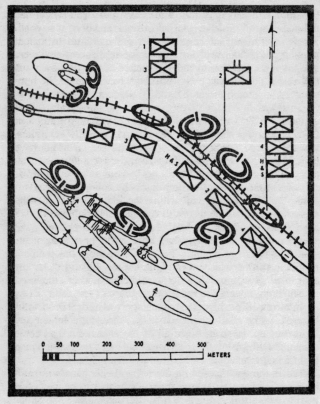

Map 18. Ambush and Reaction

initiated, and the enemy had succeeded in splitting the marine battalion into two parts, each about 500 meters from the other. Their defensive perimeters were not mutually supporting, and the loss of the entire command group had cost the battalion its tactical integrity and made it incapable of employment as a cohesive organization.

But now a US light aircraft with an artillery observed aboard appeared over the scene of the ambush; within ten minutes he was bringing in on the enemy the fires of a US Marine artillery battery which was only four kilometers away and which had been supporting another Marine operation. Soon, too, a US Air Force forward air controller arrived overhead in a light airplane, and began directing air strikes on the enemy positions. The enemy's reaction to the appearance of the two light airplanes was violent, and both were subjected to intense fire from weapons emplaced along the high ground to the southwest of the road.

Some 20 to 25 minutes after they had initiated the ambush, the Viet Cong forces began breaking contact. The air strikes, the artillery fire, the heavy volume of small arms fire laid down by the South Vietnamese marines from their two perimeters all had had their effect.

Forty-five minutes after the initial contact had been reported, a US Marine rifle company arrived by helicopter and took up the pursuit of the withdrawing enemy. By noon, another US Marine company was in the area, together with three South Vietnamese Army (ARVN) battalions. A large portion of the Viet Cong force trying to get away to the west was trapped, and in the reaction part of the engagement which last for the next three days, more than 200 of the enemy were killed.

The ambush was another demonstration of the ability of an enemy force in Vietnam to conduct this type of operation without prematurely disclosing its positions. This particular one had been conducted in broad daylight, by a large force which was encumbered by heavy, crew-served weapons, and positioned within four kilometers of a potential reaction force.

While the Viet Cong commander in this engagement must be given credit for establishing a classic ambush, he made two glaring errors that resulted in his unit taking heavy casualties during its withdrawal. The first error was in initiating the ambush when a reaction force was relatively near—both in time and distance—the ambush site. This might have occurred because the enemy commander was unaware of the presence of major US and ARVN units in the vicinity. It seems more likely, though, that this incident epitomizes the inflexibility of the enemy: the ambush had been planned, it had been laid, and, therefore, it had to be executed despite the presence of forces that would certainly come to the aid of the ambushed unit.

The Viet Cong commander's second error was his failure to provide an adequate and covered route of withdrawal for his units which made up the attack force that struck the marine convoy from the southwest. Those units had to withdraw over open terrain for almost 3,000 meters, thereby providing a lucrative target to air strikes and artillery fires. His units that withdrew to the north and northeast did not have to run this gauntlet of fire, for their withdrawal route passed through a dense forest, under the canopy of which they were able to get away relatively unharmed.

The fact that the South Vietnamese marines had had no prior warning of the presence of a large enemy force waiting in ambush was due largely to the expert camouflage measures employed by the Viet Cong force. Each man wore the standard Viet Cong fiber helmet covered with freshly gathered vegetation; each had a long, cape-like garment made of camouflage material which he used to cover himself from the views of the observer in the light airplane—with the cape in place, he could not be seen from the air at altitudes as low as 500 feet.

The immediate elimination of the battalion command group deprived the South Vietnamese marines of any overall control for the first 15 minutes of the engagement, and the battle quickly evolved into two separate and distinct actions. The southern element, under the command of the battalion's executive officer, fought a rugged, face-to-face battle with a dug-in, determined enemy, and managed to hold its own. The northern element was out of the main killing zone, and did not have to contend with a close-in enemy; nevertheless, that force did take the bulk of the enemy's recoilless rifle and mortar fire—which it did in good fashion—and managed to return a heavy volume of rather effective fire of its own.

For a time it appeared that the marine battalion would suffer an almost complete disaster. What saved the battalion were certain key events: the maintenance of tactical unity by the rifle companies; the skillful employment of those companies by their commanders; and the determination and courage of the individual Vietnamese marine.

avoid the ambush

Another favorite tactic of the enemy in Vietnam is the baited ambush—the jumping of a small force in order to lure larger relief units into another and more deadly ambush.[3] While counterambush techniques are often effective in overcoming such an ambush, the greatest successes against the baited ambush have been enjoyed by those units which used proper formations and security measures when going to the relief of an ambushed unit. This fact was amply demonstrated by the 2nd Battalion, 44th Regiment, 23rd ARVN Infantry Division in February 1966.

At 0730, 21 February 1966, a small convoy of three civilian trucks and two jeeps left Thien Giao, its mission: to pick up supplies and the monthly payroll at Phan Thiet, the capital of Bien Thuan province, about 100 kilometers east of Saigon. The district chief moved with the convoy, which was under the guard of a reinforced platoon of 40 men armed with carbines, automatic rifles, submachineguns, and two machineguns. It was expected that the security of Highway 8, over which the convoy would travel, would be furnished by Popular Force (PF) units stationed along the highway and by the 1st Company, 2d Battalion, 44th ARVN Regiment, whose base camp was about halfway between Phan Thiet and Thien Giao. Air cover for the convoy was provided by a VNAF forward air controller.

In actuality, effective ARVN control over the highway and the surrounding area extended only a short distance from both Phan Thiet and Thien Giao, and the area in between was secure in theory only. The terrain through which Highway 8 passed was open, consisting mainly of rice paddies which were dry at this time of the year; small villages dotted the area at every few kilometers between the district and provincial capitals. All of the bridges along the highway had been partially or completely demolished, although in the dry season usable bypasses had been constructed around the bridges and the streams themselves were fordable. But convoys using the road had to travel at slow speeds and to even halt at times while vehicles individually negotiated the obstacles.

The convoy traversed the 16 kilometers of Highway 8 between Thien Giao and Phan Thiet without incident; shortly after 1300, it departed Phan Thiet for the return journey. Two hours later it was ambushed at a point about four kilometers from Thien Giao. The district chief, still with the convoy, called his

[3]Combat experience submitted by CPT James F. Arthur, Jr.

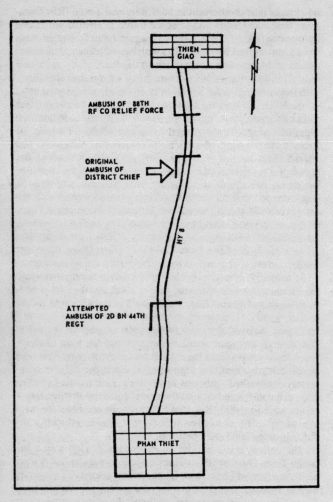

Map 19. Avoid the Ambush

headquarters and ordered the 88th Regional Force (RF) Company based in Thien Giao to come to the aid of the ambushed convoy. (*Map 19*) The 88th Company quickly loaded onto trucks and dashed pell mell into the jaws of a second ambush, which had been set up for just this purpose.

At 1600 the 2d Battalion, 44th ARVN Regiment, the headquarters of which was located in Phan Thiet, was alerted to go to the relief of both the convoy and the 88th Company; and although trucks were made available to lift the battalion, the battalion commander preferred to make the move on foot. He knew that the road was difficult to traverse in places and that there were numerous good ambush positions along the highway which the enemy might occupy. Since he also knew that two forces had already been ambushed that afternoon, and since he had been a Viet Minh in his youth and understood well the idea behind the baited ambush, the battalion commander preferred to sacrifice speed for security. As he left the environs of the city of Phan Thiet, the commander deployed his battalion so that his 2d Company and his Heavy Weapons Company moved off the left side of the road, the 3d Company off the right side of the road. In the various small villages through which the column passed, he dropped off stay-behind patrols to prevent the enemy from encircling his flanks while on the march.

It was at about 1720, as the battalion cleared the village of Tan Dien, that the battalion began receiving fire from its front. Immediately the lead companies went to the ground, the men crawled behind the rice paddy dikes, the enemy fire was returned, and units began to maneuver to flank the enemy. The Viet Cong, expecting a relief column to come up Highway 8 in trucks, had established an L-shaped ambush along the west side of the road, with the base of the L facing south. (*Map 20*)

A dry stream bed 75 meters from the road ran roughly parallel to the highway, and another crossed under a partially destroyed bridge. A bypass had been constructed around the west side of the bridge, although traffic had to descend nearly 15 feet from the level of the road into the stream bed and back up again on the other side. Some 150 meters from the bridge, an irrigation canal ran perpendicular to the highway. These natural terrain features and the obstacle presented by the bypass had provided the Viet Cong with a ready-made ambush position, one that provided them with excellent fields of fire, ob-

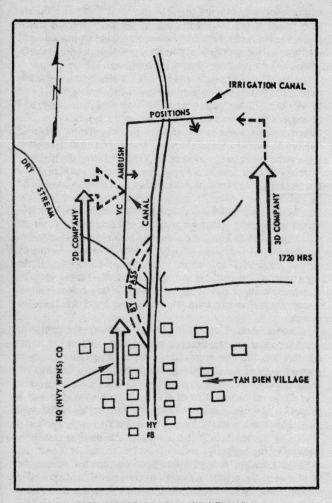

Map 20. Movement of 2d Battalion

servation, cover, and concealment.

The South Vietnamese battalion commander grasped the situation almost instantly, and he directed his 3d Company to concentrate its fire on the Viet Cong units which occupied the irrigation canal to the company's right front and to try to maneuver around the enemy's right flank. Then he instructed his still undetected 2d Company to move forward and into a position behind those enemy soldiers who were firing at the 3d Company from positions along the dry stream bed.

When the 2d Company was in position, it executed a right flank movement and then charged—from just 100 meters away—yelling and screaming toward the Viet Cong positions, overrunning the enemy and engaging them in hand to hand combat before they could turn their weapons around to meet the charge.

Across the road, sensing a reduction in the volume of enemy fire coming from his left flank, the commander of the 3d Company established a base of fire with one platoon and then led his two remaining platoons around the east flank of the Viet Cong positions. As the two platoons closed with the enemy and began to roll up the enemy's flanks, the Viet Cong units tried to break contact and withdraw to the northwest. But from overhead, their movement was detected, and a US Air Force forward air controller, who had been circling the scene of action waiting for just such an opportunity, brought in a flight of F100 jets and decimated the retreating enemy force.

At about the same time, the battalion's 1st Company, which had been performing road security north of the scene of battle, entered the battalion's radio net. Hearing the sound of battle to the south, the company had begun moving toward it and was then located less than a kilometer away. The battalion commander sent the 1st Company westward to intercept the remnants of the Viet Cong force, and then began the task of reorganizing his battalion.

The 2d Battalion, 44th ARVN Regiment thus had successfully thwarted a carefully planned enemy ambush and spoiled what otherwise could have been a clean sweep for the Viet Cong force, a reinforced company from the main force 602d Viet Cong Battalion. The Viet Cong unit had successfully ambushed a small resupply convoy, and this they used as bait to lure reaction forces—which they knew would be sent to the scene—into other carefully planned and prepared ambushes.

In one instance, the enemy was successful, and the 88th Regional Force Company was rendered ineffective within a short time; in the other instance, the enemy was unsuccessful, but only because a smart battalion commander refused to put his units on trucks but rather deployed them wide on each side of the road. From this formation, he had been able to flush out the enemy ambush force, and to flank the enemy position, causing the latter serious losses while taking only light casualties in return.

counterambush

A US unit from the 173d US Airborne Brigade also had good fortune in fending off an enemy's ambush attempt when it, too, properly used security measures and reacted vigorously to the enemy threat.[4]

Just before the arrival of the 1st US Infantry Division in South Vietnam in 1965, US units already in the country were given the task of clearing the base camp areas and the routes that would be used by the division upon its arrival. The 173d US Airborne Brigade was one of the participating US units.

During the latter part of October 1965, the 2d Battalion, 503d US Infantry, then a part of the 173d US Airborne Brigade, was engaged in clearing a section of the road which ran between Saigon and Phu Loi. This road had been closed by the enemy and had become infamous for the numerous ambushes which had been successfully executed along it by Viet Cong units.

Throughout the morning of 17 October, the 2d Battalion's Company C moved northward on the west side of the road, systematically clearing the area within effective ambush distance of the road. The high temperature and humidity made movement through the thickly interlaced vegetation a demanding and punishing struggle.

But the men of Company C, veterans of six months of combat in South Vietnam, moved steadily if cautiously, prepared for any sudden enemy attack.

Because both the platoon leader and platoon sergeant of the company's 3d Platoon had been wounded during a previous operation, Staff Sergeant Edward A. Franklin was acting as

[4]Combat experience related by Staff Sergeant Edward A. Franklin to CPT Anthony E. Hartle.

the platoon leader. He knew that Company B was clearing along the east side of the road in a similar fashion, and kept his platoon in a column formation, with his 3d Squad leading and with his 1st Squad well into the jungle to protect his flank.

Near noon, Franklin's 3d Squad reached a large open area; the squad's point man cautiously raised his hand, the signal for a halt. Franklin moved forward to survey the area and saw, to his front, that heavy vegetation bordered a nearly 60 meter wide open area that was covered by waist-high bushes and vines. The open area extended northward almost 100 meters and then widened into large, level rice paddies. The right side of the clearing appeared to be a solid wall of vegetation extending along a ridge line; running parallel and to the right of the ridge line was the road to Phu Loi. Franklin was uneasy; he knew full well that he was looking at a likely ambush site as he gazed at the ridge sloping up to his right front and the heavy vegetation.

But he had to keep his platoon moving, so he called forward his 2d Squad, attached to it a machinegun, and told Sergeant Nicholas Mrsich, the squad leader, to establish a base of fire at the edge of the open area. (*Map 21*) He then sent one of the 3d Squad's fire teams along the left side of the clearing and, keeping his 1st Squad as a ready reaction force, led the other 3d Squad fire team along the right side of the clearing. This pattern was a familiar maneuver for the 3d Platoon: one squad checking out a danger area, one squad providing fire support, and one squad ready to react as needed.

The fire teams of the 3d Squad proceeded about 100 meters, but found nothing, so Franklin motioned the fire team on the left side of the clearing to join him, and then he and the two fire teams worked their way slowly across the lightly overgrown area adjacent to the rice paddies. Still finding no sign of an enemy unit in the area, Sergeant Franklin signalled the 1st Squad to move along the left side of the open area; he planned to proceed with the 2d and 3d Squads on the right side of the clearing and the 1st Squad on the left. As the 1st Squad moved forward, the company First Sergeant, Desmond Jackson, joined Franklin, and as the two men stepped out into the open to get a better view of what lay ahead, small arms fire erupted from the near woodline; the range was close, Jackson went down, and Franklin leaped for cover. The 3d Squad had run into an enemy ambush.

Map 21. Counterambush

The enemy's fire was so close and intense that Franklin had little time to think. He did estimate that an enemy platoon was firing from the tree line along the ridge, and without hesitation brought the 3d Squad on line and moved it forward in a vigorous assault. Within a few steps the 3d Squad had overrun a foxhole position and killed two Viet Cong soldiers; within another 12 steps, it had overrun another two-man position. Listening to the firing, Franklin could tell that his men were assaulting the flank of the enemy unit. The 3d Squad drove on, cleaning out four more enemy positions before the Viet Cong unit realized its flank was under attack.

As suddenly as it had begun, the ambush was over—the Viet Cong unit, realizing its predicament, began withdrawing from the scene of action.

Because Sergeant Franklin had been ambush conscious, and because his unit had been trained to react rapidly, his platoon had been able to defeat an enemy ambush which had been established to deny use of a main road. When the ambush did take place, Franklin employed his squads in a systematic manner, and conducted an immediate and vigorous assault against a dug-in enemy. Even if his assault squad had not been adequate to do the job, Franklin retained sufficient flexibility to regroup his forces and try again. The proper employment of security measures, immediate action upon contact, aggressiveness, fighting skill—these the 3d Platoon possessed in abundance. Because it did a deadly enemy ambush had been eliminated.

ambush patrol

The enemy in Vietnam are not the only ones who conduct ambushes, for the free world forces often carry out ambushes and ambush patrols that are most successful and result in the destruction of enemy units of all sizes. The advantages that can be gained from the employment of friendly ambushes were highlighted during Operation COCOA BEACH in March 1966, an operation that was a search and destroy mission conducted by the 2d Battalion, 28th US Infantry, then part of the 3d Brigade, 1st US Division, in the Ben Cat district of Binh Duong province.[5]

The 2d Battalion, under the command of Lieutenant Colonel Kyle W. Bowie, moved on foot on 3 March from the brigade's base camp at Lai Khe to the Lo Ke rubber plantation just west of Highway 13, and established a tight defensive perimeter in terrain that was flat and devoid of underbrush except for scattered patches of elephant grass and a few small hedgerows. Although the area to the west of the plantation was thick jungle,

[5]Combat experience submitted by CPT Tyrone P. Fletcher.

there were no apparent major obstacles in the immediate surroundings and the weather was good.

The next day, 4 March, Captain Raymond Blanford's Company A was sent to check out some intelligence reports which had stated that a Viet Cong base camp was located in the dense jungle about two kilometers west of the battalion's perimeter. Captain George Dailey's Company B, at the same time, began search and destroy operations three kilometers north of the battalion's base, while Company C, commanded by Captain Tyrone P. Fletcher, remained in reserve.

At 1140, Company A located the reported Viet Cong base camp and a short fire fight ensued. With assistance from Company C, Company A was able to overrun the camp, inside of which were five small huts, warm rice and fish, and seven large underground cooking stoves, indications that about 60 enemy had only recently occupied the camp.

In the meantime, Captain Dailey reported only negative results during Company B's search and destroy mission but reported that on its return the company had come across a huge trench that extended for several kilometers west of Bau Bang. The trench was deep and had holes in the sides for protection from air attack; fresh dirt and earthworks indicated that the trench, like the base camp, had recently been occupied by a rather large enemy force.

Because of these discoveries, Colonel Bowie, feeling that a large enemy force was in his immediate vicinity, coordinated with the headquarters of the 3d Brigade to insure that the supporting air force and artillery units were well aware of his battalion's exact perimeter and the location of the enemy trench. He also made certain that his men's fighting positions were deep and well constructed. Colonel Bowie also established a four-man listening post at the edge of the thick jungle to the west, and set up three 15-man ambush patrols; these patrols would make the difference in the battle that followed. (*Map 22*)

Thirty minutes after midnight, Bowie received a radio call from the 3d Brigade notifying him the Ben Cat district advisor had reported that a Viet Cong regiment was located four kilometers northeast of Bowie's perimeter. Remembering the trench off in that direction that Company B had located the previous afternoon, Bowie personally alerted all of his companies and told them to conduct a stand to at 0530; this would get the

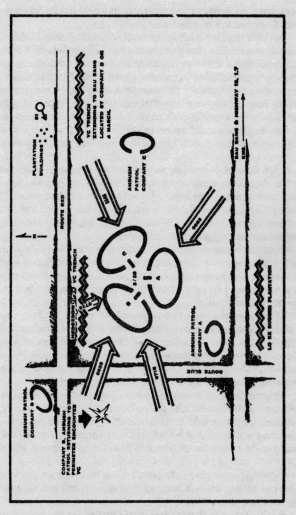

Map 22. Ambush Patrol

battalion fully prepared for the early morning hours, when the Viet Cong normally attacked.

At About 0545, 5 March, Second Lieutenant Robert J. Hibbs, with Company B's ambush patrol at the crossroads of Routes Red and Blue, reported noises from the east; thirty minutes later he reported that a group of women and children were approaching his patrol's position from the east, moving along Route Red. They were moving slowly, Hibbs reported, and some of the women were carrying weapons while almost all of the children carried ammunition. The group halted within 100 meters of the patrol, but without noticing the US ambush unit.

With the aid of a night viewing device, Hibbs could now see a Viet Cong company running towards his position from the north along Route Blue. This enemy unit halted about 50 meters from the patrol, and a man in a white robe, together with two of the Viet Cong soldiers, joined the civilians waiting on Route Red in conversation.

While this conversation was taking place, Hibbs had his men reposition their claymore mines to fire down Route Blue at the Viet Cong company; he also passed the word to his men that they should be prepared to throw hand grenades when the claymores went off.

The man in the white robe rejoined the enemy soldiers, and that force began moving down Route Blue towards the US battalion. As soon as a majority of the enemy soldiers were in the killing zone of the prepositioned mines, Lieutenant Hibbs detonated the claymores; the men in the patrol also began throwing grenades, and the enemy suffered severely.

Hearing the explosions, Colonel Bowie ordered Hibbs to bring his patrol back into the battalion's perimeter, and the young lieutenant made haste to comply. But when his patrol reached a position some 500 meters from the perimeter, Hibbs' men ran into the rear of another Viet Cong company which was even then deploying to attack the battalion. Taking the new enemy under fire, the patrol launched another grenade attack, fighting through the enemy company and reaching the perimeter at about 0630.[6]

While Company B's ambush patrol battled the enemy, Com-

---

[6]Lieutenant Hibbs was killed during this action, but for his outstanding performance of duty was posthumously awarded the Congressional Medal of Honor.

pany A's patrol operating to the south of the perimeter had also spotted Viet Cong soldiers who, the patrol reported to Colonel Bowie, were all around the patrol's position and moving towards the battalion's perimeter. In the darkness, the patrol mingled with the Viet Cong unit, joining onto the tail of a passing enemy squad. As the enemy unit neared the perimeter, the US patrol opened fire on the nearby enemy soldiers and began tossing grenades at others. The patrol was further aided in its return to the friendly perimeter by rounds from Viet Cong mortars which, fired from the vicinity of the plantation buildings, mistakenly fell among the enemy soldiers.

Colonel Bowie knew that his battalion could soon expect an all out enemy attack, so he called in Company C's ambush patrol from the east and the four-man listening post from the west. By 0630, all of the patrols and the listening posts were back and the battalion was intact in its perimeter.

The first wave of the main Viet Cong attack was launched from the northwest at 0635; a second wave came ten minutes later, this from the northeast; still a third wave attacked from the east at 0655. Fighting became continuous, and the enemy threw in a fourth attack, from the southwest, just after 0700. Every attack was thrown back although one resupply helicopter which managed to reach the battalion with badly needed ammunition was shot down by the enemy as it attempted to take off.

But help was on the way as the 3d Brigade commander sent the 1st Battalion, 16th US Infantry by helicopter to cut the enemy's withdrawal routes to the north and east and to take some of the pressure of Bowie's battalion. This was the 3d Brigade's ready reaction force, and its appearance served to distract at least some of the enemy's attention from the 2d Battalion's perimeter near the rubber plantation.

By 1200 the firing had subsided, and Bowie had Company A send out a patrol to the south to maintain contact with the withdrawing enemy. The patrol did meet up with a Viet Cong company preparing positions from which it could ambush any relief force that moved by ground from the 3d Brigade's base at Lai Khe. Company A's patrol, after fixing the enemy's position, backed off, but called in heavy artillery fires that caused the enemy company a number of casualties and forced it to withdraw from the area. From documents recovered at the battle scene, the enemy unit which attacked Bowie's men was identified as the 272d Regiment reinforced by units from a heavy weapons battalion.

Colonel Bowie's ambush patrols, positioned along likely avenues of approach, provided him with early warning of the approach of a large enemy force. His patrols were able to inflict heavy casualties on the approaching enemy and disrupted and disorganized those enemy units which had thought, until that time, that their approach had been undetected. The Viet Cong attack, when it came, was no surprise to the 2d Battalion and the enemy was met with heavy fires from the US infantrymen and from their supporting artillery and aircraft.

The danger of ambushes and hit-and-run sniping actions make even more necessary SOPs, rehearsals, battle drills, alertness, and swift reactions. There is no magic formula for counterambush success. Rather, success depends on a unit's ability to recover from the shock of a violent initial contact, on the unit's ability to build up an immediate and heavy volume of fire, and on the unit's ability to maneuver under rapid, close enemy fire, and on the unit's ability to repel an enemy's assault. A good tactic in Vietnam has been for an ambushed unit to immediately assault in the direction of the ambush.

While relatively open terrain may seem to be unsuitable for an ambush site, the enemy has the boldness and camouflage skills necessary to conduct ambushes in even the most unlikely areas. Regardless of the nature of the terrain, the commander in Vietnam cannot afford to relax his guard.

The enemy's main limitation is his inability to react to US mobility and firepower. His natural oriental tendency to operate in patterns is reinforced by his severe lack of communications, and once committed to a plan, he rarely adjusts it as the battle develops.[7]

A leader must insure that each of his soldiers is well trained and has developed good habits—habits so deeply ingrained that even under the strain of battle, each soldier, automatically, will do the right thing.

[7]LTC David H. Hackworth, "No Magic Formula," INFANTRY, January–February 1967, pp. 32–37.

V

Attack

DECISIVE RESULTS IN any war are obtained only by offensive action, action in which a commander exercises his initiative and imposes his will on the enemy. Offensive action demands the highest order of training, leadership, and morale, and places great reliance on the professional competence of all commanders to arrive at sound decisions.

The will to win is the essence of the spirit of the offensive; it is a source of strength for the attacker. The infantry attack, or the attack of a combined arms team, rests on the twin pillars of the fighting spirit and aggressiveness of officers and noncommissioned officers—on courageous, intelligent leadership—and upon the individual initiative of the private soldier. For all, it is the continuing determination to take one more step, to fire one more round.

Offensive operations are undertaken to carry the battle to the enemy with the ultimate purpose to destroy the enemy's forces. On occasion, an infantry force in the offense will be assigned other missions: to seize specific territory or terrain, to develop the enemy's dispositions, to deprive the enemy of required resources, or to divert the enemy's attention from other areas. But the ultimate purpose of the offense should never be forgotten.

The fundamentals of offensive tactics—general rules evolved from logical and time proven applications of the principles of

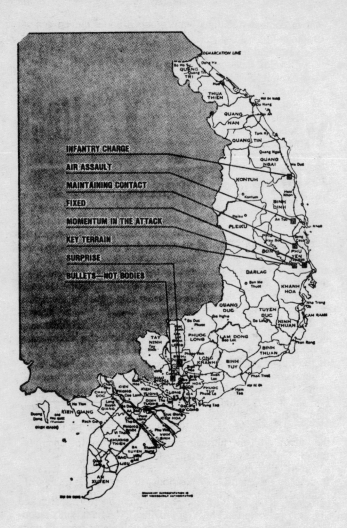

INFANTRY CHARGE

AIR ASSAULT

MAINTAINING CONTACT

FIXED

MOMENTUM IN THE ATTACK

KEY TERRAIN

SURPRISE

BULLETS—NOT BODIES

war in combat situations—are grouped under eleven general headings

• Gain and maintain contact.
• Develop the situation.
• Exploit known enemy weaknesses.
• Seize or control key terrain.
• Retain the initiative.
• Neutralize the enemy's capability to react.
• Advance by fire and maneuver.
• Maintain the momentum of the attack.
• Concentrate superior combat power at the decisive time and place.
• Exploit success.
• Provide for the security and integrity of the force.

The degree of success obtained by an infantry commander from the use of these fundamentals will depend, of course, largely on his imaginative and reasoned application of them to specific situations. In Vietnam, flexibility and speed in the employment of combat power are paramount, every effort is made to drive forward at those points where the attack has been successful. And pressure applied night and day denies the enemy respite from battle, the ability to execute an orderly withdrawal, the opportunity to recoup losses, and the opportunity to gain the initiative.

maintaining contact

The importance of maintaining contact with the enemy in a jungle environment cannot be overemphasized. Vegetation, the terrain, natural obstacles, darkness, all make this a difficult task at best. Many times a unit will make contact only to discover that the enemy has disappeared into the jungle to choose his own time and place for the next engagement.

Such was the case on a hot, humid day in March 1966, as the 1st Battalion, 327th US Infantry, then a part of the 1st Brigade, 101st US Airborne Division, conducted a search and destroy operation in Phu Yen province. The battalion's reconnaissance element—two platoons of volunteers from all units of the battalion under the command of 1st Lieutenant Norman L. Grunstad—moved well ahead, proceeding cautiously through open rice paddy country toward ambush positions to be set up on routes leading into a village suspected of being a Viet Cong headquarters.[1]

Just after noon, the reconnaissance unit reached a large stream. Lieutenant Grunstad moved one of his platoons into a covering position and then crossed the other at a fording site; he realized that the platoon making the crossing would be vulnerable to any enemy fire as it waded through the water to the other side. (*Map 23*)

Lieutenant Grunstad's fears were well founded, for as soon as the platoon began its crossing, it received sporadic enemy fire. The platoon leader, Lieutenant John D. Howard, dashed forward and led his platoon to cover on the far side, his crossing aided by the covering platoon's machinegun and M79 grenade launcher fires. He then began an often used maneuver: he shifted his M79 grenade launchers to the left flank and then sent a squad around to the right to eliminate the enemy position. The enemy force that had been opposing the crossing withdrew into the jungle, and Lieutenant Howard's squad found only bloody clothing to indicate that the enemy had sustained at least one casualty. The squad did determine that the enemy force had moved away over a well used trail.

Suspecting that his men had hit an early warning position, Lieutenant Grunstad pushed on with his pursuit to maintain contact with the enemy. He maneuvered with extreme caution, though, for he knew that his small force at any time could be ambushed or overwhelmed by a larger enemy force.

A few minutes later, the platoons broke out of the heavy brush through which they had been moving into rice paddy terrain and observed a squad of enemy soldiers running across their front about 300 meters away. Grunstad brought his leading platoon on line and had the men open fire on the enemy; at the same time he sent the other platoon to establish flank security. Several enemy fell, but were carried away by their companions.

Lieutenant Grunstad moved out again to take up the pursuit, and, just after 1500, the enemy soldiers were again seen, this time running into a hamlet which was known to be a Viet Cong sanctuary. As Grunstad's platoons moved toward the hamlet, they were taken under fire. As the enemy fire increased, he

[1]Combat experience related by LT Norman Grunstad to CPT Anthony E. Hartle.

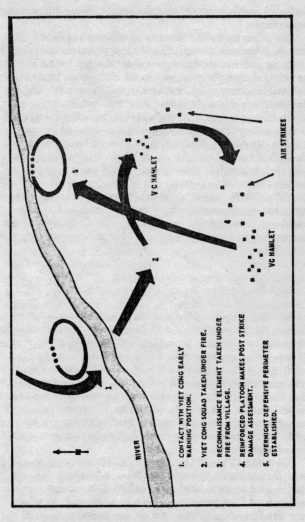

1. CONTACT WITH VIET CONG EARLY WARNING POSITION.
2. VIET CONG SQUAD TAKEN UNDER FIRE.
3. RECONNAISSANCE ELEMENT TAKEN UNDER FIRE FROM VILLAGE.
4. REINFORCED PLATOON MAKES POST STRIKE DAMAGE ASSESSMENT.
5. OVERNIGHT DEFENSIVE PERIMETER ESTABLISHED.

RIVER

VC HAMLET

VC HAMLET

AIR STRIKES

Map 23. Maintaining Contact

called for an immediate air strike before proceeding to enter the village.

Darkness was only an hour away at the end of the air strike, but as there was no sign of enemy opposition, the two US platoons moved into the heavily cratered target areas. The enemy had again withdrawn, although a much larger number than before—captured documents indicated that a Viet Cong battalion had been caught in the air strike, and heavily trodden paths leading into the surrounding jungle were littered with torn and bloody clothing, small items of equipment, and blood trails.

The day ended with Lieutenant Grunstad's men policing the battlefield and securing for the night. His reconnaissance force had been successful in maintaining contact with an enemy force and causing that force a number of casualties with a well directed air strike. The decision to fight or run had been wrested from the enemy commander—he was forced to flee with his dead and wounded, leaving behind valuable documents that contributed to a subsequent defeat of his unit by a larger American force.

fixed

While finding the enemy in the jungle is not always easy, fixing him in position is as difficult and often fraught with frustrations. Company C, 2d Battalion, 502d US Infantry, discovered just how frustrating fixing the enemy can be.

In early February 1966, the 2d Battalion, commanded by Lieutenant Colonel Henry Emerson, initiated a search and destroy mission through a series of company sized helicopter assaults in the Tuy Hoa district of Phu Yen province near the coast in central Vietnam. First contact with the enemy was made by the battalion's Company B. Company C was ordered into the area to assist.[2]

En route to assist Company B, Captain Robert Murphy, who commanded Company C, sent one squad from his unit to take a look at the hamlet of My Canh 2, a security measure he felt would justify the time and effort involved. As it turned out, his squad made contact at the northeastern limits of the hamlet and two of the men were wounded by small arms fire.

[2]Combat experience related by CPT Robert Murphy to LT Terry H. Reilly.

Unfortunately, Captain Murphy did not have the time to send over a larger force, but had to go on and link up with the other US company. This was accomplished without further incident and faced with two US rifle companies, the Viet Cong force that had been harassing Company B broke contact and withdrew into the jungle. Contact could not be reestablished.

On the next day, the battalion turned west and returned to a field base camp. Captain Murphy was still concerned about My Canh 2, though, and asked Colonel Emerson to let him take his company out the following day to conduct a further reconnaissance of the hamlet. Emerson approved, thinking that a smaller force might have a better chance of finding the enemy.

When Captain Murphy left the base camp on his reconnaissance mission, he took with him only his 2d and 3d Platoons; his 1st Platoon and Weapons Platoon had been designated to provide security for the battalion command post area and were not available.

The two platoons reached the hamlet at 0900, and Murphy sent the 2d Platoon to occupy a blocking position 250 meters northwest of the hamlet with an alternate mission of acting as a maneuver element if any contact developed. When that platoon signalled it was in position, Captain Murphy and the 3d Platoon began moving toward a large irrigation ditch which ran between them and the hamlet.

The ditch was crossed without incident, but on the other side the platoon began receiving heavy fire from the hamlet. As Captain Murphy ordered his machineguns to deploy, an enemy squad 50 meters to his left also opened fire. Because he and the 3d Platoon were now pinned down, Murphy radioed his 2d Platoon to attack the hamlet from the north. (*Map 24*)

Lieutenant James Beitz, the 2d Platoon leader, immediately began moving his men forward, noticing that the enemy firing on the 3d Platoon occupied a number of well constructed bunkers reinforced with sandbags and with overhead cover. As his men opened fire on the bunkers, they, in turn, began receiving fire from other bunkers which had been undiscovered up to this time. Beitz radioed this information to Captain Murphy. The latter, realizing he was up against a large enemy unit, called Colonel Emerson for reinforcements, and called in an air strike and supporting artillery fires to soften the enemy's hold on the hamlet. Despite the effectiveness of the supporting fires, the enemy threw back every assault tried by the company.

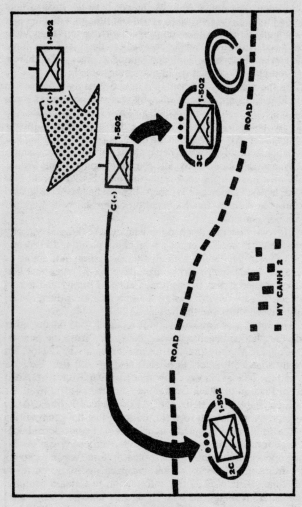

Map 24. Fixed

At noon, other units from the battalion began moving into the area by helicopter. Company B established a blocking position south of the hamlet, while the battalion's Tiger Force, a reinforced reaction platoon of nearly company strength, knocked out the enemy squad that had been firing into the 3d Platoon's left flank, and then blocked the eastern approach to the hamlet. (*Map 25*)

It was not until late afternoon that all of the units of the battalion were properly positioned; but night was coming on and the decision was made to postpone the attack until the following morning. Since all of the routes out of the hamlet were apparently blocked, the enemy could not get away undetected during the night. Unfortunately, all of the routes were

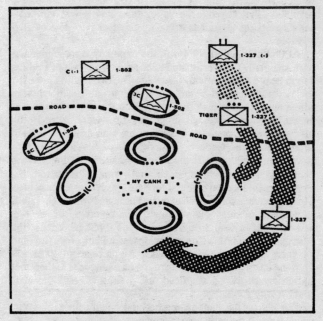

Map 25. Closing the Gap

not blocked, and the enemy did manage to get out. The next morning the US battalion found only a number of enemy dead.

momentum in the attack

Company B, 2d Battalion, 7th US Cavalry, part of the 1st US Cavalry Division, was more successful in demonstrating another important offensive fundamental—maintaining the momentum in the attack—in an action in which it participated in early 1966 during Operation EAGLE CLAW.[3]

The operation itself took place in the Son Lon valley complex along the central coast of Vietnam and involved a company sized search and destroy operation by Company B, then commanded by Captain Myron Diduryk. Intelligence reports had spotted an enemy unit of unknown size in the dense jungle vegetation that covered the valley floor and it was the company's mission to find that enemy force and to destroy it if possible.

At 0825, 15 February 1966, the company came under fire from an enemy force estimated to be about a platoon of soldiers dug in near a small stream. (*Map 26*) The two leading platoons returned the fire and began maneuvering into positions from which they could assault the enemy. But the enemy's fire continued at a heavy rate and supporting fires were called in; by 1100 the enemy position was being hit with artillery fire and an air strike, and Captain Diduryk ordered his 3d Platoon to assault immediately after the air strike had been completed.

At 1145 the air strike ended, and, without hesitation, the men of the 3d Platoon charged forward, even before the echoes from the bomb explosions had died. The squads moved in rapid, coordinated bounds, maintaining a heavy volume of fire. As half of a squad would dash forward for about 20 meters, the other half, from prone firing positions, would place its fire onto the enemy. When the platoon reached a point about 40 meters from the enemy entrenchments, the men clambered to their feet and charged forward at a dead run, yelling as loudly as they could. (*Map 27*)

But before the platoon reached the enemy lines, the Viet Cong force—actually two companies of a main force regi-

[3]Combat experience related by CPT Myron Diduryk to CPT Anthony E. Hartle.

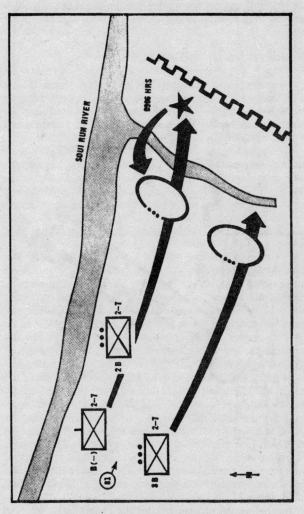

SQUI RUN RIVER

0996 HRS

2-7

2 B

2-7

B(−)

B1

2-7

2-7

2 B

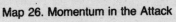

Map 26. Momentum in the Attack

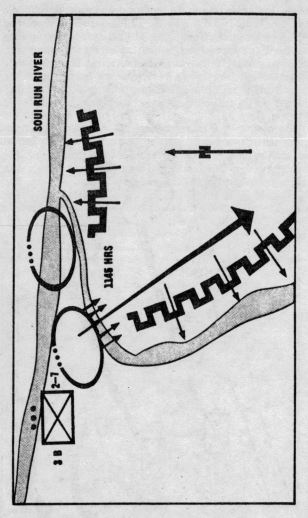

Map 27. Assault by 3d Platoon

ment—broke and ran to the south and southeast, directly into the fires being laid down by the 2d Platoon and a supporting aerial rocket artillery unit. The 3d Platoon drove on, rolling up the entire enemy line, which extended far to the south, adjusting artillery and mortar fire as it advanced. Diduryk brought in his 2d and 1st Platoons to increase the momentum of the assault and to exploit the 3d Platoon's breakthrough, and they fanned out to the east and drove south just behind the 3d Platoon. (*Map 28*)

By now, the enemy's resistance was completely disorganized, and at 1450, broke contact; Diduryk called his platoons to a halt so that they could be resupplied and reorganized. The enemy battalion commander had been captured, together with considerable materiel and documents.

The assault by the 3d Platoon, launched immediately after heavy air and artillery fires had been placed on the enemy's

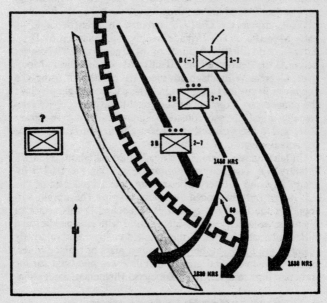

Map 28. Driving Forward

positions, capitalized on the psychological effect of fixed bayonets, fierce shouting, speed, and violence, as well as on a heavy volume of supporting small arms fire; its momentum had been strengthened as the other two rifle platoons of the company swept into the breach in the enemy lines and broadened the base of the attack, keeping the enemy in a disorganized state and preventing him from organizing another defensive line.

bullets—not bodies

On other occasions in Vietnam, bullets, not bodies, have been used quite successfully to develop a situation that has about it an aura of uncertainty and potential doom. For an assault against an undetermined force in an undeveloped situation can result in unnecessary losses. When firepower is available, it should be used to neutralize the enemy first before a unit is committed to an assault that could prove its undoing.

The first United States Army unit to deploy to the Republic of Vietnam was the 173d US Airborne Brigade (Separate) in early May 1965.[4] The Brigade was then commanded by Brigadier General Ellis W. Williamson, who emphasized whenever he could the deliberate and effective use of firepower. Moreover, General Williamson advanced the concept of using this firepower in any and all situations where its use might preclude the unnecessary exposure of personnel to hostile fire. He continually urged his subordinate commanders to use firepower first, and to use as much as necessary in lieu of or to precede the actual advance of the troops.

In late January 1966, the Brigade's 2d Battalion, 503d US Infantry was assigned the mission of securing the 1st US Infantry Division Artillery's base camp, located just east of Phu Loi on an old abandoned Japanese airstrip. The terrain surrounding the base was typical of that found in this sector of Vietnam: secondary jungle interspersed with rice paddies and rubber plantations. While the jungle's canopy was relatively open, at ground level the jungle was a mass of tangled vines, bush, scrub trees, and grass. Visibility was poor and for the most part limited to less than 10 meters. Movement, navigation,

[4]Combat experience submitted by CPT Romie L. Brownlee.

and control would be difficult and complicated for any unit committed to action in this area.

Prior to taking on this assignment, the battalion had been conducting operations in the remote and sparsely populated jungles of War Zone D to the south where restrictions on the use of firepower were few. But the area around Phu Loi was more densely populated and several villages dotted the area; these conditions placed restrictions on the use of firepower; and the units had been instructed not to fire unless fired on or unless they observed a hostile act.

Units from both the 173d US Brigade and 1st US Infantry Division had conducted several clearing operations within the area, and the influence exerted by the US troops was everywhere apparent. But while intelligence reports pointed out that there were seldom any large size enemy units that moved through the area, there still remained a strong political infrastructure and associated small, hard core units. The latter operated usually as squads and were notoriously adept at ambushing and in employing command detonated mines.

The men of the 2d Battalion knew that the best way to secure the base camp was to search aggressively and to patrol the surrounding areas. It came as no surprise, therefore, to Captain Romie L. Brownlee, commanding Company B, when an order came down for his unit to conduct a search and clear operation in the jungles northeast of Phu Loi.

The unmistakable sound of a rifle shot cracked through the jungle, and the combat experience of the men of Company B was apparent as they dropped instantly to the ground. Captain Brownlee's first impression was that one of the men in the 2d Platoon—the base platoon on the left—had accidentally discharged his weapon. The company had been moving in its usual company formation with two platoons forward in column, followed by the Weapons Platoon and the other rifle platoon; in effect, the company formed four separate files moving parallel and adjacent to each other. In the dense jungle, the files were seldom more than 50 meters apart.

Since the shot had sounded as though it had come from his left front, Brownlee called Lieutenant George Reynolds, the 2d Platoon leader, and asked for some sort of explanation. Reynolds, also suspecting that one of his men accidentally might have fired his weapon, was in the process of checking on the mystery of the lone round. But before he could reply to Captain Brownlee's query, another rifle shot sounded. There was no mistaking this one—it was incoming.

Staring hard at the dense, green jungle foliage in front of him, making one more vain attempt to peer through it and failing, Brownlee eased back down against the ground. It was the same old problem: one just could not see a thing!

The radio operator chose this moment to hand his commander the radio handset. Lieutenant Reynolds' voice was calm as he reported that the last shot had been an incoming one, and that none of his men had been responsible for either of the rounds. The platoon leader also reported that the shots had come from his left front and asked if Captain Brownlee wanted him to take some of his men to check out that area.

Brownlee decided against this course of action, for things hadn't gone smoothly all day. Earlier that day—it was now 1455—his company had joined with Troop A, 1st Battalion, 4th US Cavalry for the movement to the objective area. The plan had called for Troop A to transport Company B on its personnel carriers to a dismount point in the area in which the company was to conduct its search and destroy operation. The rifle company would then search an area of dense secondary jungle while the troop swept the abandoned rubber plantations which occasionally broke up the dense jungle. Both units would then rendezvous at a designated point early enough to make the trip back to the base camp prior to darkness—Troop A had an important mission scheduled for the next day and needed some time for preparation.

Company B had loaded on the personnel carriers at daybreak and the combined force started the move along the road that ran northeast from Phu Loi. Captain Brownlee had decided that his men would ride on top of the carriers rather than inside the iron boxes, for in this area the greatest danger was not from small arms fire but from mines buried in the road that detonated as vehicles passed over them. A mine exploded underneath a personnel carrier would probably kill all of the men riding inside. Men riding on top, though, stood a good chance of being blown clear.

But the movement did not go as planned, for on four separate occasions the column had had to halt while thrown tracks were replaced. These delays placed units far behind the schedule they were supposed to be following; they had expected to arrive in the objective area no later than 0930—it had been 1230 before the dismount point had been reached. The units had split then, agreeing to meet again four hours later. *(Map 29)*

For the first two hours after leaving the dismount point the trek had seemed to be just another walk in the woods. A point squad had been pushed well out to the front, and to prevent losing the squad, Captain Brownlee had had the squad halt at frequent intervals until the company could close on it. The company had just made contact with the point squad, and the latter was just preparing to move out again, when the first shot had banged through the jungle.

Now the men of Company B lay on their stomachs in a dense, silent world of green. For Captain Brownlee, with only two hours left in which to complete his mission and rejoin Troop A, the time for decision had arrived. Was his company faced by a sniper? Or were there more enemy out there waiting to ambush his unit if it moved any farther into the jungle?

He remembered some earlier battles in which his company had participated—when Company A had pursued several Viet Cong soldiers into a mined area, and when Company B itself had been ambushed not from this very same spot several months earlier. Brownlee felt that his company was being enticed into an enemy trap, and this he was determined to resist at all costs.

It was then that he thought of General Williamson's phrase: "Use bullets, not bodies." He remembered the General stressing the point for his units not to send men into an area where bullets could be sent first. He began issuing orders to his platoon leaders: the 2d Platoon would form a base of fire oriented toward the area from which the shots had come; Lieutenant Jim Stanford's 3d Platoon would put two squads on line at a 30-degree angle from the right flank of the 2d Platoon's base of fire; the remainder of the 3d Platoon and Lieutenant Tom Dooley's 1st Platoon would provide security for the flanks and rear. All movement was to be made with extreme stealth. The Weapons Platoon leader called in then and reported that he had located a bomb crater and was emplacing his one 81mm mortar in the crater and would be prepared to give supporting fires in just a few minutes.

Captain Brownlee had also instructed his artillery forward observer to notify the supporting artillery battery of the situation and to furnish the battery the necessary firing data for it to

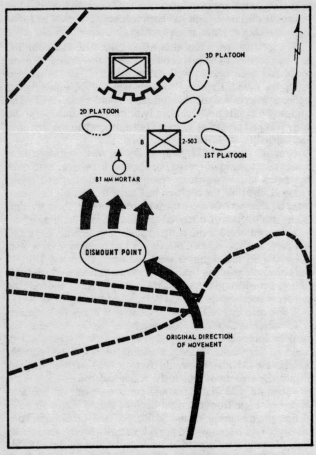

Map 29. Bullets—Not Bodies

place a marking round some 600 meters to the front, and to be prepared to walk in its fire from that point onto any enemy positions that might be encountered.

As the platoons reached their designated positions, the platoon leaders called in. It was Captain Brownlee's plan to have the 2d Platoon open fire on the area to its front—a reconnaissance by fire—while the 3d Platoon's squads would assault the area from the right or provide additional fire support if an assault were not feasible.

At 1520 Brownlee gave the order to open fire, and the jungle silence was shattered by the noise sent up by the 2d Platoon's 30 M16 rifles and two machineguns. Almost simultaneously, the jungle to the front erupted violently with several earth shaking explosions—the enemy had detonated several buried mines.

The 2d Platoon's firing slackened noticeably for a moment or two, and then resumed in full volume. The men had been lifted off the ground by the violent explosions, and Captain Brownlee felt certain that the platoon had suffered casualties. He knew, though, that his platoon leaders would give him casualty reports as soon as possible, so he turned to his artillery forward observer to request the artillery to begin firing. But the forward observer had already called for the marking round, and as he located it, began adjusting his artillery in closer to Company B. Thus far, the company had received only a few rounds of small arms fire from the enemy.

Brownlee called Lieutenant Colonel George E. Dexter, the battalion commander, to inform him of the company's situation. Dexter, who was in the air in a command and control helicopter, instructed Brownlee to move the company back about 200 meters and to walk the artillery in closer than before. This would take care of any enemy immediately in front of the company.

As the forward observer continued to adjust the fires of the artillery battery, Captain Brownlee pulled Company B back into a company perimeter. From his helicopter, Dexter could see red smoke in the area where the artillery was impacting, and knowing that the enemy on several occasions had used smoke as a signalling device to deceive US units, called Brownlee to make certain that company B had been pulled back—if the smoke was not being used by the company, then the enemy was using it in an attempt to get the artillery fires stopped.

Assured that the company was indeed out of the area, Dexter ordered Brownlee to assemble Company B and move to the rendezvous point to join up with Troop A. He also called for an air strike to take place just as soon as the company cleared the strike area.

On the ground, Company B started moving to the rendezvous area; from behind came the sounds of the air strike. Just a short time later, the men saw the tanks and personnel carriers of Troop A break out of the jungle.

The few rounds of small arms fire that the company had received during the engagement indicated that Company B was dealing with only a small force of enemy soldiers, possibly only two or three people. These few, though, intended to lure the US unit into the killing zone of several command detonated mines, probably artillery and mortar rounds that had been collected, fused, and buried in the ground or hung in trees. Had Captain Brownlee permitted any of his platoons to charge blindly forward, Company B would have taken numerous casualties. As it turned out, the heavy volume of fire laid down by the company caused the enemy to trigger his mines prematurely and before any US soldiers had arrived in the killing zone.

air assault

Both flexibility and speed in the employment of offensive combat power have received a tremendous impetus from the introduction of the airmobile concept, a concept that was only a wishful dream until advances in aviation technology over the past several years brought it to fruition. And because the concept is no longer a dream, today's airmobile units can go from one operation to another with great speed and flexibility, while multiple operations can be conducted with less individual preparation, great immediacy, and more continuous action.

The Ben Khe operation conducted by the 1st Battalion, 8th US Cavalry between 18-20 December 1965 can stand as a classic example of the flexibility inherent within an airmobile infantry battalion and its supporting forces.[5] The operation itself

[5]Combat experience submitted by LTC Kenneth D. Mertel, USA.

was planned with little available intelligence, under adverse weather conditions, and with actual ceilings at about 200 feet and visibility about three-fourths of a mile. Thus, the weather precluded normal tactical air support, while the nature of the operation—an airmobile brigade sized operation with three participating assault infantry battalions—denied all but the minimum of artillery support.

In spite of these obstacles, morale and enthusiasm in the 1st Battalion ran high during the days before the operation. The battalion had only recently completed a 14-day action in an area 15 miles south of An Khe, and while little enemy contact had been recorded, the battalion did achieve a high degree of polish and professionalism in airmobile techniques.

Commanded by Lieutenant Colonel Kenneth D. Mertel, the 1st Battalion was alerted on 17 December to join the 3d Brigade, 1st US Cavalry Division to take part in Operation CLEAN HOUSE scheduled to take place near Ben Khe, a little town just north of Highway 19 and about midway between Qui Nhon and the An Khe pass. In a heavy rain, the battalion moved by truck to an assembly area east of the pass to complete its preparations for the air assault the following day; it rained for the remainder of that day, with only intermittent breaks, and would rain for the next three days.

The brigade plan allotted the 1st Battalion certain additional supporting units, among which were an engineer platoon, two platoons of transport helicopters, and a South Vietnamese Popular Force platoon. The battalion could also expect additional transport helicopters as the time came for it to be airlifted into its objective area.

Intelligence about the enemy was vague, although it was believed that a main force Viet Cong battalion would be in the vicinity of the battalion's landing zones; several local force Viet Cong units were also believed to be in the same general area. Excellent maps were available, as was an extremely good aerial photograph that had been taken by an Army OV-1 Mohawk aircraft forty-eight hours earlier. The photograph gave excellent details of the battalion's objective—a small hill about 75 feet higher than the surrounding rice paddies—and helped confirm the primary landing zone. It was also apparent that some recent work had been done by an enemy force in constructing some sort of fortification complex on the hill.

Despite the rain, Colonel Mertel and a number of his staff

officers made a limited aerial reconnaissance of the objective during the afternoon of 17 December, making two high level passes over the general area to pinpoint the objective, landing zones, and likely enemy targets. Just prior to dark, after he had issued his battalion order, Mertel made one more flight over the objective, this time with his rifle company commanders so that the latter could see the terrain on which they would be fighting the next morning. Both aerial reconnaissances were of limited duration and were flown at an altitude of 2,500 feet in an attempt not to alert the enemy to the impending air assault.

Mertel's order called for an air assault, the seizure of the objective, evacuation or destruction of all enemy supplies, destruction of Viet Cong structures and defenses, and the evacuation of all civilian male personnel of military age. The battalion would be relieved on 20 December and would then revert to the control of its parent unit, the 1st Brigade.

His fire plan provided for a 30-minute artillery preparation on two landing zones, Tonto and Trigger, followed by a two-minute barrage from a supporting aerial rocket artillery unit immediately preceding the landing of the first lift of 24 UH-1D transport helicopters. In all there would be four lifts of 24 helicopters each, with 30 minutes between lifts and one company to a lift. Company C would be first in, followed by Company B and then Company A. A provisional rifle company, Company D, would act as the battalion's reserve. Although a small forward battalion command post would tag along with Company C, Mertel planned to command the battalion from the air during the initial stages. With him in his command and control helicopter would be his S2, S3, S3 Operations Sergeant, artillery liaison officer, and two radio operators, in addition to the two pilots and the crew chief. A US Air Force liaison officer would be with Company C. (*Map 30*)

The assault went off pretty much as planned although the artillery preparation was sporadic, the fires having been shifted to support the first assault battalion which had run into considerable enemy opposition at another location. Company C arrived over LZ Tonto at 0900, right on schedule, and the 24 helicopters touched down simultaneously. No sooner had the company left the helicopters, though, than it began to receive enemy small arms and 60mm mortar fire from high ground to the southwest. The men returned the fire and then prepared to

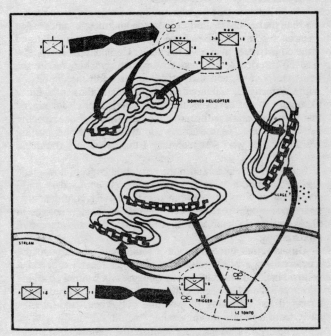

Map 30. Air Assault

carry out the planned attack toward the objective which lay some 1,200 meters away.

While his unit reorganized on LZ Tonto, Company C's commander noticed one of the helicopter gunships that had been providing fire support fall to the ground near the company's objective, apparently a victim of enemy machinegun fire. Colonel Mertel, made aware of the incident, flew to the spot, located the helicopter, but saw that Viet Cong soldiers were less than 200 meters away. The division's SOP, as well as common sense, dictated that the crew should be rescued if at all possible. But time was of the essence, and Mertel knew that some decision had to be made quickly if the crew were to be taken out of the enemy's grasp.

He also knew that his second lift—Company B—was already in the air and that the company could react to any sudden change of plans. So he radioed the company commander and directed the latter to change his plans: Company B would now land on the rice paddy near the downed gunship, rescue the helicopter's crew, and then attack to the north in conjunction with Company C, which would be pushing to the south. Since Company B was seven minutes outbound, Mertel announced that he would mark with smoke the new landing zone. Similar instructions were passed to the commander of the supporting helicopter unit who was monitoring the battalion's command net.

The flexibility inherent in the airmobile concept now made itself felt, for both the infantry and aviation commanders could accept the new orders without question, fully confident that their units would perform well despite the sudden change in plans and the lack of time in which to make any extensive preparations.

Directing his pilot to make a long, low pass around the southwest edge of the objective, Colonel Mertel dropped a yellow smoke grenade to mark Company B's landing zone; his timing could not have been better, for as his ship climbed away, he could see Company B was now only about two minutes away from touching down.

Company B's commander spotted the yellow smoke and was able to get an excellent view of the downed helicopter, the terrain, and the enemy soldiers, who were now directing a heavy volume of fire at the descending helicopters. Almost every ship in the flight was hit at least one time, but not one was disabled to the point where it could not continue the mission.

It was obvious that the enemy had expected Company B to land on LZ Tonto and had not been able to react completely to the rapid change in the tactical situation, although his reaction indeed had been strong. On landing, the 2d Platoon assaulted and carried two enemy strong points; the 1st Platoon managed to secure the hill which overlooked the downed helicopter and the helicopter itself; while the 3d Platoon took the hill to the east against almost no enemy resistance. A counterattack just before noon was easily beaten off.

Meanwhile, Mertel had landed at LZ Tonto to take charge of the battle. Company A came in just before 1000, under fire, and to it, too, Mertel gave a change in mission: to attack and seize the high ground east of the objective. That ground dominated the landing zones and objective, a fact not apparent from the study of maps and photographs or from the aerial reconnaissances of the previous day. From that hill, though, the enemy force was directing fire against all of the units of Mertel's battalion, making it hot for the US soldiers as they went about their business of organizing and preparing to carry out the rest of the assigned mission.

Once again the flexibility of command in an airmobile unit was demonstrated: Company A picked up the change of plan without hesitation, and moved off with little confusion. Shortly thereafter, Mertel's last unit, Company D, landed, thereby closing the battalion in the objective area.

By 1300, four hours after the initial landing, the situation was under control despite some earlier problems with evacuating casualties and a few civilian women and children, and bringing in some badly needed ammunition. Company D was securing the landing zones; Company A had gained the hill from which the enemy had been directing his most accurate fires; and Companies B and C were converging on the battalion's objective. A limited number of tactical air missions were in progress, along with extensive aerial rocket artillery and tube artillery support.

By 1530, Companies B and C had secured the objective, linked up, and established a defensive perimeter. The battalion was now formed into three mutually supporting perimeters, and all of the enemy forces who had opposed the landing had been eliminated or driven from the area. There would be no further enemy contact for the duration of the operation.

In the succeeding days, the battalion would be able to piece together from various sources the extent of the rather formidable enemy opposition it had encountered. The 1st Battalion had actually landed on two sides of a main force Viet Cong battalion which had numbered about 250 men. At least two, and possibly more, 60mm mortars and five machineguns had been employed by the Viet Cong unit. Company B's landing to the south of the objective had caused the enemy to fight in two directions, weakening his defensive measures and permitting the battalion to accomplish its mission with a minimum number of casualties.

Certainly if the original plan had been followed, Mertel's companies would have suffered far more heavily than they did.

It had not been all that easy for Company B, of course. One platoon leader, later talking about the landing and the ensuing battle, said: "The new LZ was hot. The CO in the lead helicopter landed near the stricken gunship, but the heavy enemy fire caused the other lift ships to scatter over a wider area than had been planned. The CO had not been able to contact me to inform me of the change in mission. On landing, I saw where he had set up his command post, next to the downed gunship. He was serving as the focal point for the reorganization and assembly of scattered elements of the company. The 2d Platoon was receiving heavy mortar and small arms fire from three sides. The fire from the enemy was effective, causing several casualties, pinning a portion of that platoon to the ground. My platoon was not engaged in the fire fight initially, so I was committed to maneuver around the south flank against the Viet Cong positions. The first attempt I made was unsuccessful because of the thick jungle which made movement difficult. I had one man badly wounded, and had him evacuated to the company CP. I then launched a second assault which was successful in relieving the pressure on the partially pinned down 2d Platoon."

Another of Company B's platoon leaders said: "We had received a report that Company C had received fire and was engaged; thus, we were forewarned to expect trouble. We lifted off for the flight to the objective. About seven minutes out, the company commander called to give me the change in the company's mission. About two minutes out our assault helicopters started receiving fire, and we could hear small arms and automatic weapons fire popping all around us. Before the ships could settle to the water-filled paddies, the troops had jumped out into a hail of enemy fire, including explosions I assumed to be from 60mm mortar rounds. Men scattered everywhere, the initiative of the air assault landing partially spoiled by the retaliating enemy force."

From this one action, Mertel's battalion took away several important lessons:

• Be prepared for changes and be prepared to take advantage of any situation that might suddenly arise in a combat operation. Change should be expected as a matter of course.

• Responsive artillery support is a must in an air assault. Every engaged infantry battalion requires some artillery support.

• Supply personnel at all levels must anticipate resupply needs and be prepared for the worst. A basic load of ammunition does not last long if a unit is heavily engaged.

• Evacuation of casualties from the battlefield without delay is of the utmost importance even though a considerable effort may be required to do this successfully.

• An airmobile force can operate in almost any kind of weather.

This had been the battalion's first major battle in Vietnam; it had drawn first blood with a minimum of friendly casualties. But more, it had confirmed the value and effectiveness of airmobile techniques, stiff and thorough training, and teamwork.

surprise

Surprise, as a principle of war, is not reserved for a particular level of command, but must be employed in the planning and conduct of operations from the highest military level to the squad level if decisive victory is to be achieved. At no time can the enemy be given the advantage of surprise, especially when the fighting takes place in his environment. For the small unit commander, the principle of surprise is of paramount importance in all operations—the offense, the defense, patrolling, marches, ambushes. He must gain the advantage offered by surprise while at the same time he denies the enemy that advantage; if he can do this, he can attain success in battle comparable to that achieved by a platoon of the 173d US Airborne Brigade in War Zone D.[6]

After participating in a successful airmobile assault just north of Ben Cat, the 3d Platoon, Company A, 1st Battalion, 503d US Infantry was ordered to move as part of the company column to a battalion helicopter extraction zone several thousand meters away. At midday, the platoon leader, Lieutenant Robert Oakes,

[6]Combat experience related by CPT Walter Daniel, USA, to CPT Anthony E. Hartle, USA.

received a further order to move with his platoon on a separate axis en route to the extraction zone and to search an area where enemy activity had been reported.

As his platoon moved through a thick jungle spotted with small open rice paddies, Lieutenant Oakes concentrated on the task of finding the enemy before the enemy found him. He would move approximately 300 meters in one of the usual platoon combat formations, employing a point element to his front and security to his flanks, and then halt and form a hasty perimeter. From this perimeter he would send out five-man fire teams to the front and flanks in a cloverleaf pattern; the fire teams would move out from 50 to 200 meters—depending on the terrain and vegetation—to search for signs on any enemy soldiers; if nothing were found, the fire teams would return and the platoon would move forward another 300 meters and repeat the process. (Map 31)

Oakes had found this method to be quite effective on previous operations, because in the dense undergrowth which limited command and control and encouraged ambush, the platoon could cover a considerably larger area during its movement than would have been the case had it employed only normal security measures and formations—the wedge, column, or vee.

At about 1400, the fire team looping to the front saw an enemy soldier in an outpost position, moving slowly and carefully; the team returned to the platoon command post and reported to Oakes what it had seen. Oakes consolidated his platoon and sent a small reconnaissance patrol forward, the members of which could see a number of camouflaged huts about 100 meters beyond the outpost. After receiving this report, Lieutenant Oakes swiftly dispatched two squads to work their way around to the opposite side of the camp to establish blocking positions on what seemed to be a possible avenue of withdrawal.

In about 30 minutes, Oakes received word by radio that the blocking squads were in place. He then led the remainder of his platoon forward, squads in column, moving quietly to avoid discovery by the enemy. As they neared the camp, the men moved on line as well as they could in the thick vegetation and launched their attack. The enemy soldiers were taken completely by surprise, and 12 of the 15 who occupied positions near the huts were killed during the first rush; the other three

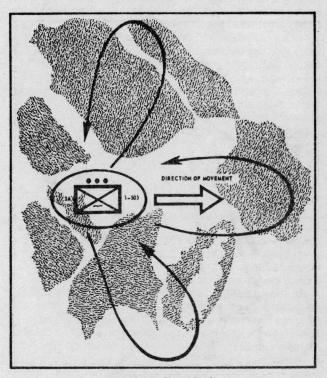

Map 31. Cloverleaf

enemy soldiers escaped the initial assault but were cut down when they ran into the blocking squads. (*Map 32*)

Oakes and his men had succeeded in surprising and annihilating an enemy unit in the latter's own base area. His initial formation proved to be effective for achieving surprise—without being surprised—in a dense jungle environment. Had a different formation been used, the 3d Platoon might well have been discovered by the enemy outpost and the element of sur-

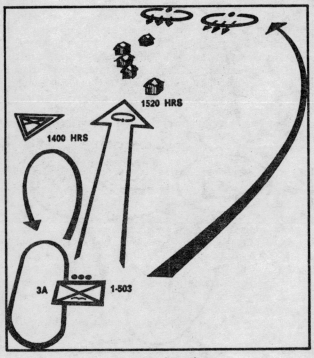

Map 32. Assault

prise would have passed to the enemy. In that situation, Oakes might have been faced with evacuating his dead and wounded and with the survival of the remnant of his command, rather than with assaulting and overrunning an enemy camp.

Realizing the futility of trying to encircle the camp with his small force, Lieutenant Oakes established blocking positions along the enemy's most likely avenue of withdrawal. By taking this action, he again achieved surprise and was totally successful in destroying an enemy force and an enemy camp.

key terrain

The lush foliage of the jungle usually conjures up thoughts of tropical monsoons, high temperatures, and high humidity. But seldom do thoughts consider the extreme dry seasons that alternate with the monsoons and make water resupply a major problem to the fighting troops who range the jungle in search of the enemy.[7]

Yet, when considered in its proper light, this other face of the jungle can be a major factor in determining key terrain and in locating the enemy.

Several months after the My Canh 2 action, in April 1966 and during the dry season along the central coastal regions of South Vietnam, the 2d Battalion, 502d US Infantry was participating in Operation AUSTIN II; its mission: find the enemy. And after a careful analysis of the area of operations the battalion commander sent Company B to seize what he considered to be key terrain—a trickling creek!

Soon, the company, led by Captain Thomas Taylor, but minus two of its platoons which had been pulled away for other purposes, was hacking a trail through the thick jungle vegetation. The Weapons Platoon—converted to a rifle platoon and acting as such—was leading, the company commander behind the point squad, and a rifle platoon bringing up the rear.

None of the men of Company B wondered why the small creek had been selected as their target. As a matter of fact, they were wondering if the two canteens each man carried would take them through the sweltering heat that parched their mouths as they moved to the oasis ahead. At first glance the men could have passed for South Vietnamese Regional Forces with their conglomeration of jungle uniforms and cellophane bags of rice slung around their shoulders. In place of the regular combat packs, the men trudged along with frameless, battered rucksacks on their backs; rather than air mattresses and sleeping bags, they carried lightweight nylon hammocks captured from the Viet Cong or purchased on the local market. Two Montagnard guides added native color to the command group.

Overhead a solitary forward air controller circled in a small,

---

[7]Combat experience related by CPT Thomas Taylor to CPT Terry H. Reilly.

high winged, O-1 Bird Dog. He was the only outside contact with Company B and periodically he could see a vivid cloud of yellow, violet, or green smoke boiling up from the background of the jungle canopy to let him know of the slow progress on the ground. Since Captain Taylor could not reach his fire direction center for indirect fire support, he was using the air controller for radio relay; in a pinch, Taylor could relay fire missions as well as direct close air support.

Hours later, Company B arrived at the objective. To the men, it was an oasis, for most of them had already drained their meager water supply. The area around the creek abounded with signs of recent use—the tell-tale signs of the deep tread of the "Ho Chi Minh scandals" were everywhere. Viet Cong soldiers, too, had been at the creek!

On a distinct trail leading from the edge of the jungle down to the creek bed, the point man—an 81mm mortar forward observer—disappeared into a shaded V-shaped glade. Standing alone in the small sanctuary, he wet his throat with the remaining water in his canteen and kneeling, refilled the canteen and almost absentmindedly replaced it in its cover. As he did so he glanced up and saw at the other end of the glade another uniformed figure step into view. He was looking at an enemy soldier! His firing of his M16 represented "enemy contact" in the wilderness, and like most meeting engagements, the time and location were unplanned and unexpected for both sides. (*Map 33*)

The enemy soldier fell and the point man ducked into the tall grass at the water hole; he was soon joined by his squad leader. No words were needed as the two men squatted and peered cautiously over the top of the grass—they knew that the enemy seldom traveled alone. Where were the others?

The two soldiers did not have long to wait for their answer—an enemy bullet whacked into the squad leader's thigh. One by one the members of the Weapons Platoon came abreast in the glade of sprayed fire on the far treeline which sloped downhill on their right flank. Automatic weapons fire broke out from the woodline on this flank, indicating that the enemy had maneuvered quickly through the trees and were apparently ready for a fight.

By this time the Weapons Platoon had set up an effective base of fire and the 3d Platoon was coming up, moving to the high ground on the left under Captain Taylor's directions. Tay-

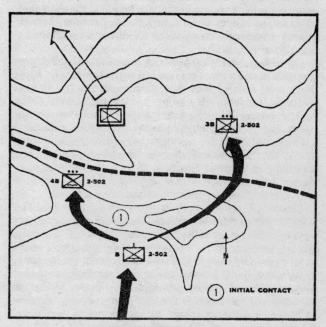

Map 33. Key Terrain

lor wanted that platoon to wheel down onto the rear of the
enemy. But as the platoon's machinegun opened fire, the enemy, sensing defeat, broke contact. A short pursuit found four
of their dead—all with empty canteens. Once again in Vietnam
the basic necessities for survival, like water, had assumed significant proportions and had become a dominant objective for
a small unit action.

infantry charge

There are times, of course, when many of the fundamentals
of offensive combat must be put aside and a decision sought
by an overwhelming infantry assault on an enemy's fortified

position conducted by an aggressive, well trained rifle company. No better example of this can be found than that illustrated by the actions of Company C, 1st Battalion, 35th US Infantry in difficult terrain about 15 kilometers southwest of Duc Pho in July 1967.[8]

On 15 July 1967, Company C was on a search and destroy operation in an area that consisted of rugged mountains whose slopes were covered with thick jungle undergrowth. In most places the double jungle canopy shut out the sunlight, while the temperatures hovered during the daylight hours near the 100 degree mark. During the previous days, the 1st Battalion had received intelligence reports that a North Vietnamese Army (NVA) battalion was operating in the area; hoping to locate the enemy and thus gain tactical surprise, the battalion commander, Major James E. Moore, Jr., had decided to send Company C to seek out the enemy unit and bring it to task.

Company C moved south on two axes: the 2d and 3d Platoons on a high ridgeline with the remainder of the company moving parallel in the valley below. Captain John H. Cavendar planned to swing his two platoons on the ridgeline down a finger a little farther on to join up with the rest of the company.

At about 1000, the two platoons began their movement downhill. The 2d Platoon was leading, with the 3d Platoon following and echeloned to the left. Thirty minutes later, the 2d Platoon noticed an enemy bunker positioned to fire east down the finger. Three NVA soldiers ran from the bunker but were quickly cut down. (*Map 34*) The platoons continued their downward trek.

Suddenly, and without warning, an enemy force hidden in the jungle opened fire—intense, deadly. Nine US soldiers went down almost immediately. But the remainder, following the orders of their leaders and reacting with machine-line precision, built up their own firepower; the LAW was used to good advantage, and the enemy firing decreased in intensity. But the 3d Platoon, trying to flank the enemy position, also ran into heavily fortified bunkers and it, too, was soon engaged in a hot fire fight with an undetermined number of enemy soldiers.

Captain Cavendar, hearing the sound of firing above him, began moving his 1st and 4th Platoons up the finger to close the pincer on the enemy force. Since the vegetation on the

[8]Combat experience submitted by MAJ Garold L. Tippin.

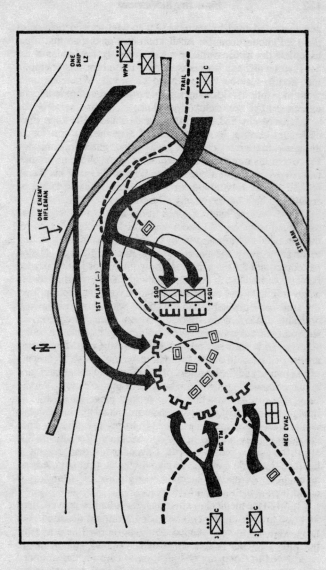

Map 34. Infantry Charge

finger was so thick, Cavendar sent the 1st and 2d Squads of the 1st Platoon toward a small knob east of the enemy to act as a blocking force, while he maneuvered the remainder of the 1st Platoon and the 4th Platoon, reorganized for this operation into a rifle platoon formation, to the north. When his units were in position, he moved forward with a squad to locate the exact extent of the enemy's positions.

Major Moore had been in the air over the battle zone since 1100 and Captain Cavendar radioed a request to him for an ammunition resupply drop and for a medical evacuation mission for two of his more seriously wounded men. In the meantime, he halted all forward movement until he could move his 90mm recoilless rifle forward to a position from which it could be brought to bear on the enemy's bunkers.

There were no landing zones in the area, so Cavendar had one squad from the 2d Platoon back off 100 meters to care for the wounded and to assist in the resupply mission; the men fell to clearing away the underbrush for the medical evacuation helicopter and for the supply drop, while Major Moore headed back to the firebase to pick up ammunition. He returned within a few minutes, and as his helicopter hovered at tree top level the ammunition was pushed out to the waiting men below.

Using LAWs again, the 3d Platoon maneuvered and destroyed the bunkers which were holding up its advance, but it soon began to receive fire from further to the east. Supporting artillery fires could not be brought in because of the denseness of the jungle and the nearness of the platoon to the enemy, and gunships could do little through the thick jungle canopy. Moore suggested to Cavendar that the company move back while he brought in an air strike, but Cavendar intimated that his platoons would sustain too many casualties in trying to withdraw since the enemy's fire was so heavy and accurate. Because he had all of the escape routes cut off, Cavendar felt that as soon as his recoilless rifle came up to take direct shots at the bunkers, he could knock out the enemy's strong point and Company C could then launch a final assault.

By 1420 the medical evacuation helicopter had arrived, used its hoist to pick up the two wounded, and had departed. But there were 14 more wounded now who needed help and the battalion's surgeon, Captain Carroll P. Osgood, volunteered to be lowered to Company C's position to care for the wounded and organize their evacuation. On the medical evacuation helicopter's third trip, Captain Osgood was lowered into the area, with much needed blood plasma. Unfortunately, the hoist on the helicopter broke, so a CH-47 Chinook was requested to hoist out the remaining wounded.

When the larger helicopter arrived, four more of the wounded were hoisted aboard, where the surgeon from the 3d Brigade, 25th US Infantry Division—Captain Dennis E. Lee—instituted further medical treatment. But since the hoist did not function properly, a total of 45 minutes was consumed in getting the four wounded up into the ship. As a fifth casualty was being lifted, the hoist stuck; unable to move the hoist either up or down, the helicopter commander decided to chance a flight to the nearest medical installation with the wounded man dangling below his ship. And so he started, but Major Moore, observing the happenings, directed the Chinook commander to proceed to an open area which he could see off in the distance. Moore then had his pilot land his ship in that open place, and dismounting, as the Chinook again hovered, removed the wounded man from the hoist. Loading the soldier into his helicopter, Major Moore delivered him to the medical evacuation center.

With Captain Cavendar, though, the recoilless rifle had not made as great an impression on the enemy as he had hoped. Although the crew of the recoilless rifle did get several direct hits, the thick vegetation hampered their efforts. The enemy's fire was extremely accurate and the company's casualties were steadily increasing—it seemed as though every time one of the men exposed himself, he was hit by an unseen marksman.

Cavendar decided that the time had come for Company C to assault the enemy bunkers—to stay where it was would only invite complete disaster. At 1600, then, using the 2d and 3d Platoons as a base of fire, Cavendar led the two squads of the 1st Platoon and the 4th Platoon in a final assault. Rising as one, shouting and screaming at the tops of their lungs, the men charged forward.

The enemy soldiers were caught unawares, and as the US soldiers closed in on them, some fled from their bunkers while others cowered behind their erstwhile protection. As the men from Company C ran forward they threw hand grenades in the enemy bunkers, and fired at the enemy soldiers who were attempting to flee. Not until the positions had been overrun did they realize there were five large bunkers arranged in a circle instead of the one or two they had expected to find.

After the battle, Captain Cavendar said: "This battle was won by the men, not artillery or airpower—but the infantrymen who were willing to close with and destroy the enemy. They did everything I asked of them and more. Once we started our assault I knew that it would soon be over, and victory was ours.

"The longer we stayed where we were, the more casualties we were taking. I have never seen enemy fire so accurate. It seemed like every time a man moved he was hit. We were too close for artillery and air, and we couldn't pull back without taking a lot of casualties. I know Charlie was surprised when we charged. His fire was still heavy—but not as accurate and we could see some of them trying to run out of their holes. When I heard the men yelling and saw the determination on their faces, I was proud to be an infantryman and their company commander. I sure would not have wanted to be in one of those bunkers.

"I still prefer to use our basic concept of finding and fixing the enemy—then use all the artillery and air we can get. However, I feel that on that day I fulfilled a company commander's dream: to lead his men in an overwhelming, successful assault of an enemy fortified position. We learned an important lesson that day—an aggressive, well trained American rifle company is the ultimate weapon."

INFANTRY IN VIETNAM

Frequent flooding turned paths into streams during the monsoon season.

An enemy base camp is routinely searched during Operation John Paul Jones (August, 1966).

VC booby traps like this were a constant source of US and ARVN casualties.

Helicopters enabled infantrymen to start search and destroy missions from high ground.

Participation in search and destroy missions was an almost daily occurrence.

Ambushes were a frequent danger for US and ARVN patrols in the Iron Triangle.

Rapid evacuation of wounded was an important morale factor.

Artillery support was essential in all ground operations.

Base camp construction required considerable engineer support in 1965 and 1966.

Terrain in Vietnam varied from dense jungle to open fields.

Men of the First Division preparing a patrol in Tay Ninh province.

A frightened child is evacuated from a battlefield.

VI
Defend

DEFENSIVE OPERATIONS WILL never win a war; only offensive operations can insure ultimate victory. But it should be recognized that many times the skillful application of the defense can keep a military force from losing a war, or a battle. Defensive operations, therefore, in the broadest sense of the term, embraces all combat actions that offer a degree of resistance to an attacking force. They are conducted to develop more favorable conditions for offensive action; to destroy or trap a hostile force; to reduce an enemy's capability for offensive action; to gain time and avoid fighting a decisive engagement; to resist, delay, and inflict punishment on an enemy force; or to deny an enemy entry into a vital area.

As there are for offensive operations, so too are there fundamentals of the defense. Among the most important of the defense fundamentals are:

- Use terrain properly.
- Provide for security.
- Insure mutual support.
- Organize for all-around defense.
- Organize defense in depth.
- Planned fires.
- Barrier plans.
- Maintain freedom of action.
- Use time available.

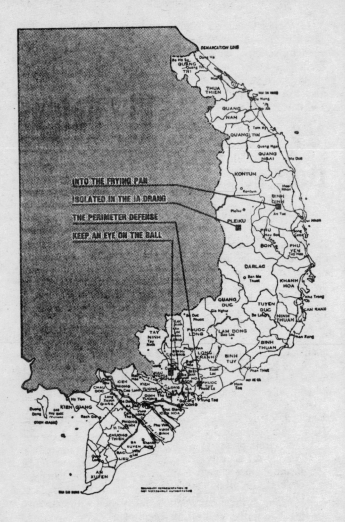

INTO THE FRYING PAN

ISOLATED IN THE IA DRANG

THE PERIMETER DEFENSE

KEEP AN EYE ON THE BALL

In Vietnam, the US Army's traditional emphasis on the "spirit of the offensive" has received increased impetus with the introduction of the airmobile assault, for a heliborne attack challenges leaders at all levels with its requirement for aggressive and rapid action and with the uncertainty that is inherent in each landing.

But reversals are sudden in combat. Particularly in Vietnam, where timely intelligence information concerning the enemy is rare and highly perishable, the hunter can quickly become the hunted, and the assault can become a defense of a piece of ground which would never be considered for that purpose under other circumstances. The most detailed plan of attack can suddenly change to a hasty defense if the enemy is not where he was thought to be. And this is what happened to the 2d Battalion, 502d US Infantry in September 1965 near An Khe.

into the frying pan

In late August 1965, the 1st Brigade, 101st US Airborne Division, then commanded by Colonel James S. Timothy, and of which the 2d Battalion, 502d US Infantry was a part, moved from the Cam Ranh Bay area to secure assembly points near An Khe for the soon-to-arrive 1st US Cavalry Division.[1] The Brigade's mission also in included the security of an An Khe pass, north of which, in the Song Con River valley, a North Vietnamese Army (NVA) battalion had been spotted.

Colonel Timothy was anxious to get at the NVA battalion, for that unit constituted a major threat to his brigade, and he set in motion a plan to destroy it—Operation GIBRALTAR. Timothy's plan called for a combined arms task force to sweep northward along the river valley to a point just opposite the suspected enemy location, then to attack to the east toward the enemy battalion. At the same time, a blocking force would be landed by helicopter behind the enemy to deny the latter avenues of escape to the east. While all of this was taking place, trails leading to the north would be interdicted with extensive air strikes to further seal off the enemy unit.

At 0730, 18 September 1965, Task Force Mark, commanded by Major Mark Hansen and consisting of Company

[1]After action report adapted by CPT James L. Shepard, USA.

A, 2d Battalion, 327th US Infantry; Company A, 1st Battalion, 17th US Cavalry; the 2d Battalion, 320th US Artillery; and a platoon of tanks from the 2d Battalion, 7th US Marines, began moving along the river, over terrain that proved far more difficult to traverse than had been expected.

Earlier that same morning the 2d Battalion, 502d US Infantry—the blocking force—had moved by motor convoy from an assembly area at the east end of An Khe pass southeast along Highway 19 to a landing zone near Khu Pho. There it was joined by a South Vietnamese Army (ARVN) Ranger company which would stay with the battalion for the operation. Led by Lieutenant Colonel Wilfrid K. G. Smith, the 2d Battalion was expected to conduct a heliborne assault to the southeast of the suspected enemy battalion near the village of An Ninh, move rapidly northwest into the mountains, and set up six blocking positions along key trail intersections. The battalion had been tailored for combat in the mountains and consisted of three rifle companies plus the attached ARVN Ranger company; mortars and recoilless rifles had been left behind because the general consensus had been that those weapons could not be carried or effectively employed in the difficult terrain in which the battalion would be operating. (*Map 35*)

The 52d US Aviation Battalion had been designated to support the airmobile assault. Eleven UH-1D helicopters from the 117th US Aviation Company, eight UH-1B helicopters from Company A, 52d Aviation Battalion, and seven CH-34 helicopters from the 7th US Marines were available for the troop life, while nine UH-1B armed helicopters were available to provide close air support. The troop transport helicopters could introduce 140 men per lift, and Smith had planned for four lifts to transport his battalion to the landing zone. The flight time for each lift would be 15 minutes.

The first lift, carrying 138 soldiers from Company C, commanded by Captain Robert E. Rawls, and a two-man air control team, touched down on its designated landing zone at 0715, 18 September. Although they encountered some resistance, the platoons rapidly assembled in predesignated areas to secure the LZ, while Rawls moved about adjusting positions to insure all-around security. Eventually, he would suffer mortal wounds while directing his 3d Platoon to move to a new location. (*Map 36*)

The second lift, with the remainder of Company C, two

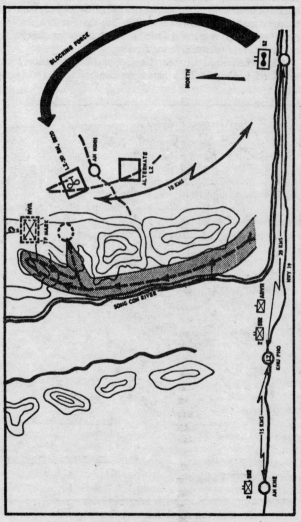

Map 35. Plan of Action

platoons from Company B, and the battalion's tactical command post aboard, approached the LZ at 0730 under intense enemy small arms and automatic weapons fire. One of the platoons from Company B failed to touch down because of the heavy fire and returned to the loading zone.

Captain Wilford E. Roe, Company B's commander, was wounded while still in a helicopter, and Second Lieutenant

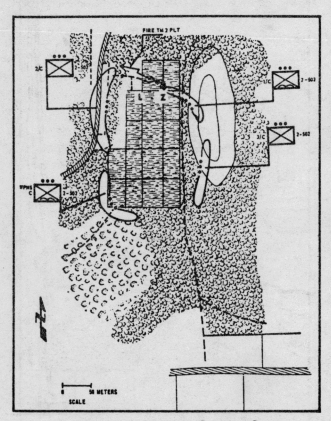

Map 36. Air Assault by Company C

Howard R. Reeves assumed command of those Company B elements that had reached the landing zone. Reeves managed to assemble the men at the northwest corner of the landing zone, and to put them into defensive positions filling major gaps in Company C's perimeter. (*Map 37*)

The heavy and effective enemy fire had also caused some damage to the helicopters—two had been downed during the landing, a CH-34 and a UH-1D, while the remainder were

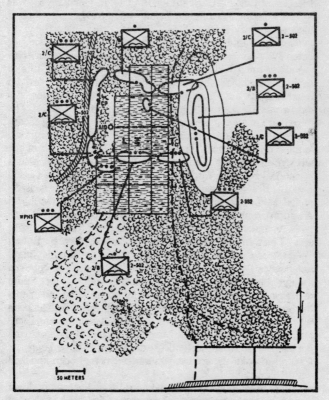

Map 37. Perimeter Defense

grounded when they returned to the loading zone because of hits they had taken. The lift capability of the supporting helicopter units thus had been reduced to about 60 men, and the armed UH-1Bs had to return to An Khe and Qui Nhon for additional ammunition before the third lift could get underway.

Just after 0800, very heavy enemy 60mm and 82mm mortar fire rained into the perimeter, and Company C's 1st Platoon was forced to pull back to more covered positions behind a paddy dike at the base of the hill. Just a short time later, Lieutenant Edward C. Schillo's 3d Platoon, Company B, was forced from the former enemy camp site it had been occupying back through Company C's 2d Platoon.

Colonel Smith with 224 men was now in a hasty perimeter defensive position surrounded by an estimated two enemy battalions. Armed helicopters were Smith's only means of fire support until 0900 when US Air Force fighter aircraft arrived overhead; the 47 sorties that would be flown throughout the day would play a most important role in Smith's plans. The initial air strikes did prevent the enemy from launching a concentrated attack, though, and at 0920 the third lift attempted a landing on an alternate landing zone 800 meters south of the airhead. On board the helicopters were 60 men from Companies A and B led by the Company A commander, Captain Gerald Landry. But once again, extremely heavy enemy fire was directed at the LZ during the landing attempt, and the 117th Aviation Company helicopters could land but 8 men from Company A, under the control of Platoon Sergeant Robert L. Jack, and 28 men from Company B, led by Platoon Sergeant Robert Wightman, at two separate locations. These small units fought independently until they were able to link up at 1200; but even though communications were established with Colonel Smith at the airhead, the 36 soldiers would remain isolated and unable to move until the next morning. Captain Landry had been wounded during the landing and had been evacuated, and Lieutenant Charlie Y. Talbott assumed command of the company back at the departure airfield. In the space of three hours, or less, all three of the company commanders had been knocked out of the action.

Three of the helicopters in the third lift had been shot down during the landing attempt, while most of the rest had aborted because of the enemy fire and returned to the departure field. There, after a quick mechanical inspection, all 26 of the troop lift helicopters were grounded because of mechanical difficulties caused by the enemy's fire at the landing zones, although five of the armed helicopters remained in action and continued to support the ground action.

On the hill, a series of enemy attack's and 2d Battalion counterattacks took place during the course of the morning, and Colonel Smith had his hands full in trying to organize the airhead. Smith did receive word that Colonel Timothy had ordered Task Force Mark to move to his relief across the mountains from the west and that every effort was being made to procure additional helicopters for resupply purposes, for medical evacuation, and to lift the remainder of the battalion to an alternate landing zone nearby.

At 1330 two helicopters from the 1st US Cavalry Division arrived with sling loads of ammunition and one 81mm mortar with 80 mortar rounds. Five wounded were evacuated on the two helicopters even though they had to make a hurried departure as the enemy began concentrating his fires on the two ships. A little later a CH-47 helicopter tried to land to evacuate more of Smith's wounded, but when the crew chief was killed and the co-pilot wounded, the mission was called off before it could be completed.

During the remainder of the afternoon, the 2d Battalion defended against periodic enemy probes. Occasionally, intense enemy fire was received, particularly when helicopters tried to land and take out the wounded. Three medical evacuation helicopters made unsuccessful attempts to lift out wounded personnel, although at 1600 a UH-1B helicopter managed to evacuate two of the wounded from the little force at the alternate landing zone.

Try as he could, Colonel Smith did not feel that he and his small force could fully stabilize the situation at his position unless he received additional help—he estimated three additional companies would be required to make the situation tenable. Timothy agreed with Smith's estimate, and made plans to dispatch another task force, this one to be led by Lieutenant Colonel Edward V. Collins, the commander of the 2d Battalion, 327th US Infantry, to Smith's aid. Task Force Mark was ordered to continue its push to the west and to get on to the heights overlooking An Ninh as soon as possible.

Collins' task force, which included the rest of Smith's battalion, one company from his own battalion, and two ARVN

Ranger companies, began loading at 1600 into 18 UH-1D helicopters, seven UH-1D helicopters, and one CH-47 helicopter borrowed from the 1st US Cavalry Division, for an airmobile assault on an alternate landing zone 5,000 meters east of Smith's besieged airhead. The assault went off without a problem, although two full lifts were required to transport the task force, and the CH-47 had to make two additional lifts to move in the last of the ARVN Rangers.

Collins started moving his men to the west immediately upon landing. Meanwhile, artillery accompanying Task Force Mark had moved into supporting positions on the east bank of the river, using CH-47 helicopters also borrowed from the 1st US Cavalry Division. Because of the difficulty in effecting a night linkup in the face of heavy enemy contact, and because of the possibility of an enemy ambush of Collins' task force, however, Timothy concurred in the recommendations made to him by both Smith and Collins that Collins' men should organize defensive positions for the night about 2,000 meters southeast of Smith's battalion.

Flareships and artillery fire provided continuous illumination over Smith's unit during the night, and in the dim light provided by the flares the men could see enemy soldiers moving in front of their perimeter collecting bodies and equipment. The enemy did probe the perimeter on six different occasions, usually when a new flareship was adjusting its pattern.

When morning came, Smith reported that only two enemy platoons remained in contact and that the rest had withdrawn during the night. At 1000, Task Force Collins linked up with the eight men from Company A and the remaining men from Company B on the alternate landing zone. Then, at 1315, Smith's men were extracted from their hill positions by helicopter, while Task Force Collins remained to search the area and later to link up with Task Force Mark.

The spirit of the offense which had characterized the 2d Battalion's heliborne landing rapidly deteriorated to a hasty defense, for the battalion had conducted its assault into the training area and base camp of the 95th and 94th Battalions of the 2d NVA Regiment and was soon surrounded by a numerically superior enemy force. In fact, the landing zone itself was later determined to be an established objective for the enemy's training exercises.

This operation was one of the first conducted by the 1st Brigade, 101st US Airborne Division in Vietnam, and the lessons learned were to pay great dividends in the months that were to come.

isolated in the ia drang

In the case of Colonel Smith's battalion, his unit—minus several of its elements—had been attacked on a landing zone by a larger enemy force. Although the attack had been unexpected, the battalion's elements that were on the ground had deployed properly in order to secure the landing zone for the remainder of the battalion, and they were in a good position to conduct a hasty defense. The 2d Platoon, Company B, 1st Battalion, 7th US Cavalry, then assigned to the 1st US Cavalry Division, discovered that sometimes even this situation may be considered a luxury.[2]

During late October 1965, the 1st Brigade of the 1st US Cavalry Division assisted South Vietnamese Army forces in lifting the siege of a Civilian Irregular Defense Group (CIDG) camp at Plei Me, a camp located some 35 kilometers southwest of Pleiku in the central highlands of South Vietnam. A North Vietnamese Army (NVA) division, consisting of the 32d and 33d Regiments, had conducted the siege; one of the regiments, the 33d, had suffered heavy casualties.

As the enemy units withdrew to the west toward the Chu Pong mountain complex where their base camp was located, and where they had not been disturbed for the past 11 years, they were continually harassed by units of the 1st US Cavalry Division. Numerous small battles were fought, and the NVA regiments suffered additional losses in men, materiel, and equipment.

Despite the harrassment, the two enemy regiments did gain the sanctuary of Chu Pong mountain and were joined there by the 66th Regiment, which had only recently arrived in South Vietnam. Within the security of their mountain fastness, the NVA units, operating under the control of a Field Front Head-

[2]Combat experience related by SSG Clyde E. Savage, USA, to CPT John F. Murphy.

quarters (the equivalent of a US Army division headquarters), regrouped and were resupplied preparatory to returning to the attack at Plei Me.

On 9 November 1965, the 3d Brigade of the 1st US Cavalry Division assumed responsibility for the conduct of operations in the Chu Pong area—the assigned mission: find the enemy and destroy him. During the next four days, the Brigade carried out extensive search and destroy operations north, south, and east of the Plei Me camp, but with little enemy contact. Then, on 14 November, the 1st Battalion, 7th US Cavalry was ordered to conduct a helicopter assault into Landing Zone X-Ray; little did the men of the battalion know that they would be landing in the direct path of the three NVA regiments who had completed their reorganization and were even now spilling off Chu Pong mountain on their way to attack the CIDG camp at Plei Me. (*Map 38*)

Company B, commanded by Captain John D. Herrin, loaded into transport helicopters at Plei Me just as an artillery preparation began on the landing zone. Aerial observers reported that the artillery rounds were being well placed, landing in the trees and high grass around the LZ and on the finger and draw leading down from the high ground to the northwest. After the artillery preparation had been completed, the gunships from the aerial rocket artillery battalion would make a firing pass over the LZ expending half of their load of 2.75-inch high explosive rockets.

At Plei Me, the pilots of the transport helicopters pulled their craft into the air at 1030 and headed for LZ X-Ray. And as the formation approached the touchdown point, escort ships darted ahead and laced the landing ground with suppressive fires from their machineguns and rockets. The door gunners of the lift ships also joined the fray, firing their machineguns in a suppressive fashion while the helicopters flared and settled down. As the helicopters departed to bring in the remainder of Company B and the lead elements of Company A from Plei Me, Lieutenant Albert Devney's 1st Platoon formed for a quick reconnaissance sweep of the landing zone.

At 1120 a prisoner was captured; he was unarmed, carried an empty canteen, and was dressed in dirty khaki clothes with a serial number on one of his shirt epaulets. When interrogated, he stated that he was a member of the North Vietnamese Army, that he had had only bananas to eat for five days, and that there

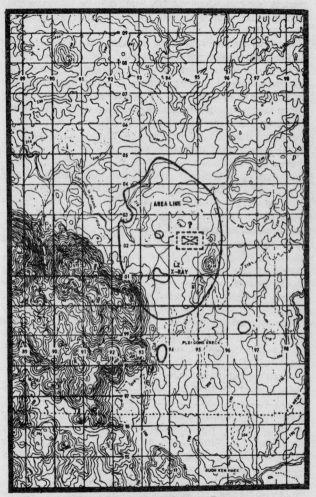

Map 38. Assault in the Ia Drang

were three battalions on the mountain above the LZ that wanted very much to destroy US soldiers. So far, he continued, they had been unable to find any Americans.

After the prisoner had been evacuated to the headquarters of the 3d Brigade, and Companies C and A arrived at the landing zone, the soldiers from Company B concentrated their efforts in the area where the prisoner had been captured—to the northwest. At 1220, the 1st Platoon, which had encountered only a few enemy riflemen, suddenly found itself pinned down by an estimated force of 40 NVA soldiers. Company B's 2d Platoon, led by Lieutenant Henry T. Herrick, maneuvered to the right flank of the 1st Platoon to take off some of the pressure. Enemy mortar fire began to fall in increasing intensity.

During its movement forward to assist the 1st Platoon, the men of the 2nd Platoon began receiving enfilading fire from the right and could see NVA troops withdrawing along a well beaten jungle path. Herrick maneuvered his squads so that they could pursue and engage the fleeing enemy soldiers along the path that crossed a dry creek bed about four feet deep and which led to a small ridge finger descending from the tall Chu Pong mountain.

The platoon advanced along the path until the 1st and 2d Squads were atop the ridge finger near a gigantic ant hill, similar to the other hills that dotted the area, and about 100 meters past the dry creek bed. The 3d Square was to the right and down the hill from the ridge finger, firing on about 20 NVA soldiers that had taken cover behind two other enormous ant hills.

Then the tables were turned as an unseen enemy force suddenly opened fire from all sides—these NVA soldiers, some 75 to 100 strong, had infiltrated down the dry creek bed to the platoon's rear, and soon had driven the 2d Platoon into a tight perimeter only 25 meters wide. (*Map 39*) The enemy soldiers proved to be well trained, for they resisted all attempts made by the remainder of Company B to reach the beleaguered 2d Platoon. Lieutenant Herrick and the men of his platoon were effectively isolated from the battalion's airhead; reinforcements could not get through as the enemy fire increased almost by the minute, lacing the perimeter at a height of twelve to eighteen inches.

At 1620 Company B, assisted by Company A, again tried to reach the 2d Platoon. But despite heavy supporting fires

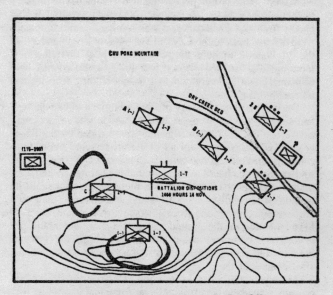

CHU PONG MOUNTAIN

DRY CREEK BED

(176-200)

BATTALION DISPOSITIONS
1400 HOURS 14 NOV

Map 39. The 2d Platoon Is Cut Off

from both artillery pieces and aircraft, the attack could progress
no more than 20 meters before both companies were halted by
the enemy, who were firmly dug into the base of trees, the
sides and tops of ant hills, and foxholes.

One platoon, commanded by Lieutenant Walter J. Marm,
Jr., advanced a bit farther than the others and was itself in
danger of being encircled. Knowing that his platoon could not
hold for long in its exposed position, he watched four of the
enemy move into his platoon's position. Marm ran through a
hail of bullets and killed all four of the enemy soldiers, then
charged 30 meters across open ground to hurl hand grenades
into an enemy machinegun position. Although wounded, he
killed the remaining enemy soldiers in that position with his
rifle.[3]

[3]For his heroic actions, 1LT Marm was awarded the Congressional Medal of
Honor.

Marm's actions did permit the two companies to make a further advance, but again they were stopped by overwhelming enemy fire. And since darkness was coming on, the companies were ordered back to the LZ, and the battalion commander told the 2d Platoon to hold its perimeter at least until the next morning. The isolated platoon was still in radio contact with Captain Herrin and reported that it was holding firm against all enemy assaults.

During the night, priority of fires was given to Company B and any call for fire to assist the 2d Platoon was immediately answered. The 2d Platoon was now commanded by Staff Sergeant Clyde E. Savage, for all of the officers and senior noncommissioned officers had either been killed or wounded. Enemy soldiers could be heard moving around the perimeter, and each time Savage sensed the enemy was prepared for an assault, he would call for artillery support. With the shells from their own artillery bursting around them, Savage's men would lay their M16 rifles flat on the ground and would spray automatic fire beyond the perimeter about two inches above the ground. Screams and shouts from outside the perimeter attested to the effectiveness of these fires.

At about 0330 the next morning, 15 November, an NVA reconnaissance element from a larger force that was on its way to flank LZ X-Ray stumbled into the platoon's perimeter. Not expecting to encounter any US troops outside the limits of the landing zone, the enemy unit was taken completely by surprise and wiped out to a man. Shortly afterwards, the sounds of a larger force moving towards the LZ could be heard and Savage alerted Captain Herrin of an impending attack.

The sounds Savage heard were made by a battalion of enemy soldiers who eventually hit the LZ perimeter in the sector defended by Company C, an attack that was launched with such force that the perimeter was penetrated and the enemy enabled to reach the company command post, 50 meters inside the perimeter. (*Map 40*) The fighting was severe, and by 0800 all of Company C's officers were casualties.

At 0910 Company A, from the 2d Battalion, 7th US Cavalry, began arriving in the LZ and by 1000 the enemy had been expelled from the perimeter and the attack defeated. The units along the perimeter swept out to a distance of 300 meters, and evidence of the damage dealt to the attackers was everywhere:

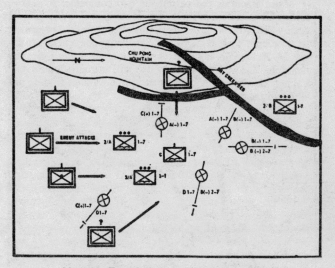

Map 40. Enemy Attacks on 15 November

dead enemy soldiers lay scattered throughout the area; weapons, equipment, and bandages littered the ground. Another new arrival in the LZ was the 2d Battalion, 5th US Cavalry, which took over the mission of screening the base of Chu Pong mountain.

With the arrival of the reinforcing units, Company B left the perimeter to extract its isolated platoon. (*Map 41*) The attack jumped off after a heavy artillery preparation, but this time the enemy offered little resistance. The 2d Platoon withdrew with all of its dead, wounded, and weapons, although only seven men remained unscathed from the 24-hour ordeal. From their tight circle, the men of the 2d Platoon had been able, with the help of supporting artillery fires, to withstand the thrusts of a numerically superior enemy force. They had sustained themselves despite heavy casualties, and had remained a thorn in the side of the enemy throughout the fight. They had demonstrated the ability of the US infantryman to fight hard and well in a most difficult defensive engagement.

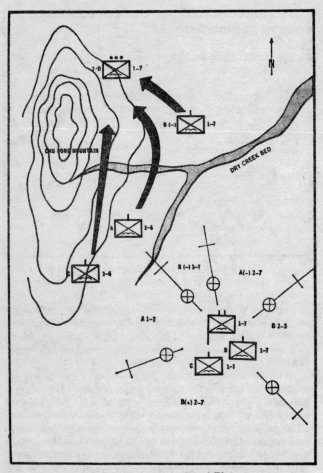

Map 41. Relief of Isolated Platoon

the perimeter defense

Six months later, in April 1966, the infantrymen of Company A, 2d Battalion, 27th US Infantry, then assigned to the 25th US Infantry Division, participated in a similar trial by fire as they were called on to defend their isolated company's perimeter against the attack of a reinforced enemy battalion in the western fringes of the Ho Bo woods 30 miles northwest of Saigon.[4]

At the time, Company A was occupying a blocking position across the axis of advance of a mechanized unit which was sweeping to the south. A warning order had been received by the company commander which told him to be prepared to move his unit by foot to an assembly area near the 2d Battalion's command post after the sweep force had made contact with the blocking position.

The commander of Company A completed his ground reconnaissance for the move and relocated most of his 81mm mortar ammunition to the new area. But as it turned out, Company A would not be moving that night—at 1700, the company was directed to establish a defensive perimeter for the night where it was then located, for the mechanized unit would not be able to complete its sweep to the blocking position before nightfall.

Because of the lateness of the hour, the company commander decided to take advantage of an old enemy trench system in the area, and used this system as a basis for his company's hasty perimeter defense for the night. Unknown to him, and to the men in the company, an enemy battalion was even then deploying for a coordinated attack on the US position.

Shortly after dark, Company A's commander established two ambushes, each of which consisted of one rifle squad, a machinegun team, and a forward observer. The northern ambush site, manned by elements of the 2d Platoon, was 150 meters forward of the perimeter; the eastern site, made up of 1st Platoon members, was located some 175 meters from its platoon.

[4]Combat experience extracted from an after action report by 1LT Terry H. Reilly, USA.

Just after 2100, the north ambush position saw four enemy soldiers coming toward them from their rear; the men manning the ambush fired at the enemy, who promptly dispersed. Since their position had been compromised, the 1st Platoon members moved about 150 meters to the west and set up a new ambush.

Shortly thereafter, the men at the east ambush site saw six enemy soldiers moving toward their positions; these enemy soldiers, too, were engaged as they moved into the rice paddies and a number appeared to be hit. The squad leader at the ambush site, together with two men from his unit, went forward to investigate, found nothing, and then started across the open field to the next wood line to the east to try to regain contact with the enemy. But as the three men neared the woods, they could hear what appeared to be a large number of men moving through the woods; they fired in the direction from which the sounds were coming, without discernible results, and then fearing being ambushed themselves, withdrew to the east ambush site. As a follow up, Company A's commander had artillery fire placed on the woods, but with unknown results.

For the next several hours, peace reigned in Company A's area. But then at 0400 in the morning, the men at the north ambush position saw what they estimated to be a column of 100 enemy soldiers moving toward them from the north, and another column of enemy soldiers approaching their ambush from the northwest. (*Map 42*) Smaller numbers of enemy soldiers were also seen moving east and west.

It was a bright moonlit night, and taking advantage of the light offered by the moon, the squad opened fire with all of its weapons. Enemy soldiers began falling faster than the squad leader could count, but the columns scattered, regrouped, and the remaining enemy soldiers began returning the fire, preventing the ambush squad from breaking off the action and returning to the company perimeter. The squad leader tried to contact his company commander, but had no success. He had no alternative now except to pace the expenditure of the ammunition his men still had—the squad had started with a triple basic load: 36 magazines for each M14E2 rifle, 300 rounds for each M16 rifle, 6 hand grenades for each man, and 2,000 rounds for the M60 machinegun.

At the same time that this action was taking place, over on the east, the squad at the ambush site there saw some 70 enemy soldiers suddenly pop out of the brush, move into the open

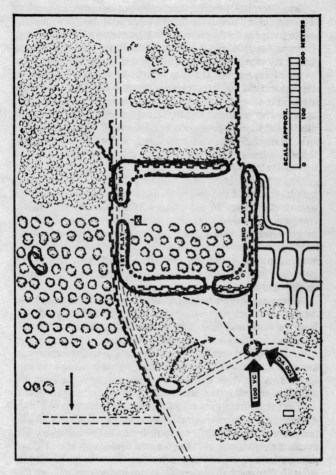

Map 42. Action at North Ambush Site

area to the squad's rear, and head for the company's perimeter. The men of the squad perforce had to hold their fire, for they did not want to hit their own fellow soldiers who were manning Company A's defenses. The enemy soldiers appeared to know where the perimeter was located, but they did not seem to be aware of the ambush site. And while the squad leader radioed this information to the company, by that time the enemy had started his attack. Artillery and mortar fire dropped in the area between the perimeter and the ambush site delayed the enemy attack, but when the enemy opened fire with a 57mm recoilless rifle, a machinegun, and with numerous and accurate mortar rounds, a few of them were able to reach the trench occupied by the 1st Platoon.

The enemy soldiers who did reach the trench fired down its length, threw in hand grenades, and directed their main efforts against the flanks of the platoon. Communication with the company command post was lost, and feeling he could no longer hold the trench line, the 1st Platoon leader gave the order to withdraw from the trench and establish a new line some 25 meters to the rear. Initially he could only account for five men; others, though, gradually appeared and regrouped on the new line.

Ten minutes after the attack on the 1st Platoon started, the 2d Platoon's defensive position also came under attack, this from the north and west. The platoon's right flank was heavily grenaded and was soon overrun by enemy soldiers who then moved down the trench toward the east. Simultaneously, an enemy force launched an attack from the west, advancing rapidly across the open rice paddy. They employed at least one machinegun, but relied heavily on hand and rifle grenades.

The 2d Platoon leader lost contact with his left and right squads, and with the squad out on the ambush site. Radio communication with the company commander was spotty and at times nonexistent, and the platoon leader feared that Company A no longer existed and that the few men still with him were all that was left of the unit. Ammunition was running low and attempts to get supporting artillery and 4.2-inch mortars to bring down concentrations were unsuccessful because of the poor communications.

By this time, all of Company A was hotly engaged with the enemy, for the 3d Platoon had come under heavy fire from its left flank at about the same time the 2d Platoon had been attacked. But the men of the 3d Platoon, despite taking heavy casualties, managed to keep the enemy soldiers out of their defensive positions. (*Map 43*) When the enemy soldiers then tried to get into the 3d Platoon's positions by way of an unoccupied continuation of the existing trench network, constant friendly fire down that trench halted them.

The company's 81mm mortar section, located in the southern portion of the company's perimeter, had been unable to fire close defensive fires or effective barrages because of minimum range limitations. The mortar pits, only hastily prepared, could not be manned because of heavy enemy grazing fire, so the section occupied defensive positions and prepared to engage any enemy soldiers who might break through the 3d Platoon.

Then, at 0530, an enemy bugler sounded an eerie call, one that was unfamiliar to the US soldiers. The surviving members of Company A readied themselves for a last ditch defense against an expected human wave attack. What little ammunition that remained was redistributed as each platoon sought to account for its personnel and reorganize its position.

But the attack did not materialize, for the bugle call had been a signal for the enemy soldiers to withdraw. They finally broke contact, although the 2d Platoon's ambush squad, which was still in position, did report that the enemy unit was going into what seemed to be an assembly area not too far from the ambush site. After calling in an artillery concentration on the suspected enemy assembly area, the ambush squad returned to what was left of Company A's perimeter.

Although the enemy force had been able to breach Company A's line in several areas, it had been unable to exploit the penetrations. Well directed artillery fire and heavy small arms fire managed to plug the gaps. Had it not been for these fires, the absence of alternate and supplementary positions—a glaring weakness in Company A's defensive posture—might well have permitted the enemy to gain a complete success. Too, communications, normally the key to a successful perimeter defense, had been practically nonexistent and therefore a critical weakness. Leaders at all levels were unaware of the overall situation, although the poor communications did point out the extent to which junior officers and noncommissioned officers were capable of independent and outstanding action in maintaining the integrity of the company's position.

A rifle company which conducts an isolated defense invites

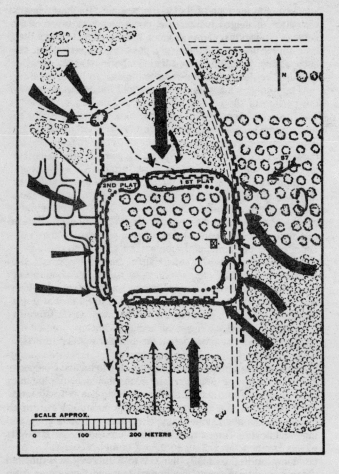

Map 43. Defense of the Perimeter

an enemy to mass and risk decisive combat. The best response to this is an aggressive defense, one which makes use of ambushes on likely enemy avenues of approach to harass and disrupt the enemy's movements; the use of alternate and supplementary positions to provide flexibility and to avoid set patterns; the use of booby traps and mines to impede the momentum of the enemy's attack; and the availability of adequate fire support.

It would appear from the actions of Company A that the defensive doctrine taught by the US Army is sound and its techniques valid. Where doctrine was violated, the defense was weak; where doctrine was followed, the defense was strong.

keep an eye on the ball

As can be seen from the preceding incidents, in Vietnam whenever a unit halts, regardless of the reason, it assumes a defensive posture. Small units in a hasty perimeter during temporary halts do not have the ability to ring their positions with combat outposts, but they can, through aggressive patrolling, protect themselves from an enemy force which is bent on surprising and overhwelming the friendly force. This was poignantly demonstrated to the 1st US Infantry Division during Operation ABILENE in the spring of 1966.[5]

During the latter part of March and early April, the Division's 2d Brigade was enjoying tremendous success in uncovering hundreds of tons of rice and other supplies while conducting search and destroy operations in Phouc Tuy province south of Highway #1. The area in which the Brigade was operating had long been the almost uncontested operational area of an enemy division, and contained various enemy headquarters and communication lines extending from the east coast into War Zone D.

On 9 April, the 2d Battalion, 16th US Infantry, was directed to conduct a company sized search and destroy operation in an area south of the Courteney Rubber Plantation and east of Provincial Highway #2. Late that same day—it was Easter—the battalion's Company C halted in a small clearing for re-supply purposes and to hold religious services.

[5]Combat experience submitted by CPT Robert E. Ward, III, USA.

At dusk, three enemy soldiers were seen and brought down with small arms fire at the north edge of the clearing. Documents taken from them indicated that they were part of a main force Viet Cong battalion, a subordinate unit of the main force 274th Regiment. Aware of the enemy's almost fanatical determination to recover the bodies of his dead, Company C's commander moved his unit into the jungle and established ambush positions around the dead Viet Cong soldiers in the hope of engaging other enemy elements who might attempt to remove their fallen comrades.

No enemy appeared during the night, however, and early the next morning Company C formed up and proceeded west towards Provincial Highway #2. After leaving the less dense fringes of the clearing where it had spent the night, the company was soon back in the sunless jungle. A column formation had been selected, for this provided as good control as it was possible to achieve. Movement was extremely slow, for a matted mesh of vines and underbrush was everywhere.

Until well after 1300 the company was harassed by small groups of enemy soldiers who would fire a few rounds at the US column and then would disappear into the jungle when a patrol was sent toward them. (*Map 44*) By 1345 all action had ceased so Company C's commander pulled his unit into a hasty perimeter to care for four of his men who had been wounded during the preceding few hours. He also needed time to formulate a plan to attack a suspected enemy position that lay to the south. From this position, too, he could request artillery support so that it would be ready to assist the company in the forthcoming assault operation.

Through an airborne relay station, the company's artillery forward observer began registering his supporting concentrations, but one of the rounds landed short, exploding in the jungle canopy above a section of the perimeter and causing several casualties. This accident compounded the company commander's problem, for now he was faced with the need to evacuate 15 wounded men out of a jungle in which there appeared to be no clearings.

With suspected enemy forces nearby, the company commander called on US Air Force helicopters operating in the vicinity for assistance and set a detail from each platoon to work to clear an opening in the canopy large enough for the rescue helicopters to lower their baskets for the wounded. Be-

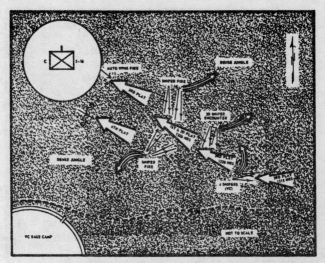

Map 44. Enemy Harassment

tween 1400 and 1600 the rescue helicopters made three trips evacuating some of the company's wounded, and one UH–1D helicopter managed to air drop some badly needed ammunition. During this two hour period no enemy contact was reported, and no movement observed by listening posts which had been set out in front of the perimeter.

As the medical evacuation helicopters returned for a fourth time, an enemy 60mm mortar, without warning and its sound covered by the roar of the descending ships, began firing into the company's perimeter. At the same moment, enemy small arms and light automatic fire began pounding the area from various positions around the perimeter. An abortive attempt by the 3d Platoon to strike back at the enemy was called off when the enemy's fire proved too heavy.

Now the battle began in earnest, as the company's perimeter was restored and all of the wounded brought back inside the defensive area. Many of the enemy soldiers had used the time during the initial engagement with the 3d Platoon to climb into trees and fire down into the company's positions. Two .50

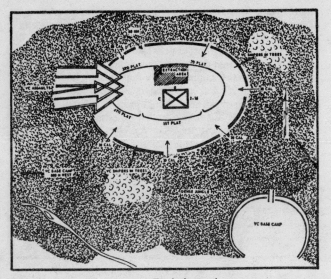

Map 45. Encirclement

caliber machineguns and at least six .30 caliber machineguns placed a blanket of fire over the perimeter. Only the thick underbrush and trees afforded Company C's defenders any semblance of protection.

An attempt by an enemy unit to penetrate the 3d Platoon's area was thrown back, and soon a game of cat and mouse developed all around the company's defensive line: the enemy would send one or two men running and darting from tree to tree to draw fire from the defenders; if any of the men from Company C fired at the running targets, thus marking their locations, the enemy would return the fire from their positions in the trees. To counter this tactic, many of the US soldiers would lie on their backs and fire back at the muzzle flashes from the invisible foes in the trees. (*Map 45*)

Friendly artillery fire also played a large role in helping Company C to hold out against what appeared to be a numerically superior enemy force, preventing the enemy from massing his force for a final assault. Then just prior to darkness, at about 1900, the enemy again attempted to breach the company's defenses. This time the assault was concentrated against the 4th Platoon. Running desperately low on ammunition, the men from the 4th Platoon threw tear gas grenades in an attempt to stave off the enemy soldiers, and a few of them had to engage in hand to hand combat with their foes to keep them out of the perimeter. The position held, though, and once again the enemy chose to withdraw as friendly artillery rounds began exploding within 30 meters of the 4th Platoon's lines.

Darkness descended, and the company was still seemingly secured in its tight perimeter; its wounded were all being taken care of by the medical aid men. Aircraft orbiting overhead illuminated the area, adjusted needed artillery fire, and guided reinforcing units that were on their way to assist the beleaguered Company C. By morning, Company C had been relieved by Company B, 2d Battalion, 16th US Infantry and Company B, 2d Battalion, 18th US Infantry, both of which had pushed forward for over 5,000 meters to assist their comrades.

During the time consuming process of air evacuation and resupply through a small hole in the jungle canopy, Company C, which had been doing a good job of tracking the enemy and keeping him in its sights, took its eyes off the ball, permitting the enemy to maneuver undetected into attack positions around a hastily formed perimeter. The ensuing attack came as a complete surprise to Company C, and only the defenders' determination and stubbornness prevented the enemy's superior forces from overwhelming the company's position.

Yet the encirclement could probably have been prevented by active patrolling on all sides of the perimeter during the company's halt. Reinforcements should have been readily available, too, or the companies within the battalion should have been mutually supporting—no more than an hour apart under the most adverse conditions.

Proper security measures have to be employed at every troop level, and the enemy must be kept off balance and unsure of the true intent of combat operations. He must not be given time to mass his forces against a small unit. An alert commander must employ all the tools available to him in fulfilling his responsibilities to look after his men; even in the most serene surroundings he and his subordinate leaders must take every possible measure to preserve the command. To do less invites disaster.

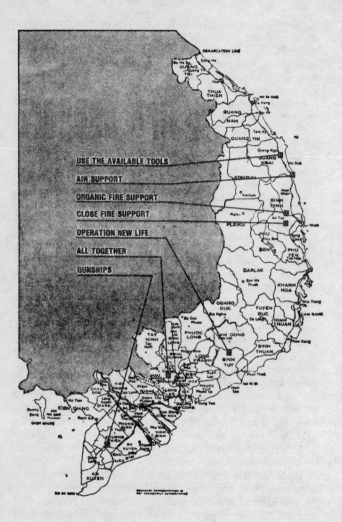

USE THE AVAILABLE TOOLS

AIR SUPPORT

ORGANIC FIRE SUPPORT

CLOSE FIRE SUPPORT

OPERATION NEW LIFE

ALL TOGETHER

GUNSHIPS

VII
Fire Support

SUCCESS ON THE modern battlefield is dependent upon fire superiority. If the coordinated fires of the attacker are more effective than those of the defender to the degree that the attacker may advance against the enemy position without ruinous losses, the attacker has fire superiority. On the other hand, if the defender's fire is so effective that the attacker will not advance against it, then the defender has fire superiority.

The roots of modern gunnery can be traced back to man's first impulse to throw missiles, and the realization that missile throwing enabled one to strike an enemy from a distant and possibly a safe point led to the development of bows, catapults, and other devices for propelling missiles. A common advantage of all of the early missile throwing devices was range: the extension of man's capability to throw an object at an enemy.

Modern gunnery is the result of the continued development of missile throwing capabilities, and the development of the various weapons of modern warfare has made firepower a primary factor to be considered when evaluating the capabilities and limitations of any force.

Enemy demoralization is the effect desired from coordinated fires; the degree to which it is achieved is usually proportional to the actual number and distribution of hits on the opposing force. Thus, fire superiority implies a large volume of accurately aimed and controlled fire, effectively directed and distributed over the objective area.

But it is not sufficient simply to establish fire superiority; once fire superiority has been achieved, it must be maintained by continuous and properly distributed fires. If fire superiority is not maintained, the ascendancy will pass to the opposing force. This, then, requires that every element of the opposing force capable of delivering or controlling effective fires must be subjected to continuous and properly distributed fire until the enemy has been destroyed or the mission accomplished. Once such fires cease on any element of the enemy force, that element can be expected to renew its fires in an effort to gain fire superiority and the decision.

Obviously no single weapon system is capable of providing continuous suppressive fires, although the wide variety of yields and effects available from modern weapons permits the application of continuous and effective fires over a period of time. But the proper employment of available firepower can only come from an understanding and the application of appropriate methods of employment, techniques of fire, and related detailed procedures applicable to the various weapon systems. Just as David preferred a slingshot to the conventional sword, so must the modern commander consider the basic characteristics and techniques of fire of the various systems when planning their employment.

all together

Individually, supporting fires are sometimes quite effective; but when those same fires are consolidated, they become devastating. A coordinated fire plan which incorporated all available fires provided the key to a successful operation for elements of the 25th Infantry Division soon after their arrival in South Vietnam.[1]

In January 1966, the 2d Brigade, 25th US Infantry Division assumed operational responsibility for the Cu Chi district, and securing the base camp—out to the range of enemy mortars—soon received the highest priority. The 1st Battalion, 27th US Infantry, was assigned the southwestern portion of the Bri-

[1]Combat experience submitted by CPT Jimmie L. Adams, USA.

gade's perimeter, and by several small unit actions it soon cleared the enemy out to the distance of friendly small arms range. As the next step in extending the band of security, the battalion planned to use its companies on search and destroy operations at a further distance from the perimeter to keep the enemy from using his mortars at effective, and deadly, ranges.

A large abandoned village some 2,000 meters west of the base camp became the 1st Battalion's objective in the extension of the close in security belt. Roughly taking the shape of an "L", with the long portion oriented north and south, the village was subdivided by many rows of bamboo thickets, each of which formed a square around a house or cultivated area. A large rice paddy lay adjacent to the village on the west and north, while a rubber plantation bordered it on the south and east.

For four days, various companies of the battalion took turns trying to clear the village, but with little success and a rather large number of casualties; Company A, for example, suffered 45 casualties during one three-hour period. The battalion had established a pattern which governed its operations against the village: air strikes, followed by an artillery preparation, and then by an infantry attack. But as a company would approach the village, enemy soldiers would place extremely accurate rifle machinegun, rifle grenade, and mortar fires on the US unit, and then would break off the engagement by splitting into small groups and fading into the jungle. Later, they would return from a different direction to harass the company as it tried to search and destroy the houses in the village, or as it returned to the base camp perimeter.

Because of the nature of the fighting, anger born of frustration was the undertone during the critiques that followed each operation. Captain Jimmie L. Adams, who commanded Company B, the next unit of the battalion scheduled to take a crack at the village, was fully conversant with the particulars of the previous attempts, and it was evident to him that the key to success lay in his use of all supporting fires—his own organic mortars; the battalion's 4.2-inch mortars; a battery of 105mm howitzers from the 1st Battalion, 8th US Artillery; helicopter gunships; and US Air Force fighters which would be standing by on ground alert.

During his briefing, Captain Adams learned from the battalion's S2 that natives had reported the existence of a major tunnel complex in the northern portion of the village. This, Adams thought, probably constituted a hangout for snipers, for the enemy soldiers could stay underground and out of harm's way until his supporting artillery fires had been lifted, when they could surface to continue their harassing tactics. One of his jobs, then, would be to locate and destroy that complex.

After he had received the battalion commander's order, Adams talked with the other company commanders who had attempted to search the village. With the knowledge he gained from these conversations, together with what his S2 had told him, Adams anticipated certain hot areas within the village where the enemy might be expected to concentrate his efforts. These he would consider when planning his artillery concentrations, and these would govern his routes into and out of the village.

Working closely with Lieutenant Ed Brinkman, the company's artillery forward observer, and with his weapons platoon leader, Lieutenant James Hill, Captain Adams developed a fire plan to support his unit. The 105mm howitzer fires would start in the southernmost portion of the village and would be slowly walked to the north. Waiting at a phase line near the objective, the infantrymen would follow the exploding artillery rounds as closely as possible all the way into the village. The company's organic 81mm mortars would fire a blocking and fire suppression mission in the northern part of the village shortly after the artillery preparation had begun; it was hoped that the short delay between the start of the two preparations would catch the enemy soldiers as they sought safety in the tunnels. The battalion's 4.2-inch mortars, meanwhile, would fire at the sniper infested patch of bamboo to the southwest of the village and across the rice paddy; that particular patch of ground had concealed the source of previous enemy fires.

Then, throughout the day and while the company was in the village, the howitzers and 81mm mortars would employ harassing and interdiction (H&I) fires in the north, while the 4.2-inch mortars would be on call after they had fired their initial preparation.

As one final step, Adams insured that the radio call signs and frequencies of the Army helicopter gunships were coordinated with those held by the US Air Force forward air controller who would be airborne over the village. The gunships could be over the objective within minutes after they had received a request for their support, for they would be standing by on ground alert at the base camp. The Air Force aircraft could be over the target within 15 minutes from their location at the Bien Hoa air base; at the first indications of a significant contact, their presence would be requested to tactically complement the other supporting fires.

Time passed slowly as Company B waited at the designated phase line. The packs on the backs of the soldiers bulged with the thermite grenades that would be used in the village in lieu of flame throwers. Then, with an all too familiar sound, the artillery shells passed overhead, landing with a roar on their target. At the same time, the exploding mortar rounds could be heard shredding the bamboo thickets. Impatient and tense from their brief delay at the phase line, the men of Company B were relieved to be moving; and as they moved forward, their faith in the supporting fires was almost boundless—they felt certain the fires would assist them in accomplishing their mission with the loss of as few men as possible.

A cry, "short round," came from the 1st Platoon as a black column of smoke drifted upward near the advancing troops. But panic was averted by the immediate yell of Platoon Sergeant Leslie Crawford—he had recognized this to be an enemy mortar round, and he knew that the explosion had been too small to have come from any of the supporting weapons. Crawford's quick thinking foiled the enemy attempt to get the supporting fires lifted. The men had been alerted to this enemy ruse while they were still in Hawaii, and Company C, just a few days before, had encountered the same trick.

By the time they had progressed 150 meters, the men could see the edge of the village and the lead elements could hear enemy soldiers yelling as they tried to get away from the curtain of steel which had descended on them. Then the low pitched explosions from the 81mm mortar rounds began testifying to the initial success of Captain Adams' plan, for the reported tunnel complex was being raked from one end to the other and any enemy soldiers who had fled there could do little to ward off the mortar fire.

Late that morning, two separate fire missions were delivered by the 4.2-inch mortars on unseen snipers who opened fire from other bamboo thickets, while the H and I fires continued

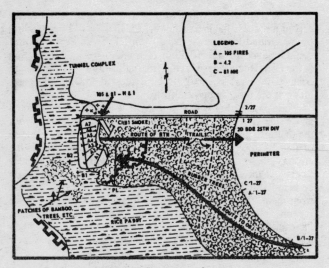

Map 46. All Together

their random method of sealing the area to prevent any enemy
from escaping. (*Map 46*) Then a little after 1200, helicopter
gunships were called in to rake the bamboo thicket to the
northwest with rocket and machinegun fire, a thicket from
which enemy snipers had fired on a medical helicopter that had
been called in to evacuate a wounded man.

Eventually, the men completed their grim tasks of searching
and burning houses, of finding and destroying booby traps,
and of maintaining all-around security. Nothing of significant
value had been found. But as seen by Lieutenant Brinkman
from above, the area was a patchwork of fires from burning
houses that had formerly given comfort to the enemy. The
small amount of rice that had been found had been dumped
down wells, while the countless booby traps had now been
reduced to the odor of burned powder, destroyed by demolitions. For the first time, a mission had been completed in the
area without a casualty from hostile fire—the wounded man
that had been evacuated had suffered a neck injury from a
wayward fragment of a booby trap demolished by explosives.
The frustration of fighting an unseen foe had been slightly eased
by the finding of blood trails left by enemy wounded, and by

the one enemy soldier that had been seen and killed.

Now it was time for the company to return to its base camp. Lieutenant Hill, in direct communication with his weapons platoon, was placed with the rear guard and as soon as the company had cleared the village he called for 81mm mortar fires. The first nine rounds were smoke, and a billowy gray cloud soon hung at the edge of the village like an early morning fog. It was a perfect screen and provided excellent concealment for the stay-behind ambush patrol, led by Lieutenant John Swenson and located just a few hundred meters from the outskirts of the village.

Then Hill began mixing high explosive rounds with the smoke to discourage enemy soldiers from using the screen to their own advantage. The movement back to the base camp proved uneventful except for an occasional explosion of demolition charges placed against newly discovered enemy booby traps found along the return route, and for the sounds of the covering fires as they passed overhead.

Captain Adams' detailed development of a coordinated fire plan allowed his company to successfully accomplish its mission. The enemy's reaction pattern had been broken, while the display of the supporting fires gave the men of the company full confidence in their leaders and in their own ability to search and destroy what had been a formidable enemy stronghold.

operation NEW LIFE

One of the striking characteristics of the war in Vietnam is the dynamic individual activity of the units up through brigade level. By the nature of the terrain and the enemy, the massive operations of division-sized units as were seen in Europe during World War II have been limited—indeed, almost eliminated. In place of these massive operations has emerged the independent maneuvering of separate brigades, with battalions actively hunting the enemy on their own and with company-sized patrols probing deep into hostile territory.

Operation NEW LIFE, conducted by the 173d US Airborne Brigade in late 1965, was a whole campaign in itself, a swing and traverse in both scope and in depth.[2] At bottom, it was not

[2]MAJ Robert B. Carmichael, USA, and LT Richard E. Eckert, USA, "Operation New Life," INFANTRY, January–February 1967, pp. 43–47.

only a military effort with a wide sweep, but it was also a true counterinsurgent effort. It was conducted to overcome the overt resistance of the Viet Cong, to counter the psychological poisons spread in the minds of the people, and to remove the social irritants—the Viet Cong cadre—who were forcing the people to take arms against allied soldiers.

Prior to launching Operation NEW LIFE, no effort of such magnitude had ever been made in South Vietnam. Earlier efforts on the part of the Brigade saw it hunting for the enemy, hitting him, extracting suddenly, and then moving on to other missions. But there had not been an operation of sufficient duration to allow exercising the complete arsenal of weapons available to a US unit in countering the psycho-sociological aspects of the counterinsurgency problem.

In this operation, then, the mission of the Brigade was to seize and secure a large, inhabited, fertile valley to the north and east of Vo Dat in Binh Tuy province. The valley contained over 28 square kilometers of rice paddies, all of which were ripe for harvest, and the Brigade had the task of ensuring that the Viet Cong did not get the crop. The crucial area of the operation, where the Viet Cong held dominant sway, fell into the tactical area of responsibility of the 2d Battalion, 503d US Infantry. The Brigade itself was augmented by two infantry battalions—the 1st Battalion, 2d US Infantry and the 1st Battalion, 26th Infantry, both from the 1st US Infantry Division—and by Battery B, 1st Battalion, 6th Artillery, a 155mm howitzer battery also from the 1st Division. In addition to the 2d Battalion, 503d US Infantry, the Brigade consisted of the 1st Battalion, 503d US Infantry; the 1st Battalion, Royal Australian Regiment; the 3d Battalion, 319th US Artillery; and Company D, 16th US Armor.

There were three key terrain features in the area of operations: an air strip at Vo Dat, interprovincial Route #3, and the inhabited village areas. (*Map 47*) A North Vietnamese Army (NVA) regiment and three main force Viet Cong battalions were reported operating in the hills to the north of the La Nga River; one main force Viet Cong regiment was reported 10 kilometers south of Vo Dat; and up to one battalion of local force Viet Cong was organized—and positively known to be operating—in the hamlets which dotted the 2d Battalion, 503d US Infantry's area of interest. Those hamlets contained exten-

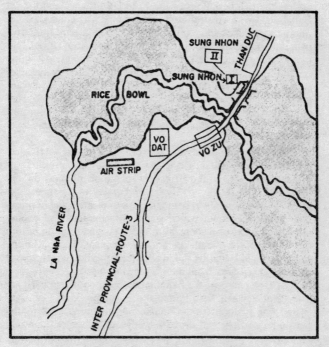

Map 47. Operation NEW LIFE

sive anti-airborne obstacles, individual defensive positions, and crew-served weapon emplacements.

The original battle plan called for the 1st and 2d Battalions of the 503d US Infantry to conduct a parachute assault on two drop zones north of the La Nga River on 25 November 1965. But when the local vendors in the Bien Hoa area began trying to sell parachute wings to the troops, it was quite apparent that the plan had been compromised. The Brigade commander, Brigadier General Ellis W. Williamson, wisely allowed this to pass as deception, and on 21 November, four days prior to the commencement of the original plan and with a minimum of notice, the two battalions of the 503d US Infantry and the 1st Battalion, Royal Australian Regiment (1/RAR) conducted heliborne assaults on the Vo Dat air strip. Concurrently, the two battalions from the 1st US Infantry Division moved out in a motor convoy from the south to link up with the assault units.

The four day jump in plans caught the enemy by surprise. In fact, roads were only half-cut by fresh ditches, while automatic and individual weapon positions, though started, were left unfinished. Sorties into the airhead, carried out by transport aircraft, soon built up and maintained a constant, five day level of supply.

The next seven days were spent in securing the vital interprovincial route to Gia Ra in the south and in patrolling aggressively to expand the Brigade's sphere of influence in and around Vo Dat. (*Map 48*) By the eighth day of the operation, the Brigade was ready to begin the task of clearing the northern half of the rice bowl, which was still in the hands of enemy units. The areas of responsibility were assigned, but to ensure the success of the overall operation, Lieutenant Colonel George E. Dexter's 2d Battalion, 503d US Infantry had to wrest control of its assigned area from the enemy. (*Map 49*)

The first phase of the battalion's operation began early on 1 December when Task Force Bravo, composed of Company B and one platoon from Company A, mounted 22 armored personnel carriers and drove a wedge of armor through and around the key southern village of Than Duc. After swimming the river behind the support of a rolling artillery barrage from the 105mm howitzers of the 3d Battalion, 319th US Artillery and air strikes flown by US Air Force fighter aircraft, the armored elements approached the village from the south and west. Enemy resistance was shattered under the savage pounding of the artillery fires and air strikes, and the enemy soon fled into the hills in disorganized bands. (*Map 50*)

The use of air and artillery preparations had presented a complicating factor in the operation, for there was always the chance that innocent civilians, mixed among the enemy soldiers, would be injured; but, fortunately, through the professional competence of the forward air controllers and the artillery forward observers, the civilians in the village were unharmed—

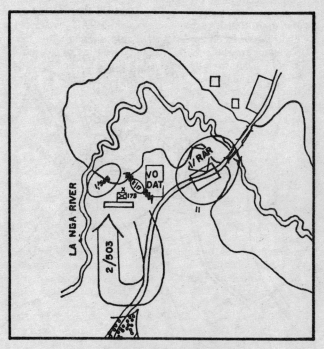

Map 48. Securing the Vo Dat Area

only the enemy, who offered resistance by manning defensive positions, were brought under the supporting fires.

Four hours after the armored assault, the remaining elements of Colonel Dexter's battalion landed in a helicopter assault on Landing Zone Silver. Company C drove at once to the northwest, cutting off Than Duc village from Sung Nhon I and taking up a blocking position to thwart any counterattack, a move also designed to cut off any remaining enemy soldiers who might be trying to escape to the north. Company A, meanwhile, moved to assist Company B at Than Duc.

Only seven and a half hours after the first attack had begun

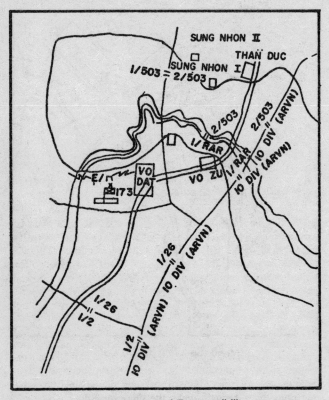

Map 49. Areas of Responsibility

all organized enemy resistance had been smashed. The village areas were searched methodically and thoroughly, and all military age males were taken into custody and evacuated to Vo Dat where they would be interrogated by the district chief. To clarify allied policy, leaflets and interpreters explained why the Americans were there and what was expected of the citizens to assure their safety.

The next phase of the operation began on 2 December, a

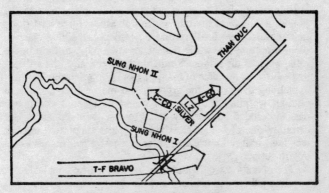

Map 50. Attack on Than Duc

phase which would see the employment of a sheer mass of
concentrated firepower to interdict and destroy the guerrillas
hidden in the hills. This rain of destruction would be followed
by combat patrols, while enemy movement to and from the
villages at night would be either stopped completely or slowed
significantly by silent and deadly ambushes. Under Dexter's
direction, the artillery liaison and air liaison officers teamed
up to develop a coordinated fire plan which would utilize all
the artillery and air support available to the Brigade. At the
same time, it was planned that Dexter's organic indirect fire
weapons: 81mm mortars, 4.2-inch mortars, and 106mm recoilless rifles, would complement the support plan by providing
close in, defensive fires. It was everyone's hope that the effects
of the coordinated fire plan would be devastating.

   And when the fire plan was put into effect, an area within
a randomly selected 1,000 meter grid square was covered in
one smashing instant by hundreds of rounds of artillery fired
by the 105mm howitzers, the 155mm howitzers, and the
4.2-inch mortars. Any area which study or intelligence indicated might be a lucrative target was given special attention.
But in bringing these fires to bear on the enemy, care was
exercised not to establish a pattern; no place within the range
of the guns could be considered safe by the enemy soldiers.

   It was not long before the results of these fires became

known. Occasionally, an enemy soldier would stumble help-
lessly out of the mountains and into the battalion's base camp.
Patrols would find fresh grave sites and blood stains in the
jungle; and, one of the ralliers from the local force Viet Cong
unit reported that artillery and air strikes had killed over 40
men in a company while they were attempting to hide in the
hills. Most of the ralliers admitted a greater fear of the artillery
and mortar rounds than of the fires from the supporting aircraft,
explaining that while the artillery and mortar rounds came in
without warning, the airplanes could be spotted and hence
partially eluded before they could release their ordnance. But
certainly one of the greatest values of the supporting aircraft
was their ability to strike at an area masked from other kinds
of fire support.

The operation would continue to a successful conclusion in
late December, and artillery and air strikes would continue to
punch at those enemy soldiers who chose not to surrender;
patrols would pick their way carefully through the valleys,
combing the mountains for the enemy units; psychological
broadcast and leaflet operations would be cast like giant nets
over the countryside.

The 2d Battalion would finally crush enemy resistance before it could crystallize, while bullets would be used to deny
the guerrilla forces freedom of action, to break up and defeat
the enemy's forces.

organic fire support

In Vietnam, where tall trees often fail to give the necessary
mask clearance needed by indirect fire weapons, units have
been prone to leave their organic mortars behind and depend
on artillery and close air support for their needs. The weight
and bulk of the mortars, the large amount of ammunition required to keep them in action, the hot temperatures and high
humidity of the country, all when combined have contributed
to this tendency to leave the mortars at home.

The problem of using mortars to support maneuvering rifle
elements has been further compounded by the lack of good
intelligence information to pinpoint the enemy, plus the danger
of leaving the small mortar section without adequate security.
Yet, on occasion, the mortars organic to every rifle company

have made the difference between success and failure for a number of units. Company B, 2d Battalion, 12th US Cavalry was one such unit.[3]

On 17 May 1966, in the Vinh Thanh valley near An Khe, Company A, 1st Battalion, 12th US Cavalry became heavily engaged with a large enemy force. Before the end of the action, all but one soldier in Company A's weapons platoon had been either killed or wounded when the enemy force overran its position. The following morning, the 2d Battalion, 12th US Cavalry was committed to act as a blocking force to the east of Company A's location. The Battalion's Company B was given the specific mission of blocking the expected eastward movement of the enemy unit which had mauled Company A the previous day.

A small clearing 600 meters south of Hill 766 was selected as the 2d Battalion's landing zone and designated as Landing Zone Horse. A visual reconnaissance of the landing zone did point up the fact that an enemy unit had covered the clearing with long bamboo poles stuck into the ground as anti-helicopter devices, and so the 2d Battalion's reconnaissance platoon went in ahead of Company B to remove the bamboo poles and to secure that area.

As soon as the reconnaissance platoon had completed its tasks, Company B landed on LZ Horse and immediately organized for the march to Hill 766, on which it would establish its blocking position. Captain Joseph Beeman, the company commander, moved his platoons as rapidly as possible to prevent the enemy's escape, but because of the difficult terrain the unit could not move as fast as he wanted. Because he had known his company would be moving through thick vegetation, Captain Beeman had decided to take only one mortar with him; the others he had ordered left at the base camp.

The ground inclined steeply upward as the company neared the area in which it was to set up its blocking position, and dark shadows were cast by the 130-foot canopy of the towering hardwood trees; the soil was wet, and the men were soon reduced to climbing hand over hand in trying to reach the crest of the hill.

The leading 1st Platoon, before it could gain the crest, was halted in its climb by light small arms fire from up the hill,

[3]Combat experience related by CPT Joseph Beeman to LT Terry H. Reilly.

but as the men of the platoon deployed to maneuver against the unexpected enemy force, the intensity of the enemy's fire increased and the platoon soon found itself unable to move. Beeman promptly ordered his 2d and 3d Platoons into the fight, moving them around the 1st Platoon to flank the enemy force. The two platoons managed to reach a small plateau below the peak of the hill from which they could bring their fires to bear on the enemy unit that had been firing on the 1st Platoon, but the enemy soon reacted to this new threat and shifted his effort to counter the fire. So effective was the counter move that the 2d and 3d Platoons were soon engaged in a stiff fight; their main disadvantage lay in the ground they occupied: a small, flat piece only 75 meters wide with steep slopes on both sides. (*Map 51*)

Unable to move any further up the hill until the enemy soldiers had been dispersed, Beeman moved his 1st Platoon into position behind the other two platoons, and sent his mortar squad back to the landing zone—which was still secured by the battalion's reconnaissance platoon—to find a cleared area from which it could register fire on the enemy soldiers who were sharing the small ridge with his company. He had been unable to find the proper clearance for his mortar on the slopes of the hill.

While the mortar squad moved to LZ Horse, the artillery forward observer with the company called for artillery support. But the only artillery fire available in the hilly terrain was high angle fire, and with the artillery tubes elevated to the degree necessary to clear a surrounding hill, the dispersion of the rounds was too great; the fire mission had to be cancelled.

Beeman then called for helicopter gunships, but from above the jungle canopy the pilots of the gunships could not distinguish friend from foe. Their fires would have to be held back until such time as a better target presented itself.

On the small plateau, Captain Beeman made one last effort to maneuver his platoons against the enemy force, but again his platoons were stopped by the intense and accurate fire. There was nothing to do now but to dig in and hold until help could arrive. As the platoons started preparing their defensive positions, setting up trip flares and claymore mines as defensive aids, the mortar squad signalled it had reached the landing zone and was ready to fire.

The mortar observer registered the first round on the sus-

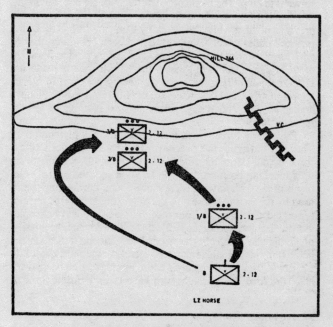

Map 51. 2d and 3d Platoons Move Up

pected enemy positions, and so successful was he that several of the enemy soldiers jumped out of their holes; for the first time, the men of Company B could actually see their enemy. No longer was he a phantom shooting from the cover of the jungle; now he was a harassed, scurrying foe, seeking cover from the lethal mortar rounds that fell on his position.

Before dawn of the next day, the single Company B mortar fired over 800 rounds at the enemy. And when the enemy soldiers attacked in waves at dawn, the mortar forward observers with each rifle platoon adjusted the mortar's devastating fire to within ten meters of their positions and denied the enemy his victory.

But help was on the way to Beeman's unit, for Company A of the 2d Battalion had landed at LZ Horse and was hurrying forward to help. The battle raged throughout the day, but night-fall found Company B in the same defensive posture as the previous night—while the attack by Company A had eased the pressure under which Company B had been operating, the en-emy force had not been dislodged and grimly held to his share of the ridge. (*Map 52*) Again, the 81mm mortar made the difference, as during the night the enemy persisted in his at-tempts to drive the US soldiers off of Hill 766. Finally, though, he had enough, and at daylight on the next morning he left the scene of battle.

The enemy force which had mauled the US platoon on 17 May had moved to the east much faster than had been antici-pated by the US commanders, and Company B, moving to set up a blocking position, had run head on into the security ele-ments of the withdrawing enemy unit. Then, the hugging tactics used by the enemy soldiers in the hilly, jungle covered terrain, prevented Company B from receiving artillery and helicopter gunship support during the battle that followed, and the mission of giving the company the needed fire support fell upon the one 81mm mortar squad that had accompanied the assault into LZ Horse. Had the company's entire mortar section been avail-able, the final results might well have taken a different turn.

gunships

One of the most significant developments in the conflict in Vietnam has been the employment of the armed helicopter and numerous reports attest to the close teamwork and the confi-dence which has developed between the infantryman on the ground and the pilots in the helicopters above who fly the fire support missions. As the war has intensified, the armed heli-copter has more and more developed into an outstanding weapon system with a wide variety of potential uses. It combines the mobility and speed of cavalry with the responsiveness and effectiveness of artillery fire. And with armed helicopters cov-ering the battlefield with observation and lethal, high volume fire, enemy soldiers often find their freedom of movement severely curtailed.

Except for enemy rounds which sometimes shatter the cock-pit's plexiglass and set off minor explosions in ammunition

Map 52. Help on the Way

trays, the world of the armed helicopter pilot is somewhat similar to that of the television viewer couched in the serenity of his own living room.[4] But even in this unreal setting, each member of a ship's crew is aware of two important factors: any mistake, no matter how small, can result in his death or in unnecessary casualties to his comrades on the ground; and he realizes that the armed helicopter is an important part of the ground commander's scheme of maneuver and fire support.

Armed helicopters provide ground commanders the firepower of 2.75-inch rockets, 40mm grenades, SS-11 guided missiles with anti-personnel warheads, 20mm cannons, or 7.62mm machineguns, depending on the weapon system mounted on the ships. This firepower, coupled with mobility and long range radio communications, enables the armed helicopters to conduct armed reconnaissances far to the front and flanks of the infantry units and materially increases the ground

[4]Combat experience submitted by CPT Frederick G. Terry, USA.

commander's sphere of influence. Yet the ships may be recalled rapidly and their firepower massed anywhere on the battlefield within minutes after a fire request has been received.

The versatility of the armed helicopter was particularly evident on 11 February 1966 when the South Vietnamese Army's 9th Infantry Division initiated a joint ground-airmobile operation in the Xom Ngoc Ty area—10 kilometers southeast of Kien Giang, the province headquarters—against elements of the Viet Cong's U Minh Regiment.

To find and destroy the enemy unit, the Division adopted a task organization. Task Force 15, consisting of the Division's reconnaissance company and the 2d and 3d Battalions, 15th ARVN Infantry Regiment, would carry out airmobile assaults into landing zones north of Xom Ngoc Ty and to sweep south and west to force the enemy unit against blocking positions that would be occupied by the 2d Battalion, 13th ARVN Infantry Regiment.

Task Force Cavalry's headquarters troop and the 2d and 3d Troops, 2d ARVN Armored Cavalry Squadron would screen the area to the north and south of Xom Ngoc Ty and, on order, support the movements of Task Force 15. The 43d RVN Ranger Battalion and the 1st Battalion, 15th ARVN Infantry Regiment at Rach Gia would make up the Division's reserve, while the 114th, 116th, and 121st US Aviation Companies and Company A, 101st US Aviation Battalion would provide the air lift and armed helicopters to support the Division's operations. (*Map 53*)

The heavy ground fog which blanketed the operational area during the early morning of 11 February 1966 did not deter the US and ARVN Air Force fighter planes from carrying out preliminary aerial strikes, and from the cockpit of his helicopter, Captain George L. O'Grady; who commanded the 3d Platoon, 114th US Aviation Company, could see the plumes of smoke rising from the napalm and bombs of the attacking aircraft. Orienting on the smoke, he set a course for the six armed helicopters of his platoon; their mission: to reconnoiter Landing Zones Tiger and Lion and to escort the troop carrying helicopters to the landing zones.

Approaching LZ Tiger, O'Grady viewed the white blanket beneath him and checked his navigational aids to pinpoint his location. The Air Force airplanes made a last strafing run on the landing zone and then shifted their fires to LZ Lion as the

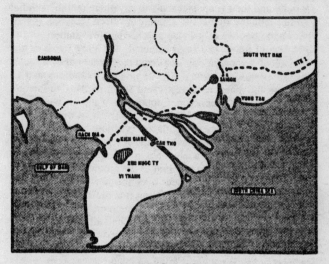

Map 53. Gunships

helicopters began their let down for the landing zone reconnaissance. As his ship broke through the fog cover, O'Grady could see the ground and noticed that the area beneath was lined with unoccupied foxholes and bunkers and that houses located along a north-south canal also appeared vacant.

After making a thorough reconnaissance of the area, Captain O'Grady sent Captain Frederick G. Terry's team of two helicopters to escort the troop carriers that were bringing in the 2d Battalion, 15th ARVN Infantry Regiment. O'Grady remained in the area and created enough turbulence with his ship's rotor to dissipate the ground fog in a small portion of the landing zone. When the first troop carrier helicopters arrived, their rotor wash cleared an even larger portion of the LZ, and the two succeeding lifts of 20 ships each landed with only minor difficulty.

As the last of the troop carriers left LZ Tiger, the gunships proceeded to LZ Lion and repeated the procedures; there, the 3d Battalion, 15th ARVN Infantry Regiment landed without incident and O'Grady took his ships back to Vi Thanh to refuel. He was careful not to leave the area, though, until a relief platoon—the 3d Platoon, Company A, 101st Aviation Battalion—had come up to provide any needed fire support.

After his ships had been refueled, O'Grady received the missions of reconnoitering suspected enemy withdrawal routes in front of the advancing ARVN infantry battalions and of screening the major east-west canal south of the two landing zones. It was not long before Captain Terry and his wing man, Chief Warrant Officer Leon K. Elding, flying at treetop level, had discovered many camouflaged positions. Reporting this information back to the base camp, Terry and Elding shifted their reconnaissance to a new area in which an enemy force of some 800 men had been reported to the ground commander by a local civilian. As they flew over the new area, the pilots could see many young men crossing rice paddies on their way toward a large number of sampans which crowded the canal.

The aviators received permission to halt all movement from the area, and were also told to select a landing zone that could be used by a blocking force which would be lifted in within the next hour. Terry and Elding stopped the sampans with a rocket across the bow of the farthest boat, but the young men noted earlier began running from the sampans across the open rice paddy field. The commander of the ground unit ordered the men halted, but though Terry and Elding tried in every way they knew to halt the men without actually firing at them, the race away from the sampans continued. Finally, the pilots told their door gunners to open fire at the young Vietnamese; after a few minutes of this, the remaining men stopped their running and stood passively waiting for the ARVN troops to come.

It was at this moment that the 3d Battalion reported that they were receiving heavy enemy fire and requested immediate fire support from the armed helicopters. O'Grady took over the mission of keeping the Vietnamese corralled in the rice paddy and sent Terry to support the infantry. As Terry arrived in the 3d Battalion's area, he could hear enemy bullets whizzing past his ship and could see on the ground scenes of violent activity. He set up an attack pattern as soon as he could definitely identify the 3d Battalion's lines, and pressed his attack to within 200 meters of the enemy; Elding followed close behind, loosing his rockets at the same enemy targets.

But on the second firing pass, the enemy soldiers were better oriented to defend against the threat from the sky and tracers soon curved up toward the attacking helicopters. Elding felt his aircraft shudder as he closed on the enemy and heard still more bullets crack around the ship. Again the two helicopters fired at the enemy at the edge of a wood line, but as they curled up and away bright yellow lights in each aircraft started to flicker on and off with their message that only 20 minutes of fuel remained. It was a crucial moment, for the pilots could see still more enemy soldiers running for the tree line. Without hesitation, they both turned back and steered their helicopters after the running foe; they knew they had to move quickly. Closing the gap swiftly but surely, the pilots fired off their remaining ordnance: a death dealing salvo directly into the running enemy unit. Then, once more climbing away, Terry and Elding turned and flew to the staging area to refuel and rearm.

When they returned to the operational area, it was obvious that the ground fighting had intensified. The 2d Battalion, 13th Infantry had occupied a blocking position along the east-west canal; the 2d Troop, 2d Armored Cavalry Squadron was advancing from the north; and the 2d and 3d Battalions, 15th Infantry were pushing toward the blocking force against moderate resistance. (*Map 54*)

Watching the 2d Troop from the air, Captain Terry could see a classic type of attack developing. Eleven armored personnel carriers in line advanced with their machineguns blazing at the tree line. But, then, without warning, two of the carriers burst into flames, victims of an enemy recoilless rifle team which was firing from well camouflaged positions.

The armed helicopters again swung into action. O'Grady, who had also refueled and rearmed by this time, overflew the tree line, spraying the area with rockets and grenades, while Terry talked to the force to set up an attack. He could hear the roar of the enemy's recoilless rifle as it threw out shell after shell, and he could see that the enemy crew had hit several other carriers.

Flying through the columns of black smoke rising from the burning carriers, O'Grady placed his fire so that initially it fell 50 meters in front of the disabled carriers; he then walked it into the tree line. He was followed closely by Terry and then by Elding, as the three ships made pass after pass against the enemy positions. O'Grady then flew directly over the enemy

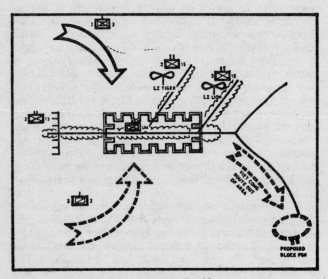

Map 54. Blocking Positions

force and placed plunging fire on its positions with his grenade launcher and with the machineguns in either door of his ship. Since he was flying along the long axis of the tree line, he was not concerned with deflection. The three helicopters continued their attacks until they were relieved to refuel and rearm.

No sooner had O'Grady's aircraft been taken care of when they were ordered back into action. During their absence, the 43d ARVN Ranger Battalion had been air landed between the 2d Troop and the 2d Battalion, 15th Infantry, had deployed, and were preparing to attack the enemy's tree line positions in conjunction with an attack that was being launched by the 2d Battalion.

Under the supporting fires laid down by the helicopters, the two Ranger companies advanced toward the enemy unit. The company on the west managed to reach the tree line, but the company on the east was pinned down 50 meters away. (*Map 55*) The only fire support available to the hard pressed ARVN units were the armed helicopters, and again O'Grady

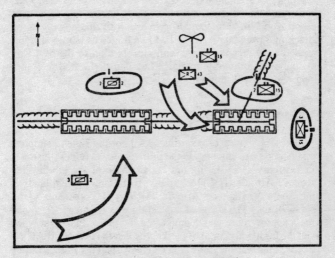

Map 55. The Rangers Attack

and his men made pass after pass until they had no more ammunition. Again, it was rearm, refuel, and back on station, just in time to escort the troop lift helicopters which were bringing the 1st Battalion, 15th ARVN Infantry to the support of the Rangers. O'Grady rendezvoused with the troop lift carriers as the latter approached the battle area and guided them in a low level approach across the rice paddies to a landing zone immediately behind the Rangers and only about 300 meters from the enemy's main battle position. But so effectively did the gunships provide suppressive fires that the troops off loaded without difficulty and the troop lift ships departed with only negligible damage.

Fighting continued into the night, and so long as the area was illuminated by flares the gunships were able to continue their fire support mission. But when the ground troops halted their attacks and began establishing defensive perimeters, the division commander released the gunships.

During this engagement, each of the armed helicopters logged over 12 hours, three of them at night. O'Grady's ships alone expended 525 2.75-inch rockets, 225,000 rounds of 7.62mm machinegun ammunition, and 2,250 40mm grenades. They had been used to conduct reconnaissances of landing zones, to escort troop lift ships, and to provide close fire support to the attacking ground units. They had functioned as a trained team, immediately responsive and consciously alert to the best way to support the infantry soldier. They had performed well in a long and difficult mission.

close fire support

The importance of coordinated supporting fires to suppress an enemy's fire and to gain the initiative was vividly illustrated in February 1965 during the initial phase of the North Vietnamese Army's (NVA) campaign to isolate the highlands in the South Vietnamese Army's (ARVN) II Corps area of responsibility.[5] The scene of this action was Highway 19, a vital main supply route which connected the port city of Qui Nhon and the highland capital of Pleiku, the headquarters of II ARVN Corps. This was the same area where in 1954 the French Group MOBILE with its famous Korean battalion had been ambushed and wiped out by the Viet Minh during the French Indo-China War. In fact, some of the fighting took place within sight of the monuments which had been erected to commemorate that action.

On 20 February 1965 the enemy, as part of his overall plan to cut off and isolate the highland plateau, launched attacks against two US Army Special Forces forward operating bases (FOB) which had secured Highway 19 midway between the Mang Yang pass and the district capital of An Khe. On hearing of the attacks by radio, the commander of the Special Forces camp at An Khe immediately dispatched his alert reaction force, a CIDG rifle company. During the fighting which followed that afternoon, the CIDG company broke through a hasty enemy ambush and reached FOB #1, which had been overrun; after gathering up the scattered garrison, the CIDG company decided to remain overnight at the camp's location. (*Map 56*)

As the CIDG was returning to the base camp the next day, it was ambushed again. This time the ambush succeeded and

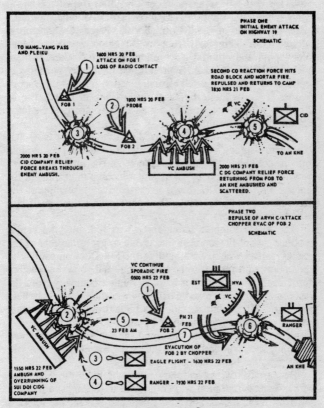

Map 56. Close Air Support

the truck column was left shattered with its vehicles burning and personnel dispersed. As soon as he heard of this incident, the Special Forces camp commander immediately sent out his last alert CIDG company. But this unit, too, ran into an enemy roadblock, and came under heavy 82mm mortar and small arms fire which destroyed the lead vehicles. Threatened by encirclement, the company withdrew to An Khe.

On the next day, 22 February, the garrison at FOB #2 reported that it was again under fire. Because of the losses already suffered by the CIDG forces from An Khe, the commanding officer of the II Corps Special Forces C Detachment alerted a CIDG company from Sui Doi camp west of the Mang Yang pass and ordered it to relieve FOB #2. Careful plans were made to furnish A1E aircraft and helicopter gunships as column cover, and a small reserve reaction force—the Special Forces II Corps Eagle Flight platoon—was also alerted to be lifted by helicopter to reinforce the CIDG company if the latter should run into trouble.

As the Sui Doi company moved past the ruins of FOB #1, the enemy sprang still another ambush, and the fires poured into the column left the trucks shattered and burning. The volley was followed quickly by an assault which so intermingled the enemy with the CIDG troops that effective close support fire from the air was impossible; the fight soon resolved itself into a hand-to-hand contest.

The Eagle Flight reaction force was sent into the battle, landing east of the ambush site, trying to get at the rear of the enemy forces which were battling the Sui Doi company. But the enemy unit proved to be too strong, and soon the reaction force itself was calling for help. A Ranger company from the last remaining corps reserve battalion was then flown in to help the Eagle Flight, but it, too, was pinned down and together with the reaction force formed a perimeter in order to survive through the night. After screening the ambush site the next morning, they withdrew to join the garrison at FOB #2. Shortly thereafter, the base was surrounded.

Because the enemy had shown great strength, the remainder of the Ranger Battalion was committed to the fight to free the garrison at the forward operating base and was moved forward to the An Khe airstrip under the cover of darkness. The next morning the Rangers moved out to relieve the encircled units, but not long after leaving An Khe they encountered a dug-in enemy force which occupied positions blocking the road. They were also counterattacked by an estimated two enemy battalions and driven back with heavy casualties. This enemy unit was identified as belonging to the North Vietnamese Army and its men were armed with the latest military weapons. The military authorities in Saigon were immediately notified of this threat and of the fact that II Corps had nothing left to throw into the fight—more air support was needed, and the Corps wanted the ARVN Airborne Brigade moved into its area to assist in the fighting that lay ahead.

Since the Airborne Brigade would take several days to close into An Khe, it was suggested that the troops at FOB #2 should try to break out and infiltrate in small groups either to Mang Yang or to An Khe. At the same time, though, permission was given to use US Air Force fighter aircraft and bombers to support the ARVN troops fighting along Highway 19. This commitment of US aircraft changed the picture and the morale of the South Vietnamese rose sharply. This commitment also changed the idea of having the garrison break out; now thoughts turned to possibly lifting the garrison out by helicopter.

Eventually a plan was drawn up which called for the use of extensive close support fires by Air Force aircraft on both sides of the embattled outpost to suppress the enemy's fires, while helicopter lift ships, guarded by gunships, would land beside the outpost and lift out the garrison.

The matching of speeds, firepower, and other capabilities of the helicopter gunships with the US Air Force F100s, A1Es, and B57s in a single integrated operation required centralized planning and split second execution. Fortunately, the operation went off like clockwork, and the detailed timing schedule and plans worked like charms. The heavy aerial strikes so blanketed the enemy forces that it was only on the last helicopter lift that the ships began receiving any enemy fire at all, and this was only sporadic fires from small arms and mortars.

Throughout this action, the importance of supporting fires had been vividly illustrated. In the case of the ambush of the CIDG company from Sui Doi, the sudden assault by the enemy and the closing with friendly troops kept the supporting fires from being properly used, even though gunships and fighters circled overhead. Patrols deeper into the jungle would have discovered the enemy and permitted the orbiting ships to bomb and strafe the enemy soldiers before they could have closed with and overrun the main body.

In the relief of the units trapped at the forward operating base, all of the available fires—from F100s, A1Es, B57s, helicopter gunships—were used in a comprehensive fire support plan which depended on careful timing to insure that the area surrounding the base was kept under constant bombing and strafing attack to prevent the enemy troops from placing heavy fires on the troop lift helicopters or onto the landing zone from which the friendly troops were being extracted. The importance of coordinated supporting fires to suppress enemy fires and to gain the initiative had been reaffirmed.

air support

A repeated Viet Cong and North Vietnamese Army tactic is to mass and attack during the hours of darkness and to disappear before daylight. Usually the objective of the attack is the destruction of a smaller force which mans an isolated defensive position. Timely reinforcement of those positions at night by units moving overland is usually difficult and dangerous, since the enemy almost always establishes ambushes along the approach routes, while reinforcement by heliborne units is at least as difficult because of reduced visibility, vulnerability to enemy fire, and limited landing zones. Under these conditions, the defending force must hold out against the enemy's onslaught with its immediately available artillery or close air support.

During June 1966, Task Force 140, Army of the Republic of Vietnam, was dispersed along the coastal plain north of Bong Son.[6] Its mission was to establish government control over the area secured in two previous operations, MASHER and DAVY CROCKETT. Although local force Viet Cong and some NVA forces had suffered heavy casualties during those operations, a major threat still existed from a number of NVA units which remained in the Bong Son area.

At the time, the task force consisted of two ARVN battalions, one troop mounted in armored personnel carriers, two Regional Force companies, six Popular Force platoons, and two 105mm howitzer platoons. The task force's base camp was on the northern edge of Tam Quan, along National Route #1, and was a permanent defensive position having an adequate trench system, protective wire, and some mines.

Shortly after 2200, 19 June 1966, the stillness of the night was shattered when heavy enemy 81mm and 82mm mortar rounds began exploding inside the defended area; moderate casualties were inflicted on those troops who had been sleeping

[6]Combat experience submitted by CPT Richard S. Kent, USA.

in the open or in uncovered trenches. Within five minutes, probing attacks had begun from three directions. Immediate illumination and fire support against the attackers was provided by the task force's mortars and artillery, as well as from other artillery located in De Duc, some eight kilometers to the south, while the call went out for a flareship and for immediate close air support. (*Map 57*)

For the next 45 minutes the enemy's mortar attack continued, although somewhat lessened in intensity. The ground attacks picked up, though, as enemy units probed for weak spots in the defensive perimeter. Within the perimeter, armored personnel carriers moved about, countering the enemy assaults, while the local artillery pieces bolstered the defense by using their direct fire capability. From the volume of fire received, however, it was soon apparent that the defenders faced a large enemy force and that the base camp was in serious danger of being overrun.

At 2300, the pilot of a US Air Force AC-47 aircraft called in, reporting that he was ten minutes out with an hour and forty-five minutes of continuous illumination and a gatling gun with 15,000 rounds of 7.62mm ammunition aboard. He was briefed on the ground situation and a mortar flare was fired to assist him in locating the defensive area.

Once he had picked up the camp, the pilot began a slow orbit over it, dropping flares, and located the features he had received during the in-flight briefing. During his first circle, the pilot was able to identify nine enemy mortars by their muzzle flashes; these he promptly reported and received permission to suppress them. His first two passes put four of the mortars out of action and started ammunition burning at one of the sites. Although the other mortars continued to fire, the pilot was able to give warning whenever rounds were on the way, giving friendly troops time to take cover.

In spite of these suppressive fires, the enemy was able to land a concentration of 82mm mortar fire in the task force's artillery position, killing several men, including the battery commander, and starting a serious fire in the ready ammunition pit. The local artillery, which had been shooting effective direct fire missions, was now completely out of action, while a series of huge explosions from the burning ammunition pile caused enough damage to the north side of the perimeter to seriously weaken the defenses on that side.

Map 57. Attack at Tam Quan

Sensing this, the enemy increased the intensity of his attack from the north. But at this critical point, the airborne forward air controller from Qui Nhon called in and reported a flight of A1E fighters on their way. He was briefed by the AC-47 pilot, and in agreement with the ground commander, selected the remaining enemy mortar positions as the first targets. Within ten minutes, the fighters were diving in to attack, and the last of the enemy mortars was soon destroyed.

The ticklish job of striking the attacking enemy infantry, who were then assaulting the northern portion of the perimeter, remained, a task complicated because the assaulting enemy soldiers were in close proximity to the friendly positions and within 150 meters of the village of Tam Quan. Precision control was absolutely necessary if the village was not to be destroyed.

At first the ground commander attempted to designate targets by relating them to points on the defensive perimeter: for example, troops in the open 150 meters from the northeast bunker. While this system would not have been adequate under most conditions, the enemy cooperated and revealed the position of his supporting automatic weapons by firing tracers which were visible from the air. This, then, gave both the ground commander and the forward air controller a common reference point and a workable system from which to adjust strikes and disrupt the main enemy attack.

The remaining threat was a secondary enemy attack from the southeast. Close air strikes were also adjusted on that enemy force, this time by using the intersection of a line of palm trees and a rice paddy as a reference point. The strikes were accurate, and by 0130 the enemy had disengaged, leaving behind a few small elements to cover the removal of his dead.

A North Vietnamese Army soldier, separated from his unit during the attack, surrendered at an ARVN outpost, and from information he divulged, the attacking force was determined to have consisted of two NVA infantry battalions, two main force Viet Cong companies, some local force Viet Cong soldiers, and an NVA heavy weapons battalion; he also reported that his unit had suffered heavy casualties.

The quick response to the immediate request for close air support undoubtedly assisted this isolated ARVN battalion to successfully defend itself against a larger enemy force, and showed again that in Vietnam support is not limited by range and is not subject to the hazards which face a reaction force in trying to reach a battle area.

use the available tools

Naval gunfire support has also proven to be a valuable adjunct to the operations conducted by free world forces in South Vietnam. In all of the corps areas it is possible to engage many enemy targets with naval gunfire from ships at sea, and it has become the rule rather than the exception for US, South Vietnamese, and their Allies to plan for and employ this fire when operating near the coast. With the help of naval gunfire, two ARVN Popular Force platoons not only defended their outpost at My Trang, they were able at the same time to inflict grave damage on a reinforced enemy battalion bent on the destruction of their position.[7]

The My Trang popular force unit had been given the mission of protecting a segment of National Route #1 in the coastal lowlands of Quang Ngai province and of supporting the pacification program in that area. For his headquarters, the force commander had selected an old primary school building, around which he had his men construct a communications bunker, four personnel bunkers, a trench filled with punji stakes, and three fence lines of pointed bamboo. Since the defensive complex was situated on relatively high ground, his unit had good all-around observation and fields of fire. He also had his men integrate the lakes and ponds to the south and east into the outer fence to create moat-type obstacles. (*Map 58*)

Personal contact with the local population by the outpost commander succeeded in procuring local labor and materials for the array of barriers that surrounded the position. The local inhabitants also provided a combat youth organization to provide early warning and to cause the premature deployment of any attacking enemy force. The outpost commander also coordinated the fires of those artillery units within supporting range.

The 3d Battalion, 4th ARVN Infantry Regiment, minus one

---

[7]Combat experience submitted by CPT Ralph E. Inman, USMC, and CPT Ernest G. Rivers, USMC, and adapted by CPT Arthur R. Littlewood, III.

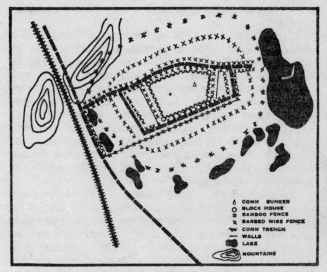

Map 58. My Trang Outpost

rifle company but reinforced by two 105mm howitzers, was located in a static defensive position on high ground at Nui Dau, about four kilometers to the southwest. One company of the battalion, reinforced with two 155mm howitzers, was also in a static defense position, on the high ground at Nui Dan, approximately two kilometers to the northwest. Both of these positions overlooked the outpost of My Trang.

Early in December 1965, intelligence reports received by the 2d ARVN Infantry Division indicated that a large enemy force would attack somewhere in the Duc Pho area in the near future. Because the enemy could and did interdict the lines of supply to Nui Dan and Nui Dau, both outposts had to be resupplied by helicopter. As a result, neither position had a large number of artillery rounds on hand. To overcome this deficiency, the commander of the 2d ARVN Infantry Division asked that a US Navy destroyer be positioned off the coast near

Duc Pho to provide additional fire support. His request was approved, and the USS *McKean* soon took station off the threatened area.

Captain John Hey, a US Marine Corps officer serving as advisor to one of the South Vietnamese battalions of the 4th ARVN Infantry Regiment at Nui Dau, was responsible for calling and adjusting any needed naval gunfire.

Although the most likely targets for an enemy attack seemed to be the villages of Nui Dau and Nui Dan, the popular force commander at My Trang was determined not to be taken by surprise. He carefully insured that his understrength unit of 68 men, armed with US-manufactured M1 rifles, carbines, and Browning automatic rifles, was thoroughly rehearsed, and that each man understood his mission and area of responsibility within the defensive position.

As darkness fell on the My Trang outpost on 14 December, the combat youths took up their positions on the edge of the village in much the same manner as they had done every night since their organization. But this night would be different, for shortly after midnight, concealed by the inky blackness of an overcast sky, the entire main force 9th Battalion of the 18th Regiment, 325th Viet Cong Division, reinforced with a heavy weapons company, crept into the area and prepared to attack the My Trang outpost. Outnumbering the outpost defenders by almost eight to one, the Viet Cong sensed an easy victory as they made final preparations for the attack.

Two rifle companies were sent to prepare ambush positions north and south of the outpost along Highway #1, these designed to intercept and destroy any reinforcements that might be sent from the 3d Battalion at Nui Dau and Nui Dan; the enemy's command post and supporting heavy weapons company were established on a hill to the northwest overlooking the popular forces outpost. When the command and support elements were in position, the enemy commander sent his assault troops—two rifle companies—silently toward My Trang. But before they reached the village, a shot from one of the combat youth ripped into their formation and alerted the outpost, forcing the attacking companies to deploy long before they had planned. (*Map 59*)

Immediately the outpost commander ordered the defenders into position to cover the withdrawal of the combat youth and notified the Duc Pho headquarters of the situation. He did not

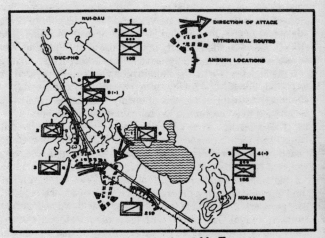

Map 59. Enemy Attacks at My Trang

know at this time the strength or size of the force making the attack.

Discovered, but still sensing victory, the enemy companies launched their assault behind a barrage of 60mm and 81mm mortar rounds directed at the outpost. The popular force commander immediately called for and received his preplanned concentrations around his perimeter and as the first volley of 105mm and 155mm rounds exploded among the assaulting enemy soldiers, the mortar fire momentarily ceased.

Following a 15-minute lull, the mortar fire began again, this time more accurately, and the attackers crossed the first fence. The defenders illuminated the night with their final protective fires, but the small garrison could not long deter the Viet Cong soldiers from pressing home their attack to the second fence line. Realizing his difficult position, but determined to do all that he could to stop the enemy, the outpost commander requested an Air Force flare ship and naval gunfire support.

As the enemy companies penetrated the second fence and began the final assault on the third and last fence in front of the trench line, Captain Hey began calling for and adjusting the USS *McKean*'s fire. Knowing that the naval gun is extremely accurate in deflection and that the position of the ship was to the northeast of the target—providing a gun-target line roughly parallel to the friendly lines—Hey was able to bring the naval gunfire in to within 50 meters of the trench line. The 5-inch rounds landed directly in the midst of the attacking Viet Cong soldiers and their explosive effects succeeded in driving off the attackers. With the iliumination now being provided by a US Air Force AC-47, Hey shifted the artillery and naval fires to cover the suspected routes of enemy withdrawal even as he continued to place fire on the retreating enemy soldiers.

The defenders were critically low on ammunition by this time, and the commander, who did not think his men could stand off another enemy attack without some sort of resupply, ordered his soldiers to move outside the fences to pick up all of the weapons and ammunition that the Viet Cong soldiers had abandoned during the fight. Once back inside the outpost, the popular force soldiers waited for the gray dawn and a relief force from Nui Dan; armed with the weapons of their enemy, they prepared again to give a good account of themselves should the enemy force return.

But the 9th Battalion did not return to the fight, for with the coming of dawn tactical aircraft arrived overhead searching for the small bands of fleeing enemy soldiers and striking at every target of opportunity. The enemy had paid a high price in both men and materiel while the team work exhibited by all of the friendly forces had been largely responsible for the enemy's defeat. The popular force commander, knowing his unit was understrength and poorly equipped, had made use of every available military tool to accomplish his mission. His good judgment and detailed planning prior to the action not only enabled him to maintain control in his assigned area, it rendered an enemy battalion ineffective for a considerable period of time.

VIII
Combat Support

AN OUTSTANDING LESSON learned—or relearned—in Vietnam is the fact that combat support and combat service support are of extreme importance to the successful conduct of offensive or defensive operations, and that the movement of troops and supplies to the critical point at the critical time has been, and will continue to be, the dominant factor in winning a battle, or a war. Conversely, it has been learned that the loss of one's ability to move troops and supplies entails the loss of initiative and a limitation of action which can only result in final defeat.

Under the US Army's present organizational concepts, the combat support and combat service support structures can be tailored to support differing sizes and types of combat forces. But each structure, no matter how tailored, must contain those support elements most appropriate to the requirements of the combat force. For example, in a division, the organic combat support elements consist of the division artillery, the aviation battalion (or aviation group, if an airmobile division), the engineer battalion, the signal battalion, and the military police company.

Combat service support elements, on the other hand, provide logistic, personnel, and civil affairs support and may be found within the division's support command. Primarily administrative in nature, combat service support functions specifically

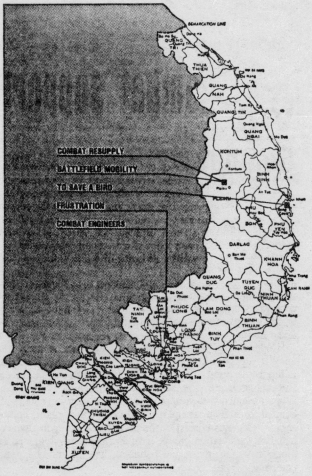

COMBAT RESUPPLY

BATTLEFIELD MOBILITY

TO SAVE A BIRD

FRUSTRATION

COMBAT ENGINEERS

include supply, transportation, maintenance, labor, and medical activities.

combat resupply

The many successes enjoyed by the free world forces in Vietnam certainly stand as a tribute to the unheralded men behind the scenes who provide the necessary combat and combat service support to the man up front. Although many of these men operate behind the scenes, they do not necessarily operate behind the lines, for often they face the same dangers as the infantryman, and at times are placed in positions even more precarious than those held by the men or units who ask for their support.

During the afternoon of 30 March 1966, the Rifle Platoon, Troop A, 1st Battalion, 9th US Cavalry conducted a heliborne operation onto a landing zone from which it quickly moved to investigate earlier sightings of enemy troops and to capture a prisoner if at all possible.[1]

Moving to the northeast portion of the large L-shaped clearing, the platoon was taken under fire from enemy soldiers manning positions to the north and northeast. After sustaining several casualties and engaging in hand-to-hand combat with the enemy soldiers, the platoon managed to break contact, and the men withdrew to the southwest corner of the clearing to await extraction. (*Map 60*)

The extraction helicopters were quick to arrive, and the lift off was almost completed when an extremely heavy, concentrated volume of enemy fire brought down four of the loaded helicopters. Immediately the ready reaction force—Company A, 1st Battalion, 12th US Cavalry—waiting at a base camp at Pleiku was alerted and airlifted to the scene; arriving at LZ Eagle, some 500 meters to the south, at 1600, the company moved rapidly to secure the area around the downed ships. When the company was in position, the evacuation of the dead and wounded was completed.

After the evacuation, Company A swept to the north in search of the enemy unit which had engaged the Rifle Platoon; it moved only a short distance, though, when it came under

[1]Combat experience submitted by CPT Tom Caraballo, USA.

Map 60. Rifle Platoon in Action

heavy fire from two directions. Caught in the open the company sustained several casualties, including the company commander, Captain John E. Drake.

Commanded now by Lieutenant Lawrence Britten, the company began withdrawing toward LZ Eagle for a helicopter pickup. Britten sent his 1st Platoon and his Weapons Platoon ahead to secure the landing zone, while he with the 2d and 3d Platoons turned to fight off the enemy and to launch an unsuccessful assault to recover the dead and wounded soldiers. Britten went down, a casualty to the enemy's fire, and the 2d Platoon leader took over the command. Under his urging, the platoons finally retrieved the dead and wounded, and then withdrew towards the landing zone. Aerial rocket artillery helicopters and other helicopter gunships pounced on the pursuing enemy force, showering down machinegun, grenade, and cannon fires and causing untold casualties. Under the umbrella, Company A arrived at LZ Eagle at 1900, and began preparing for a night extraction.

Pathfinders called in medical evacuation helicopters to take out the casualties, placed a lighted "T" on the landing zone, and began directing the first extraction ship—a CH-47—to the ground. But as it attempted to land, and while it was still 30 feet in the air, the giant craft took about 50 direct enemy hits and the pilots had to execute an emergency landing in the very center of the landing zone. Because the LZ was small, no other helicopters could land; the remaining 100 men of Company A consolidated around the disabled helicopter while its commander requested a flare ship and informed his battalion commander that his unit had to have more ammunition if it was to get through the night.

The company's request ended up in the headquarters of the division's Support Command, where it was determined that the best way to accomplish the critical resupply mission was by a 400-foot, medium velocity air drop from a CV-2B Caribou aircraft. The 1st Forward Support Element at Oasis Strip, 12 kilometers southwest of Pleiku, was alerted to prepare 2000 pounds of small arms ammunition and 2000 pounds of rations in two A-22 containers for loading into the rear of a Caribou and delivery to Company A; the aircraft would execute a sharp climb when directly over LZ Eagle, and the loads would slide out of the cargo compartment and float almost straight down. The 17th US Aviation Company at Pleiku was charged with providing the aircraft and crew for the mission. By 2215, the aircraft, piloted by US Army Captains Tom Caraballo and Ken Hultz, was on its way to Oasis Strip.

At the strip, the two pilots received a final briefing. From their point of view, the resupply mission was going to be a difficult one, for the drop was to take place over a small clearing in a jungle southeast of the Chu Pon mastif; the night was dark, without moonlight; and they had to find a spot pointed out on a map without a visual ground reference point.

In actuality, navigation at night in the Pleiku area could be relatively simple. The US Air Force radar facility at the New Pleiku Air Base could furnish accurate radar vectors to position any aircraft over any point within a radius of 150 kilometers. Too, all US Special Forces camps were located on the Air Force's radar scope to facilitate emergency aircraft and air supply missions to the camps. But to request this radar guidance—from Oasis Strip to a grid coordinate point in the jungle—would take time—too much time. The surrounded company could not wait.

At 2325, the ammunition and rations had been loaded and rigged for the drop, and Captain Caraballo and his crew took off to deliver them as best they could. From 20 miles away they could see flares illuminating the area south of Chu Pong, and without a radar vector to guide him, Caraballo decided to use the flares as a guide. Levelling off at 4,500 feet, thereby giving a ground clearance of about 2,000 feet, Caraballo, who was flying the ship, and Hultz, who was operating the radios, discussed the forthcoming drop. The crew chief stood between the two pilots providing a third set of eyes to monitor the myriad of red dials and gauges blinking in the darkness of the ship's cockpit.

By this time, a US Air Force flare ship had arrived over the landing zone, and its flares were illuminating an area up to three miles around the target and giving a ghostly appearance to the scene. As the Caribou arrived over the company's position, Caraballo and Hultz could see that a firefight was taking place: endless flashes of weapons, belonging to both friend and foe, lit up the darkness and added a touch of ugliness. Caraballo and his crew had never had to descend to tree top level to drop supplies during a fierce firefight, and the probability of being hit was great. But the supplies were desperately needed, so down they went.

After several minutes, the pilots could see the lighted "T", aided in their search by pilots of helicopter gunships in the area and by the pilots of the Air Force flare ship. And as he flew his aircraft from north to south and one-half kilometer to the west of the marker, Captain Caraballo tried to spot the points from which the heaviest enemy fire seemed to come. From the Pathfinders on the ground, he was told that the heaviest enemy fire was from the north and south and that the aerial rocket artillery ships were shooting their rockets along the south edge of the landing zone.

Now, too, additional guidance was being received from both the Pathfinders on the ground and from the pilots of the gunships, the latter stating they would try to keep the faster Caribou on line with the landing zone. Caraballo initiated a left turn on the final approach and rolled out of the turn about one mile from the lighted "T". He had his ship at the correct drop altitude: 400 feet, and Captain Hultz gave the crew the one minute signal and flipped on the red drop light in the rear of the aircraft.

At this altitude, though, the tall trees around the landing zone blotted out the marker and the drop zone was invisible to the pilots of the Caribou. A rocket helicopter pilot gave a radio correction of 5 degrees right turn to keep the ship on its proper line—the Caribou was now headed due north and traveling at an indicated speed of 85 knots.

To the front, Caraballo and Hultz could see white flashes in the jungle, and then almost immediately after picked up the lighted "T". Hultz gave the crew a 30-second standby call and leaned over in front of Caraballo to reach the cargo release switch; on the ground, a Pathfinder called in that he had visual contact with the Caribou. And as the marker passed directly under the nose of the aircraft, the Pathfinder radioed: "Execute! Execute! Execute!"

Hultz hit the release switch as Captain Caraballo pulled the aircraft up into a steep climb at maximum power. The 2000 pounds of ammunition rushed out of the rear of the ship, dropping straight down and onto the landing zone, as the Pathfinder gave a "Roger" on the load's arrival within the company's small perimeter.

The Caribou levelled off about two miles north of LZ Eagle and Caraballo prepared to play the game again. The crew chief reported all well in the rear—no hits, damages, or bruises. It was four minutes before another drop would take place as the

Caribou banked in a turn and started descending to drop altitude for the second run. Neither of the pilots had heard any firing when they had made the first drop, but they had seen gun flashes. Apparently they had caught the enemy by surprise; things could be different the second time around, and both Caraballo and Hultz knew it.

This time, though, Caraballo decided on a slightly different procedure, in the hopes that the enemy soldiers again could be caught off guard. When he passed to the left of the landing zone, he made a 90 degree left turn while still within sight of the LZ; he held this course for about 40 seconds and then made a standard rate right turn of 270 degrees. Caraballo hoped that the first turn—to the left—might confuse the enemy soldiers as to the direction the Caribou would take on its next approach; the right turn should have brought his ship back around to a point directly south of the landing zone, heading north. As it turned out, Caraballo was slightly off course as he brought the Caribou level after the last turn, but a nearby rocket helicopter pilot watching the maneuver radioed the necessary corrections.

Once again Caraballo piloted the ship inbound until he again established visual contact with the "T"; once again, Hultz gave the one minute and 30-second warnings to the riggers; and once again the drop was made on command from the Pathfinder on the ground. This time, however, Caraballo heard ground fire and as he pulled up over the "T" maintained his climb power for an additional 1,000 feet. Although the rations landed to the south of the marker in no man's land, the Pathfinder reported that the container was being kept under observation and covered by fire; at least the troops of Company A were assured of a morning meal.

This mission had amply demonstrated that a soldier engaged in active combat can fight only as long as his "bullets and beans" hold out. For Company A, an alert supply system had planned for contingencies and for resupply missions, determined that the fighting man would not have to surrender the battlefield because he lacked the necessary support. The ammunition resupply and the sight of the rations in no man's land helped turn the tide of battle for the men of Company A, and just prior to sunrise the enemy force withdrew from the fight and disappeared from sight.

battlefield mobility

Company A, the rapid reaction force, had been carried into battle in a number of unarmed helicopters. And although the conflict in Vietnam has often been referred to as the "small unit leader's war," in reality the helicopter has provided the means by which a commander can centralize his reserves and rapidly reinforce small units which get into trouble and need quick help. Without this capability, support could not have been given to the Rifle Platoon, which had made the initial contact with an enemy force, and the platoon might well have suffered a grievous defeat.

As it was, "slicks"—so named because of their complete lack of armament in order to increase their lift capability and to make room for more troops and supplies—were available, and Company A was picked up and flown in to help, a maneuver which has become standard throughout South Vietnam.

For a few of the helicopter crewmen who participated in the action, the call for help came at 1600, 30 March 1966, when Captain Ralph V. Moffitt, section leader, 4th Platoon, Company C, 227th Assault Helicopter Battalion, 1st US Cavalry Division, was called away from giving logistical support to a company that had been landed earlier near the Cambodian border and told to report to his battalion commander, Lieutenant Colonel Jack Cranford, at the "Turkey Farm," the battalion's forward base near Pleiku.[2]

When Moffitt landed his UH-1D helicopter at the "Turkey Farm" he saw that Colonel Cranford had gathered together all of the uncommitted crews of his battalion, plus one CH-47 crew borrowed from the 228th US Transportation Battalion, and had assembled 19 "slicks," four UH-1B gunships, and the one Chinook to provide a lift capability for an infantry company assault unit—Company A, 1st Battalion, 12th US Cavalry.

The mission was urgent, Cranford pointed out. Out of range of any artillery, a rifle platoon from Troop A, 1st Squadron, 9th Cavalry, was engaged with a dug-in enemy force, apparently part of a battalion from the 18th North Vietnamese Army Regiment. Rescue attempts by 9th US Cavalry "slicks" had

---

[2]Combat experience submitted by CPT Ralph V. Moffitt, USA.

failed: four ships had been shot down and most of the others riddled with bullets. One pilot had been killed and numerous casualties had been sustained among the crew members. One ship had been flown back to its base by the crew chief, who made his first landing because both his pilot and co-pilot had been seriously wounded.

Cranford went on with his briefing, telling the assembled aviators that they would lift Company A, 1st Battalion, 12th Cavalry into Landing Zone Eagle, south of the Chu Pong mountain and near the Cambodian border. Company A, once it had been landed, would link up with the threatened platoon from the 9th US Cavalry, while the helicopters would extract both groups as soon as the rescue had been accomplished. Pathfinders would go in with the first lift to mark the landing zone for the pickup in case the extraction could not take place before dark.

Moffitt's section—two helicopters—was assigned the last two slots in the lift formation because he had been the last to arrive at the rendezvous. He knew that his section's position was a hazardous one for any extraction, day or night; his previous experiences had taught him that enemy snipers around a landing zone would hold their fire until all of the infantry had loaded and were airborne, then would open fire on the last of the aircraft as the latter lifted from the ground. This was especially true at night since the escorting gunships could not pinpoint the enemy's positions to deliver effective suppressive fires.

By the time Colonel Cranford had completed his briefing, Company A had been loaded. The order was given to "start engines." And the last elements were still completing their radio checks when the lead ships pulled pitch and became airborne. As soon as all the ships were in the air the formation turned south for LZ Eagle. (*Map 61*)

Minutes later, Cranford made radio contact with the platoon leader on the ground, who reported sporadic enemy fire from the northeast. The latter went on to describe the landing zone as being small and covered with many small stumps, but felt that it could handle two helicopters at a time for as long as the daylight lasted.

With this information, Cranford ordered his helicopters into a "sections trail" formation; since each section consisted of two helicopters, this formation would permit one section at a time

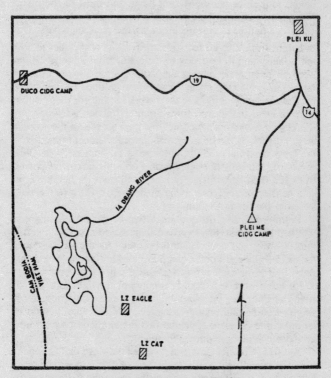

Map 61. Pick up at LZ Eagle

to discharge its loads on to the small landing zone. He then
maneuvered the formation to the southwest so that it would
approach toward the northeast to avoid overflying the reported
snipers.

Captain Moffitt was downwind at an altitude of 1,500 feet
as he watched the helicopters ahead of him, two by two, complete their final approach, discharge their troops, and lift out;
he also noticed that there was no enemy fire, and breathed a
sigh of relief. If a landing zone were hot, the first two or four
ships in could expect to draw some fire.

As Moffitt made his final approach he could see that the LZ was indeed small, completely surrounded by tall trees and almost entirely covered with slender sharp stumps which ranged in height from 2 to 20 feet. He notified his crew chief to alert the infantrymen to be ready to dismount from a hover—there were no open areas among the stumps large enough to allow him to take his ship all the way to the ground. He knew that the Pathfinders would have their work cut out for them if they were to clear the stumps for a future extraction attempt.

As he lowered his helicopter to within six feet of the ground, he felt it rock as the infantrymen jumped. Almost immediately the crew chief called "Up," indicating that the ship was clear of troops, and Moffitt made his take off with maximum power. But even then he barely cleared the tall trees on the northeast side of the landing zone as he made a sharp turn to the right to rejoin the lift formation.

Pulling out, Moffitt could see two of the four helicopters that had been shot down earlier; they were but a few hundred meters away and one was still burning. As the ships headed for the US Special Forces camp at Plei Me, where they would stand by for the extraction try, Moffitt noted that the time was 1715; there were less than two hours of daylight left. On arriving at Plei Me, the aviators soon learned that Company A was in trouble and taking casualties, and that there would be an indefinite delay; it appeared that the extraction would now take place sometime during the night.

At 2015, Colonel Cranford received the word that Company A had rescued the remaining members of the platoon, had made it back to LZ Eagle, and was ready for pickup. Because the company reported a number of wounded men needed immediate evacuation, Cranford decided to bring in the Chinook second, behind his lead ship, to take out the wounded and the survivors of the platoon. The other helicopters would then have to concern themselves only with getting out the able bodied infantrymen who would be able to load quickly and without delay.

In five minutes the entire flight was airborne and enroute once more to the landing zone. As he approached the LZ, Captain Moffitt could see armed rocket artillery helicopters and US Air Force fighter aircraft making their strikes a few hundred meters to the north and northeast of Company A's position. Although the ground was obscured by smoke and darkness, Moffitt could catch occasional glimpses of the dimly lit "T" which had been placed in the center of the LZ by the Pathfinders.

Colonel Cranford changed the formation to a single file with enough space between ships to permit single helicopter landings. From his position at the rear, Moffitt watched Cranford's helicopter turn into a final approach and begin the descent to the landing zone; he soon lost sight of the ship's lights as it disappeared into the darkness and smoke.

The Chinook was trailing close behind when Cranford radioed to the flight that he had lost the "T" in the smoke and was attempting a go around, thereby giving up his place at the head of the formation and joining on to the rear. The big helicopter continued its approach to within about 50 feet of the landing zone when enemy automatic weapons fire flamed up at it from two directions. The enemy's tracers seemed to light the entire area as the Chinook rose slightly and then dropped rapidly to the ground, almost in the dead center of the small clearing.

Cranford was left with no choice—he had to abort the extraction attempt because there was no room left in which even one of the smaller helicopters could land. He turned the flight towards the "Turkey Farm." There was nothing more he could do unless new plans were drawn up to lift additional troops into the fight.

On the ground, plans were being drafted to move a company of infantrymen into another area near LZ Eagle to secure a landing zone on which an artillery unit could be emplaced to provide fire support to the surrounded Company A. At 2300, just shortly after his helicopters had settled down, Cranford once again called his aviators together: the battalion had been ordered to make a night assault, lifting Company A, 1st Battalion, 8th US Cavalry into LZ Cat, several thousand meters southeast of LZ Eagle. After the infantrymen had secured the new landing area, CH-47s of the 228th US Transportation Battalion would bring in the 105mm howitzers of Battery A, 19th US Artillery. It would be a difficult assault: the landing zone had been picked from a map reconnaissance and a few available aerial photographs furnished by the 1st Squadron, 9th US Cavalry; the pilots would not have the benefit of a day reconnaissance to familiarize themselves with the terrain.

At midnight, two "slicks" escorted by a platoon of gunships from Company D, 227th US Assault Helicopter Battalion, departed the "Turkey Farm" for LZ Cat; the unarmed ships carried Pathfinders and combat engineers, the latter from Company A, 8th US Engineer Battalion and equipped with chain saws and axes. Surprisingly, the pilots had little difficulty in picking out the landing zone and soon the Pathfinders and engineers were on the ground and working. While the Pathfinders put in the lighted landing "Ts", the engineers began felling enough of the large trees to permit the helicopters in the main lift to make their landings.

Thirty minutes after midnight on 31 March, the 227th left the base airfield with the infantry company securely aboard the lift helicopters. This time Captain Moffitt led the trail section which carried the sling loads. As he reached the landing zone, a defensive perimeter was already being formed, and the Chinooks with the artillery were only a few minutes out. The lift was successfully completed without incident or enemy contact and by 0300 the infantry defending on LZ Eagle could count on the support of six 105mm howitzers. They would play an important role in the battle which raged throughout the rest of the night, and would still be furnishing fire support when the enemy broke contact just before sunrise and withdrew.

frustration

Throughout this action, the importance of taking care of the wounded had been emphasized. This fact is true in all of the other actions that have taken place, or will take place, in Vietnam. And the prompt, efficient evacuation of casualties and the giving of emergency medical therapy without detracting from the accomplishment of the tactical mission falls upon the shoulders of a little known individual: the Battalion Surgeon. At times, his job is a frustrating one, for the conditions under which he is required to work are seldom ideal. This was graphically pointed out to Captain Isaac Goodrich, US Army Medical Corps, the battalion surgeon of the 1st Battalion, 28th US Infantry, in the jungles of Vietnam during Operation ADELAIDE I when he realized that he was near, and yet so far, from multiple casualties in the jungle below his helicopter.[3]

During Operation ADELAIDE I, search and destroy oper-

---

[3]Combat experience submitted by CPT Isaac Goodrich, USA.

ations were conducted along Interprovincial Route #16 north of Tan Uyen by the 1st Battalion, 28th US Infantry, commanded by Lieutenant Colonel Robert Haldane. The battalion was also called on to provide security for elements of the 1st Engineer Battalion, 1st US Infantry Division, which was improving Route #16 from Tan Uyen to Phuoc Vinh. Too, a long term project was begun which aimed at the complete penetration and reduction of the Ong Dong jungle adjacent to Tan Uyen, an area that had been traditionally a safe haven and operating base for enemy units: the area was to be defoliated and systematically sliced into checkerboard squares by the engineers' bulldozers, providing pioneer roads for the Division and for ARVN forces to move rapidly through the area to encircle and eliminate enemy forces.

On 2 June 1966, the 1st Battalion was spread thin. Company B, commanded by Captain Peter Bouton, was securing an engineer work party improving a bridge several thousand meters north of the battalion's base camp. Company C, led by Captain Arnold Larsen, was securing some engineer tank dozers as they cut wide swaths into the Ong Dong jungle. Minus one of its platoons, Company A, under Captain Jack Wooley, was in the jungle on a search and destroy operation and by 0630 had established a command post in the heart of the thick woods. His 2d Platoon, commanded by Lieutenant Keith A. Wilks, was still back at the battalion's base where it would remain until 1200 to rest up after an all night ambush patrol mission; the platoon was scheduled to rejoin the company sometime that afternoon.

Captain Wooley sent Lieutenant Paul Trost's 1st Platoon to the southeast, and Lieutenant Henry Krasneski's 3d Platoon to the northeast in search of enemy soldiers in areas adjacent to the engineer work sites. Wooley intended to accomplish two things with this move: his units could clear the area of mines and booby traps at the same time they prevented an enemy force from ambushing the work teams.

At first the 3d Platoon had an easy time moving through a slightly overgrown rubber plantation; it was spread out, covering a large area, and there was no chance of a surprise enemy attack. Then the relatively open area petered out, and the platoon entered the murky depths of the jungle. In actuality, the transition from plantation to jungle was not abrupt, for between the two areas lay a stretch of secondary jungle that caused

Lieutenant Trost to change the formation from widely dispersed squads on line to a tight column with less than a meter between the soldiers. With machetes hacking a narrow path through the thick foliage, the men of the platoon advanced slowly into the welcome shade of the tall trees which constituted the main jungle. The canopy several hundred feet overhead blocked all other growth, and walking would become easier.

After a short pause, the platoon pushed on with its mission. Once more two squads were on line, one in reserve. But the jungle did not permit the squads to spread out as far as the symmetrically planted rubber trees had permitted, and the platoon's formation more closely resembled two squads abreast with each squad in column.

And then, before they knew it, the platoon arrived at an enemy base camp. The lead soldiers were almost on top of the enemy's positions before they were fired on, and although the platoon managed to breach the first enemy line, it suffered several casualties. This was the enemy's home, and he knew the ground well. Each time one of the members of Trost's unit raised his head, he would be shot by an unseen enemy. Soon the number of casualties had multiplied, and Trost sent out an urgent call for assistance. (*Map 62*)

Captain Wooley received the call and sent Lieutenant Krasneski and the 1st Platoon, nearest the action, to help out. At the same time he spoke with Colonel Haldane who told him to alert the 2d Platoon and who also said that Captain Larsen's Company C and the tank dozers would be on their way to help within the next few minutes. Haldane told his S3, Major William E. Panton, to request troop transport helicopters and to accompany Captain Bouton's Comapny B in an airmobile assault into a landing zone southeast of where Trost's platoon was then fighting.

As the various units began their movements, Company A's 1st Platoon arrived on the other side of the enemy camp where it, too, was stopped by heavy enemy fire. Although they were between the two US platoons, the enemy soldiers held the advantage: everyone was so close that the supporting US artillery and gunships could only fire blocking fires and the US platoons were in constant danger of firing into each other.

The 1st Platoon had also taken a number of casualties during the opening minutes of its engagement and Lieutenant Krasneski himself had been hit twice. Despite the enemy's fire, the

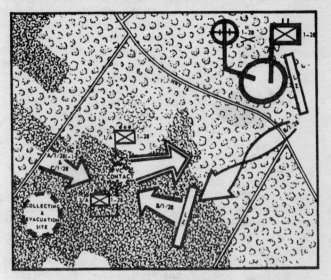

Map 62. Frustration

platoon's medical personnel were running from casualty to casualty giving emergency medical treatment—a bandage here, an IV there, a single word of encouragement. One was shot twice through his helmet, sustaining a severe skull fracture and minimal brain damage. A doctor was urgently needed.

At the battalion's base camp, Haldane ordered his executive officer, Major Robert J. Allee, to commandeer the next helicopter that arrived and to introduce Captain Goodrich and two medical aidmen into the battle area to care for the wounded. Haldane himself went aloft in a two-place OH-13 helicopter to establish an airborne command post over the scene of battle; as his ship arrived over the area, Haldane could see Company C and the tank dozers making slow progress through the thick trees on their way to help Company A.

In the meantime, Major Allee, Captain Goodrich, and the artillery liaison officer had managed to divert a UH-1D supply helicopter to their needs and arrived over the battle area at 0945; they soon discovered that the jungle foliage was too dense to permit a helicopter landing. For the next two hours, the three officers and Colonel Haldane tried to figure out a way of getting Captain Goodrich and the aidmen into the fight, but the best that could be done was to send a troop from the 1st Squadron, 4th US Cavalry, which had been attached to the battalion for this operation, to use its vehicles to push open a clearing in the jungle to within 500 meters of the fight so that Goodrich could reach the casualties.

Two hours later, this had been accomplished; now the armored personnel carriers could be used to transport the casualties to Captain Goodrich's collection and evacuation site— a small hole in the jungle not much larger than the size of a helicopter's rotor blade.

During the next three and a half hours, 45 casualties received primary medical therapy—bleeding stopped, open airway insured, intravenous fluids started—and were evacuated to the 93d Evacuation Hospital at Long Binh, 25 kilometers from the point of contact. Meanwhile, the tanks, tank dozers, armored personnel carriers, and the infantrymen all took part in driving enemy snipers from the area.

At his collection and evacuation site, Captain Goodrich had to face many acute problems during a relatively brief period of time: would it be necessary to triage, to classify casualties as to priorities for treatment based on the type and urgency of the conditions presented? Under mass casualty conditions such as Goodrich faced, it was necessary for him to reach a decision as to whether or not to treat the least seriously wounded in order to return them immediately to battle, or, if the situation were not quite so critical, to treat the most seriously wounded in order to save life. He had to determine, too, how best to conserve his limited amount of medical supplies, and how best to treat and evacuate the most seriously wounded in the briefest period of time.

On two occasions Captain Goodrich flew to the evacuation hospital with seriously wounded soldiers to insure appropriate and continuous medical therapy. On one of these occasions the command helicopter of the assistant division commander, who had set his ship down in the small jungle clearing, was utilized for casualty evacuation.

As Captain Goodrich continued to work over the wounded, the troop lift helicopters finally arrived at the battalion's forward base, and Major Panton led Company B in an airmobile assault into a landing zone in a rice paddy southeast of the enemy's camp. Captain Bouton quickly assembled his company and the unit began moving toward the enemy position. As soon as the leading platoon had entered the jungle the word was quickly passed back and accentuated with automatic rifle fire that several fleeing enemy soldiers had crossed the open area on the company's right flank. While Major Panton directed the fire of the gunships into the area, Captain Bouton's artillery forward observer directed the fires of the supporting artillery to seal the narrow finger of jungle into which the enemy troops had fled. It was growing dark, and bright tracers from the gunships and the bursting artillery shells provided a kaleidoscope of color to the scene.

In the main battle area, the enemy positions were taken by the advancing tanks, tank dozers, and infantrymen. The final shots were heard as the helicopter assault force ran into the retreating enemy's flank security—a long rapid burst delivered by one of Company B's riflemen.

From Captain Goodrich's standpoint, the first few hours of the operation had been frustrating ones, for while he had arrived over the battle area within minutes of the first shots, there had been no landing sites available near the embattled platoon and the wounded had had to wait until all the battalion's resources could be thrown into the battle to relieve the pressure and to prepare a clearing in the dense jungle.

It was comforting to the men in battle to know, however, that medical personnel were nearby and that every effort would be made to reach and to care for them if they were hurt. This knowledge—that the best medical care in the world was only steps away—enabled the men of Cranford's battalion to concentrate their thoughts on the job that had to be done, and to do the job in a competent and professional manner.

combat engineers

Several months before, the combat engineers of the 1st US Infantry Division had been called on to perform an almost herculean task of road building and mine clearing under the most difficult of circumstances.[4]

---

[4] Combat experience submitted by CPT George P. Johnson, USA.

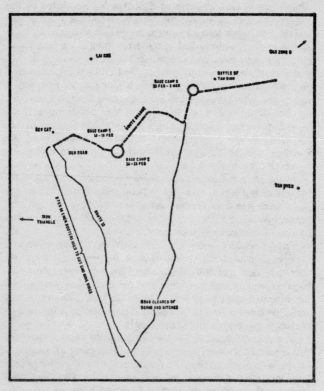

Map 63. Engineers in Combat

It was during Operation ROLLING STONE in February 1966 that the 1st US Engineer Battalion, 1st US Infantry Division was ordered to construct an all weather, bridge-free road to connect Route #13 near Ben Cat to Route #16 south of Phuoc Vinh in conjunction with search and destroy operations that were to be conducted by the division's 1st Brigade. (*Map 63*)

The general concept of the operation called for moving elements of the engineer battalion from their locations at Di An and Lai Khe along Route #13 to a base camp near Ben

Cat, there to open a laterite pit and start construction on a new two-lane road east towards Route #16. Thereafter, using other base camps near sources of laterite (if laterite could be found), construction would proceed easterly until Route #16 had been reached. And although the new road would be of great military significance because it would connect the two forward brigades, its greatest value would be to open the area to Republic of Vietnam economic and military influence.

Several months before Operation ROLLING STONE, extensive engineer reconnaissance missions had been conducted to locate laterite deposits and to determine a route for the new road. A unique method had been devised to locate the deposits, one that was particularly effective in enemy infested areas: heavy bombs had been dropped over an area and any of the resulting craters that revealed the typical red color of laterite had been investigated; the others had been left alone. In late January 1966, samples of laterite had also been obtained by what amounted to an aerial assault, when five armed helicopters provided covering fire for an engineer reconnaissance team that had landed at the site of a red colored bomb crater.

Then, just one week prior to the start of the operation, an engineer ground reconnaissance team had located a bridge-free route for the new road that would bypass the partially demolished bridge just east of Route #13. But shortly after the team had left the bridge site, an enemy unit further demolished it with explosives, as if emphasizing the enemy's interest in the road and his ability to move in swiftly to blow up bridges or to mine roads.

On 9 February 1966, Company A, 1st US Engineer Battalion, commanded by Captain Charles R. Kesterson, began mine clearing operations to clear Route #13 from Phu Loi north to Ben Cat, while Company C, commanded by Captain Robert Zellinski, started similar operations as it moved south from Lai Khe. It was intended for the two units to clear Route #13 of all mines before the remainder of the battalion and its equipment moved into Base Camp #1 near Ben Cat.

The two companies, in a typical mine clearing operation, each used five mine clearing teams, teams which consisted of nine men: three mine detector operators with metallic detectors, and six probers. Two bulldozers towing rooters preceded the clearing teams, one on each side of the road, so that the teeth on the rooters, capable of penetrating three feet of soil, could cut any wires leading to command detonated mines. Tank dozers and other engineers provided the necessary security; on several occasions the mine clearing teams were fired on by enemy soldiers, but the incidents were quickly terminated when the tank dozers returned the fire with canister rounds and machinegun fire.

To facilitate control, the men would place a marked wooden stake at the edge of the road at each tenth of a mile; each of the five teams would clear one-tenth of a mile of road and would then leapfrog forward four-tenths of a mile to a new sector. In this manner, the clearing teams did not take up more than three-fourths of a mile of road space, easing the security burden of those men charged with that responsibility.

By late afternoon the route had been cleared, and the battalion closed into Base Camp #1 completely unhampered by mines. This move contrasted sharply with previous ones in which a considerable number of US personnel had been killed in mining incidents along Route #13.

The following morning, 10 February 1966, mine clearing teams left the base camp to clear along the route of the first leg of the new road. No sooner had they cleared the base camp's perimeter, though, than the teams discovered US fragmentation bomblets emplaced by the enemy as antipersonnel mines in an area that had been completely cleared just the day before. This was further evidence that enemy units in the area would take every opportunity to mine roads that were used by US forces, and particularly those under construction where it was difficult to detect visually the presence of a concealed mine.

For the rest of the operation, mine clearing teams would be dispatched each day from the various base camps to clear both the area to be worked that day and the completed portion of the road back to its starting point at Ben Cat. Significantly, for the first four days, mines were detected and destroyed in areas that had been cleared the previous day.

By 16 February the first leg of the new road had been completed and the battalion moved to Base Camp #2. In spite of the battalion's precautionary efforts, on the first day of the operation out of Base Camp #2, Staff Sergeant Clyde C. Foster, while improving a secondary road to a laterite pit with his bulldozer, detonated two mines in rapid succession. Fortunately the bulldozer absorbed much of the blast and Sergeant Foster was unharmed. But once again, the ground along which Foster was operating had been previously checked and cleared. On the same day, clearing teams working on the completed portion of the road located six antipersonnel mines and two pressure-activated antivehicular mines which had obviously been put in the preceding night after construction activities ceased.

The new road—now known as Route Orange—was completed on 3 March, despite a number of other mining incidents that plagued elements of the battalion during the latter part of February. And as it prepared to move back to Di An, the battalion sent out mine clearing teams to sweep the road ahead of the leading units. Company C began moving out of Base Camp #3 at 1000 and managed to travel some distance without incident. But then, just east of the old Base Camp #2, two pressure-activated mines were detonated and an armored personnel carrier and a tank damaged. The road had been checked and cleared not more than a few hours earlier.

Fortunately, no further incidents marred the battalion's return march, but what the battalion had encountered this day pointed up the fact that mine clearing operations in a guerrilla environment can never be considered as being completed. Unless every inch of ground can be put under constant observation—a physical impossibility—the enemy guerrillas will take their toll of friendly soldiers.

to save a bird

While it is almost a foregone conclusion that the use of helicopters in conjunction with air power has greatly enhanced the battlefield prowess of the ground commander in Vietnam, the rotary wing ships have introduced certain support problems of their own, the most notable one being what to do when one of the helicopters has been downed in hostile territory. Should it be destroyed, or should it be lifted out to fight another day? In October 1965, units of the 1st US Cavalry Division made the decision to save a downed helicopter, thereby triggering a logistical problem of some magnitude.

The division had been in Vietnam almost two months by this time and most of its units had received their first taste of battle. But they were still learning about their new airmobile concept, and discovering again that routine administrative problems could sometimes loom larger than anyone had a right to expect.[5]

The mission was to be a "milk run" for the two crews from Company B, 229th Assault Helicopter Battalion. Two helicopters were always dispatched on any particular mission that left sight of the "Golf Course"—the division's base camp near An Khe—just in case one of them ran into any trouble. These two particular ships—UH-1Ds—were on the daily courier run from An Khe, with stops at Cheo Reo, Ban Me Thuot, Tuy Hoa, and several isolated CIDG and ARVN outposts along the route.

Little out of the ordinary occurred during the early part of the flight, although the cloud level lowered considerably and the tops of the mountains became obscured. The two ships were proceeding in a loose formation up a long, narrow valley about 15 miles southwest of Qui Nhon at 1,500 feet when they encountered enemy fire coming up at them from a stream line below. Neither of the crews could pinpoint the exact locations of the enemy weapons, and each ship took evasive action to dodge the bullets. When they had flown out of range of the enemy weapons, the two aircraft joined up again and made a quick check for damage; neither crew felt that they had received any hits, although the lead helicopter seemed to be streaming fuel from its belly. A check of the fuel quantity gauge confirmed the rapid loss of fuel, as well as the fumes that began to fill the cockpit.

Since there was an immediate danger of an explosion or fire aboard the helicopter and because the remaining fuel would be exhausted long before a safe landing area could be reached, the flight leader elected to land his ship with power while he still had some fuel; the other ship could then land nearby and pick up him and his crew. They would figure out what to do with the downed helicopter after the pickup had been accomplished.

The only acceptable landing zone was a small cleared area near the foot of a small hill close to the village of Canh Hung (2). A successful landing was accomplished, and the crew hurriedly dismounted the two M60 machineguns, the machinegun ammunition, and all of the courier material and personal weapons. The second craft then came in, picked up the downed crew, and took off immediately, for the landing zone was not

[5]Combat experience submitted by MAJ James R. Loudermilk, USA.

too far from the area where they had been fired on just a few minutes earlier. As soon as he reached sufficient altitude, the pilot radioed his battalion operations room at An Khe and told the personnel there what had happened; he did not have sufficient fuel remaining to fly cover until help arrived, so he gave the exact coordinates of the site and continued his flight to An Khe.

At the base camp, the operations personnel knew immediately that if the helicopter was to be recovered it would have to be done fast or the enemy would have it stripped or destroyed before a recovery force could reach the scene. They decided to extract the UH-1D by Chinook helicopter, with ground security being provided by two infantry squads flown into the site by other helicopters.

A call to the headquarters of the 11th Aviation Group received quick approval, and a CH-47 was made available from the 228th Assault Support Battalion for the recovery attempt. Coordination with an infantry brigade made the infantry squads available, while four UH-1B gunships from Company D, 229th Assault Helicopter Battalion and two UH-1B rocket artillery aircraft from the aerial rocket artillery battalion were procured to furnish close air support. A call from division headquarters to the US Air Force element at Qui Nhon also scrambled two A1E fighters which would provide coverage over the downed helicopter until the rescue team could arrive.

The recovery team completed its makeup at the "Golf Course," as six helicopters took aboard the infantry, and another was loaded with the rigging crew. The formation made up over An Khe pass and then headed east toward Qui Nhon.

Meanwhile, the two US Air Force aircraft had spotted the downed ship and circled the area for a closer look when the pilots saw several people running from the helicopter and reported that they had been fired on. The two A1Es immediately ringed the downed aircraft with 20mm cannon fire in an attempt to drive the people—assumed to be enemy soldiers—farther away.

As the recovery formation arrived, the A1Es were joined by the helicopter gunships and rocket artillery aircraft, and together placed a wall of suppressive fires on all sides of the disabled helicopter. Then, as the infantry squads were landed, they quickly formed a perimeter around the ship. Next the rigging crew came in and started checking the UH-1D for booby traps; finding none, the crew secured the main rotor blade and placed the lifting straps around the rotor head. A loop on the end of the strap would be hooked to the Chinook's cargo cable.

When the rigging crew had completed its task, the Chinook arrived to do its part. This was the most critical time of the recovery for the stationary Chinook presented a vulnerable target as it hovered over the disabled ship. While the hook up was being made, small arms fire did break out from the vicinity of a small village near the point of recovery, but immediate return fire from the ground security force and two bombs from the A1Es silenced whoever had opened fire.

No hits were taken by either the infantrymen or the Chinook, and the extraction went off without further incident; one final firing pass was made on the site as the infantry squads and the rigging crew loaded into their helicopters.

From the moment the disabled helicopter had landed until it was extracted just one hour and thirty minutes had elapsed. The air distance from An Khe had been about 45 miles. Complete cooperation and the mutual understanding of aerial support techniques by all of the members of a heterogeneous force had proven that even the most unexpected logistical mission could be accomplished in a most acceptable manner.

IX

Special Operations

SUCCESS IN COUNTERGUERRILLA warfare is not merely a matter of observing rules or applying standing operating procedures that have proved effective in certain instances, for the unpredictable guerrilla does not conform to any hard and fast tactical doctrine or principles in his operations.

In Vietnam, imagination and foresight have played important roles in developing new tactics and techniques and adapting them to combat under unusual conditions to meet and defeat an unusual enemy. Lieutenant Colonel David H. Hackworth, a highly decorated, former commander of an infantry battalion in Vietnam, puts it this way:

"Jungle warfare demands a complete reorientation from conventional thought and tactics. Don't throw away the book, but a flexible fresh approach to tactics and operations must be developed. As I see it, a new book is being written by the units fighting in Vietnam."[1]

When United States troops joined those of the Republic of Vietnam in 1965, and when the far reaching US B52 bombers initiated their tremendous bombardments at the same time, the enemy embraced the earth and burrowed beneath it for protection. His building of underground emplacements intensified as

[1] LTC David H. Hackworth, "No Magic Formula," INFANTRY, January–February 1967, p. 36.

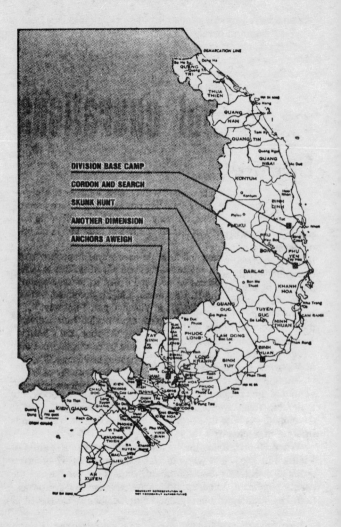

DIVISION BASE CAMP

CORDON AND SEARCH

SKUNK HUNT

ANOTHER DIMENSION

ANCHORS AWEIGH

teams were formed, allocations of work output made, and tunneling begun in earnest. In many cases it was a question only of reopening or extending underground facilities which had been dug in the latter days of World War II during the development of the Viet Minh movement in Saigon. During those days, the Viet Minh had been well indoctrinated in the use of "spider holes" and other underground positions, and had used those positions to great advantage.

another dimension

The air bombardments and the increased use of artillery concentrations had little effect on most of the completed tunnels, and a new problem faced the US infantrymen who would participate in Operation CRIMP: find the enemy's tunnel complexes, clear them, and insure that the enemy could not use them again; until this had been accomplished, no area could be considered safe.[2]

Operation CRIMP was a joint operation—it involved elements of the 1st US Infantry Division, the 173d US Airborne Brigade, and the Royal Australian Regiment and took place in January 1966 in a search of the Ho Bo woods north of Cu Chi for the politico-military headquarters of the Viet Cong's 4th Military Region. Intelligence reports had pinpointed that headquarters as the one which controlled Viet Cong activities in a large part of South Vietnam.

The area in which the operation took place was a rich farming region of Binh Duong province just west of the Iron Triangle. Numerous farms and rice paddies were intersected with hedgerows, rubber plantations, streams, and thick jungle. Since the operation would be conducted during the dry season, the farm land, and even the rice paddies to some extent, provided good cross country mobility for the heavy tracked vehicles that would participate.

Civilians in the area had lived under Viet Cong rule for many years; they had been thoroughly indoctrinated and willingly supported the enemy. Because this was so, one of the early US decisions made was to evacuate the population to a secure location where the people could not interfere with or

[2]Combat experience submitted by MAJ William E. Panton, USA.

betray the operation. After an initial interrogation, those civilians not confirmed as Viet Cong members, would be further evacuated to a refugee processing center at Trung Lap.

On 7 January 1966, the 1st Battalion, 28th US Infantry, 1st US Infantry Division, was air lifted from Phuoc Vinh to Phu Loi by US Air Force transport aircraft. From Phu Loi, the battalion conducted an airmobile assault into Landing Zone Jack on the heels of the 1st Battalion, 16th US Infantry; the two battalions had the mission of blocking along Phase Line Pecan until the 2d Battalion, 28th US Infantry could be introduced into an area to the north. *(Map 64)*

As the 1st Battalion, 28th US Infantry, settled down on the landing zone, the men of the battalion could see that the 1st Battalion, 16th US Infantry was in trouble and receiving fire from the north edge of the landing zone, from the same place

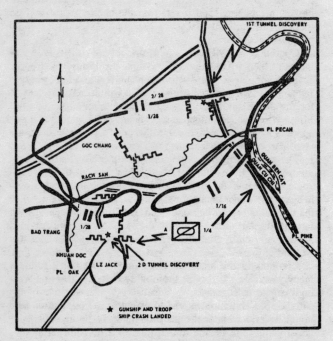

Map 64. Another Dimension

that they had to go. The battalion commander, Lieutenant Colonel Robert Haldane, could see that his men were apprehensive, particularly when they saw soldiers from the lead battalion fall under the enemy's fire and grenades.

Because of the firing, Captain Terry Christy, commanding Company B, knew that he had to get his unit off the cleared zone and into the tree line quickly and shouted orders to his platoon leaders and noncommissioned officers to get moving. His orders moved the company into the tree line, but the enemy had suddenly disappeared. Where?

Just a few meters inside the tree line at the edge of a rubber plantation, Christy's men located a large trench, the start of the most elaborate underground fortification complex that the men of the batallion would see for the next several months. But the battalion's mission was to reach a blocking position, and Haldane did not have sufficient time to check out what appeared to be a regimental sized position. Yet it was hard to believe that the enemy soldiers who had engaged the 1st Battalion, 16th US Infantry could have fled undetected through the relatively open rubber trees. Haldane planned to check on this later because his unit would operate in this very same area for several more weeks until the newly arrived 25th US Infantry Division could establish its base camp north of Cu Chi.

As the battalion advanced with three companies on line toward its assigned blocking position overlooking a small stream, reports started filtering into the battalion's command post that cache after cache of rice, salt, and other foodstuff were in the area, enough to feed at least an enemy regiment. That the battalion was, in fact, in a large enemy base complex was further confirmed when the three leading companies reported an extensive mine field across the wooded north end of the area. Apparently, the enemy had planned the area as a permanent complex.

After breaching the mine field, the battalion reached its blocking position where it remained until the 2d Battalion, 28th US Infantry pulled abreast. Then, leaving its blocking position, the 1st Battalion shifted direction and moved to the east, on line with the 2d Battalion.

As the 1st Battalion moved toward Phase Line Pine—the Saigon River—what was once thought to be an enemy regimental camp took on the dimensions of a division base, for during the next two days its soliders reported foxholes, trenches, mines, caves, and well used trails—but no people—all across the battalion's 1,500 meter front. The march was not completely without incident: soldier after soldier was hit by fire from enemy snipers; Haldane hoped that his men could pin the enemy unit against the river and there take retribution for their losses.

But when the battalion arrived on 9 January at the wide expanse of rice paddies that linked the dry ground with the Saigon River, his soldiers had seen only one or two fleeting enemy soldiers. That night they occupied a deserted village surrounded with foxholes, bunkers, trenches, and mines. Without boats the battalion could not move further to the east.

Then a breakthrough was announced—the 173rd US Airborne Brigade and the Royal Australian Regiment to the north had located the Viet Cong, underground!

On the morning of 10 January, the 1st Battalion began retracing its steps, and two hours later one of the companies reported finding a 100-man classroom that had been missed on the previous day's sweep. Fortified with the knowledge of the known successes of the units to the north, Haldane halted his battalion and after establishing all around security, started a detailed search for tunnel entrances. *(Map 65)*

Finding a tunnel entrance, however, proved not to be easy. A few soldiers—reluctantly—lowered themselves into a trench which ran the length of the classroom and then took a sharp bend to the west. Seconds later they reported that the trench led to a hole in the side of a slight rise of ground to the west. Returning to their start point, the soldiers were given flashlights to assist in their further exploration efforts; but they still could not find the sought after tunnel complex. The hole, although extensive, and with steps and a room large enough to contain 100 occupants, was no more than an elaborate air raid shelter. It seemed time to move on to renew the search in another area.

But then it came—the sought after opening! Platoon Sergeant Stewart L. Green, a wiry 130 pound soldier, jumped from the ground with a curse, thinking that something had bitten him. The country was full of aggravating scorpions and snakes so Green had good reason to jump. But as he disturbed the dead leaves on the ground with the muzzle of his rifle, he saw what had "bit" him: a nail! A further search disclosed a wooden trap door perforated with air holes and with beveled sides that kept it from falling through into the tunnel below. The long sought after tunnel had been found, and the shout of discovery brought Colonel Haldane on the run.

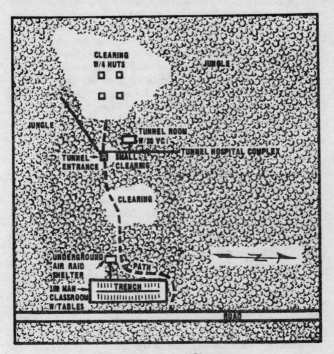

Map 65. Underground Classroom

The question Haldane had to answer was: what should he do now? The battalion had trained for combat at Fort Riley under an intensified combat training program, but the program had not covered tunnels. Sergeant Green provided the answer to the question as he stepped forward and volunteered to be lowered into the dark depths of the black hole he had so recently uncovered. Like a contagious disease, others standing around the hole volunteered to help Green. Several men followed Sergeant Green down into the hole and within minutes supplies started flowing up from the very bowels of the earth, and bag after bag of supplies were soon on their way to the classroom where Haldane had established his command post.

Captain Marvin Kennedy, the battalion's S2, after inspecting the supplies determined that the unit had uncovered a major hospital complex. Even as Kennedy looked over the captured booty, a sudden cry turned him around in time to see the soldiers who had entered the small entrance to the underground hospital pop out to the surface as if shot from guns. Sergeant Green was the last out, and he told how he had seen a side passage leading off the main run; as he had looked into the smaller passage, Green said, he first heard and then saw about 30 Viet Cong soldiers in the dim light of a candle that one of them held. He said that the enemy troops had seen him at about the same time and extinguished the candle.

Calling to one of his interpreters, Captain Kennedy asked him to go with Green back into the tunnel to tell the enemy soldiers to surrender. The interpreter agreed and the two men soon disappeared from sight, on a mission that lasted but a few minutes; for when the two men had returned, Green told Kennedy how the interpreter had refused to talk to the enemy troops. The interpreter retorted that he had had to hold his breath in the tunnel because there was no air and he would have died had he started to talk.

Colonel Haldane decided to seek a different solution and ordered a small, lightweight, gasoline powered blower to be brought to the tunnel entrance and turned on. One of the soldiers then dropped several red smoke grenades into the entrance hole while others stuffed their jackets around the air hose of the blower to seal the tunnel entrance as the smoke was pumped down. The soldiers providing security around the area were instructed to look for any sign of the smoke.

For several minutes nothing happened. Then reports came in from every direction of red smoke appearing from numerous holes in the ground. But now a new problem arose: Colonel Haldane had just received orders to destroy the tunnel and to regain contact with the 2d Battalion to the north which was outrunning its flank security, Haldane's unit.

Almost in desperation, CS, a nonlethal, riot control agent, was pumped into the tunnel to rout out the enemy soldiers; but the latter still refused to abandon the tunnel. For a third time Sergeant Green entered the tunnel, this time accompanied by a demolitions specialist. The men placed charges with short fuses in the main tunnel on each side of the secondary tunnel passage, and then made a rapid withdrawal to the surface, warning away all who stood nearby. The earth erupted and an ear-splitting explosion shook the ground; with this accomplished, Haldane moved his unit to catch up with the 2d Battalion.

But the story was not finished. Two nights later, on 11 January, the battalion returned once more to the rubber plantation on the northern edge of Landing Zone Jack and established a tight defensive perimeter. All of the units participating in the operation—the name of which had been changed from CRIMP to BUCKSKIN—had suffered casualties from random enemy bands who had continued to appear and disappear almost at will. This time, the 1st Battalion occupied the trenches which had been dug by the enemy and which overlooked the landing zone; ambush patrols were put out and the area inspected. *(Map 66)*

The trench work was quite extensive and ringed the battalion. At the north edge of the perimeter, the trench was fortified with antiaircraft firing positions; a huge crater caused by a bomb dropped from a B52 bomber raid—50 feet across and at least 15 feet deep—had hardly damaged the trench or the gun emplacements. In fact, it had collapsed only about a meter of the main trench system.

By now tunnel conscious, the men of the battalion were quick to check out any suspicious looking holes. One of the soldiers pointed out a hole about a foot in diameter which descended into the ground at a 45 degree angle. Some thought it might be an air hole for a tunnel; others thought it might have been caused by a bomb dropped from a B52 which had failed to explode. The hole remained a curiosity until the following day.

It was in the late afternoon when Captain Arnold Larsen radioed that his Company C had discovered an American soldier's helmet at the bottom of a trench and that the helmet covered a booby trapped mortar round. In a small wooded glade, his soldiers had also found two booby trapped 105mm artillery rounds and a cave with another booby trapped 105mm round in the entrance. Captain Larsen had his soldiers detonate the booby traps by exploding charges placed next to them. He also reported that the first soldier to enter the cave had seen a trap door in the floor, but since darkness was coming on he had decided to place a guard on the door and continue the search in the morning.

The battalion was not to be allowed to rest this night, however, for in the gloom of the rapidly fading light several grenade

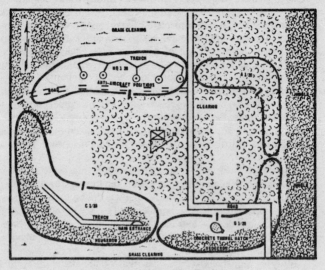

Map 66. Defensive Perimeter

explosions were heard followed by several quick shots from a carbine. Viet Cong soldiers used carbines and since the shots had come from within the battalion's perimeter, the enemy was inside, too. But how? And how many were there? Running over to where the action had taken place, in Company B's sector, Colonel Haldane and several members of his staff were met by Sergeant Green and a number of other Company B soldiers, who were standing around a small concrete hatch, shaped like a commode seat on a hinge and perforated with air holes. One of the soldiers said to Haldane: "We were sitting there almost on top of the damn thing heating our C rations, when it sprang open and this Charlie popped up. He threw two grenades, and reached down, grabbed a carbine, and sprayed a full magazine at us before we could even lift our weapons. Then he went back down into the ground."

Sergeant Green once again led a team into an enemy tunnel, and did not surface again for two and a half hours. When he did return, Green reported that he had not been able to find the end of the tunnel; he described it as having an uneven floor which would provide protection should anyone fire down it, and that there were many vestibules in the walls, apparently put there for further protection. Green estimated that he had traveled at least a mile and a half underground before returning. He also requested that he and his men—now called "The Tunnel Rats"—be given several doughnut rolls of communication wire, a telephone, gas grenades, gas masks, flashlights, pistols, and compasses.

When Green was asked whether he wanted to wait until morning before going underground again, he demurred, pointing out that it made no difference in the tunnel as to whether it was day or night on the surface. After a quick meal of rations, Green took his men back into the enemy's tunnel. But this time he could talk with the battalion, and his progress could be measured by the wire as it rolled out. Another group was stationed at the entrance to record Green's progress. Thus, while most of the rest of the men in the battalion slept, Green and his "tunnel rats" were engaged in the hazardous task of exploring the rat-infested tunnel complex.

At the mile and a half mark on the wire, Green called to say that he had spotted a light ahead. His next transmission was more urgent and he notified the anxious men on the surface that he and his group had engaged an unknown number of the enemy in the tunnel. Colonel Haldane told them to don their masks, throw their gas grenades, and return to the surface. This they did, but the firefight continued until Green and his men reached the tunnel's entrance where the soldiers gathered there could hear the dull thuds of the weapons as the men below fired at the enemy. A quick count of the "tunnel rats" caused some concern, for one of the number was reported missing. Green ducked back into the tunnel and found the missing soldier who had crawled past the exit in the dark; as the soldier made his way out of the tunnel, Green held off the Viet Cong soldiers while other members of his team re-entered the tunnel with sufficient explosive charges to block the passageway; the fuse was lit and they scampered to the top.

As the sun came up, Haldane instructed Captain Larsen to raise the trap door in the cave which his soldiers had located the previous evening. When this had been done and the men had climbed through, they saw only a large room, containing nothing more than a basket of grenades; but the soldier who removed the grenades reported that the basket covered a second trap door. This led downward to another large room which contained 148 service records of men who belonged to the

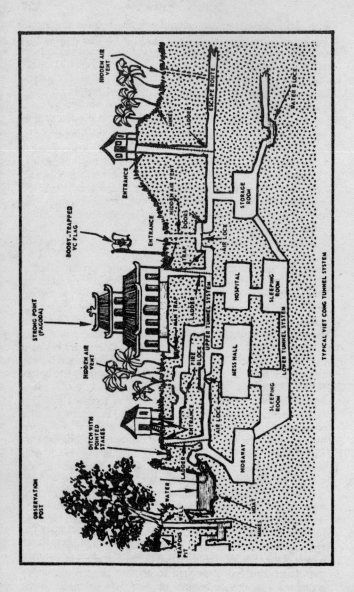

TYPICAL VIET CONG TUNNEL SYSTEM

D308 Viet Cong Company. Removing the records disclosed still another door, this one leading to a third underground level, and in which a tunnel shaft led away and then branched in two directions. The branch to the west had been rendered almost impassable, and had only a small escape hole just large enough for a small Vietnamese to squeeze through; but the other branch led to the same shaft that Sergeant Green had been in earlier. The hole in the ground discovered in the north portion of the battalion perimeter the previous day turned out to be an air hole for the tunnel.

By this time, the battalion realized that it had entered upon another dimension to the war in Vietnam, and more fully realized it when Company A found yet another tunnel complex the same day. One of its soldiers was killed by a Viet Cong soldier who shot from a small aperture in an ant hill. Several American soldiers rushed the ant hill and discovered an entrance at the rear, while an unattended weapon and a heavy blood trail told a grim story of the effectiveness of their fire. Another pack of "tunnel rats" was born as the soldiers traced the bright red blood through a three-layer tunnel complex that ended 60 feet below the level of the ground, and where a large weapons cache was uncovered as well as the camouflaged parachute from a US Air Force forward air controller who had been shot down in the area on an earlier operation.

But the wounded Viet Cong soldier made good his escape; his trail of blood led to still another opening which was too small for the American soldiers to get through. There was nothing to do but give up the chase.

The experience gained by the 1st US Infantry Division's "tunnel rats" clearly shows that an insurgent or defending force can be expected to burrow underground more and more as heavy bombardment increases. The enemy, therefore, must be cleared from below the ground as well as from the top of the ground before an area can be considered properly secured. Once cleared, the enemy's underground defensive systems must be destroyed, although an enemy can be denied the use of the positions through partial destruction and through the use of the riot control agent, CS. Essentially, though, the underground war can be won in the same manner as the war that goes on above ground: by training in, and the application of, new techniques, and by the use of initiative and sound tactical decisions.

skunk hunt

One of the most unusual but effective series of combat missions thus far conducted in Vietnam has been given the name "Skunk Hunt," a unique operational technique that combines the best features of the relatively slow but highly maneuverable armed reconnaissance helicopters of the US Army and the fast flying, destructive, heavy fighter bombers of the US Air Force.

In the spring of 1965, armed helicopters conducting daily reconnaissance missions over War Zone D received intense enemy automatic weapons fire from unseen enemy soldiers who manned positions beneath the protective jungle canopy. At the same time, the fighter bombers conducted numerous air strikes in the same area but on targets provided by forward air controllers, who in turn received most of their assigned targets through intelligence channels.

While the armed helicopters were adept at discovering enemy forces moving beneath the protective canopy, they could not muster sufficient firepower to destroy the targets. Suppress them, yes; destroy, no. On the other hand, the fighter bombers dumped most of their bombs on unseen targets with largely unknown results; since they could carry more ordnance than the helicopters their value would have been greater had they been able to take on a few of the targets spotted by the pilots of the armed helicopters.

Finally, an imaginative senior US advisor, Lieutenant Colonel John Hill—from the Phuoc Binh Thanh special zone—working with the helicopter pilots from the 197th US Armed Helicopter Company, conceived a plan to use the heavily armed fighter bombers to destroy targets developed by the helicopters.[3] His plan was simple but effective: a common frequency would be established on the UHF radios carried by both types of aircraft, and the fighter bombers would be assigned an orbit area and an altitude near the area in which the helicopters would be working. The helicopter element would consist of three ships: a light team of two armed reconnaissance helicopters, plus one aerial rocket helicopter that would fly above and to

[3]Combat experience related by MAJ Richard S. Jarrett, USA, to MAJ W. E. Panton, USA.

the rear of the reconnaissance fire team.

The plan was tested on an exceptional flying day; the skies were sunny and clear with a few scattered clouds. Visibility was good as Captain Eugene Fudge, the light fire team leader, and Chief Warrant Officer Chris Hunt, his wing man, employed nap-of-the-earth flying techniques to locate enemy targets. The skids on their aircraft barely cleared the tops of the trees while often, as they dashed across small clearings, the helicopters dropped from sight below the tops of the taller trees.

Above and to the rear, Major Richard S. Jarrett piloted the aerial rocket helicopter. With him rode Major George Bristol, a US Air Force liaison officer, who had direct radio contact with the flight leader of the fighter bombers orbiting off in the distance and above the clouds.

Then, suddenly, the day's serenity was ruptured by the sound of bullets skipping past the two ships of the reconnaissance fire team. A hidden enemy unit had disclosed itself, and the fight was on. Gone were the anticipations and tensions connected with the test; every effort could now be turned to maneuvering the fast flying helicopters into position to strike the enemy.

Captain Fudge in the lead helicopter called out the area from which the enemy fire had come, and Hunt, whose mission it was to protect the lead aircraft, responded immediately by firing a pair of rockets under Fudge's ship to suppress the enemy's fire. Then he raked the entire area with his six machineguns, all the while flying through hostile fire that grew steadily in volume.

Seconds later, Major Jarrett maneuvered his rocket ship into range and fired six pair of white phosphorous rockets into the enemy's automatic weapons emplacements. He knew that the billowing white smoke from the exploding rockets would provide an easily identifiable mark for the watchful eyes of the fighter bomber pilots when they came in to carry out their attack.

As soon as the armed helicopters were out of the danger area, the fighter bombers responded to Major Bristol's radio message and began their passes. On the first one, the stubby fighter bombers hurtled in over the positions marked by the still burning phosphorous, and their 750 pound bombs ripped the canopy from the jungle. One after another, bombs followed each other into the target area and the white smoke from the helicopter's rockets was instantly replaced by the thunder of the exploding bombs and a rising cloud of black smoke.

The fighter bombers disappeared above the clouds as they pulled out of their dives and climbed to gain altitude. Then down they came again—from a different direction—to deposit their canisters of liquid napalm onto the enemy positions through the holes blasted by their previous efforts. This time there were no thundering explosions, only the sounds of fierce fires spreading rapidly across the ground in a myriad of directions.

When the fighter bombers had finished, the armed reconnaissance ships made another low pass over the area, diving through the hole in the canopy and skimming over the ground. All was quiet—Skunk Hunt had been a success. For the time being, the problem of effectively neutralizing targets of opportunity discovered by armed helicopters in dense jungle terrain had been solved. The effective use of the support made available by the US Air Force had provided the key; no longer would the continuing reconnaissance of War Zone D be a dangerous and frustrating experience for the armed helicopters.

The initial Skunk Hunt mission required and fostered a high degree of cooperation and mutual respect between the US Army and US Air Force pilots that has continued in subsequent operations in Vietnam. To destroy an enemy force in jungle terrain by airpower required both the reconnaissance capability of the armed helicopter to find and fix the enemy and the destructive capabilities of the fighter bomber to destroy him. It recognized that in a war where there are no clearly defined battle lines, the need to respond immediately to a fleeting enemy target can be fulfilled only through cooperation and combined imagination.

cordon and search

The twin American strengths of firepower and mobility, sometimes lacking in South Vietnamese Army units, have been paired on occasion with the Vietnamese knowledge of the people to yield an effective force to destroy the enemy's guerrilla infrastructure throughout South Vietnam, a pairing that has developed search and cordon operations to an effective degree. The inherent problems of coordination and security have been overcome by US unit leaders who have had the desire and a favorable attitude to work with the South Vietnamese in joint operations.

In August 1966, two battalions of the 1st Brigade, 101st US Airborne Division deployed into the rich Tuy Hoa valley with the mission of securing the area during the coming rice harvest. Although the 95th NVA Regiment had been driven from this area during the first half of 1966 through the combined efforts of the 1st Brigade and of the South Korean Marine Brigade, the local Viet Cong infrastructure still maintained effective control over large numbers of the local population.[4]

The 1st Battalion, 327th US Infantry was assigned to secure the western valley area, and Lieutenant Colonel Walter E. Meinzen, the battalion's commander, thought he might accomplish his mission by dividing his battalion's sector into company operational areas, then conducting saturation patrolling and ambushing during all hours of the day and night.

Intelligence for a cordon and search operation was developed as Company A conducted routine daily patrolling of its sector. A platoon patrol, approaching the hamlet of Luong Phuoc, received small arms fire from the huts within the hamlet and rushed the hamlet only to find that Viet Cong soldiers who had been doing the shooting had withdrawn. Contact with the enemy soldiers was soon re-established, though, and for the next two hours four or five Viet Cong soldiers would fire sporadically at the platoon, then withdraw only to repeat the action a little later. The platoon's progress was slow, for the enemy soldiers also set out booby traps along their route of withdrawal; they knew the terrain intimately and knew how to make the best use of it; and they also knew that the Americans would not use artillery fire against them because of the rather densely populated area through which they moved.

For the men of the 1st Battalion, the problem loomed large—how could they kill or capture these local guerrillas who never really posed a serious threat but who were ever present and could effectively impose an almost total control over the people of the various hamlets in the valley?

Meinzen decided to try a joint US-South Vietnamese cordon and search operation at Luong Phuoc; his troops possessed more than adequate firepower and mobility, while the local Vietnamese forces were more effective in searching a hamlet and interrogating the people.

The plan worked out by Meinzen called for one of his rifle companies, minus two of its platoons, to operate with a platoon

[4]Combat experience submitted by CPT Dean H. Darling, USA.

of South Vietnamese Popular Force (PF) soldiers and attached National Police representatives, to seal off and search the hamlet for Viet Cong soldiers. Six UH-1D transport helicopters would be made available, as well as some armed helicopter support, while the tactics would be as simple as possible: the US force would leave its base during the night, move by foot into blocking positions around Luong Phuoc by 0500, and secure a landing zone on which the Popular Force platoon would land an hour later. When the PF platoon had landed, an American squad would join the platoon and the sweep would begin. The armed helicopters would initially support the landing, then would shift to screen a river north of the hamlet to prevent an enemy escape by boat. Meinzen's command and control helicopter would overfly the operation with the battalion's artillery liaison officer on board prepared to adjust the fire of two supporting artillery battalions.

But even before the battalion had deployed into its operational area, Meinzen had sent his S2, Captain Dean H. Darling, to make a courtesy call on the district chief, a South Vietnamese Army (ARVN) Captain. During the course of his call, Captain Darling opened the subjects of joint American-Vietnamese patrolling and the exchange of intelligence information. He came away from the meeting satisfied that the ground work for a good working relationship had been laid.

During the morning hours of the day before the operation was to begin, Darling again visited the district chief to talk over some of the various happenings which had taken place since their last meeting. The specific details of the operation were left somewhat vague for security purposes, and Darling asked that the Popular Force platoon and the National Policemen join the battalion that same evening to avoid a late start the following day. The district chief agreed, and at 1700 the PF platoon and two National Policemen moved to the 1st Battalion's command post where they were accorded a rousing welcome, given a hot meal, and assigned a sleeping area within the perimeter. Then, just before dark, the platoon was assembled and given a detailed briefing on the morrow's operation.

Most of the Vietnamese soldiers and one of the policemen were familiar with Luong Phuoc and were certain that a Viet Cong cell did in fact operate in the hamlet. The PF soldiers displayed great enthusiasm for the operation, asking numerous questions and in turn being questioned to make certain that each understood his part.

At ten minutes before six the following morning, the lift helicopters and the command and control helicopter landed on a lighted pickup site which had been marked by the battalion's communications officer, Captain Dave Tambling.

Meanwhile, Captain Jerry White, Company A's commander, had moved his unit just before midnight of the previous day across the rice paddies towards the hamlet. A short time later he had reported that his cordon forces were in their blocking positions and that the landing zone had been secured. *(Map 67)*

Precisely at 0600 white smoke was set off to mark the landing zone for the inbound helicopters, and seconds later the PF platoon was on the ground. The US squad which had been securing the LZ joined the South Vietnamese soldiers and the sweep into the hamlet began; above, the helicopter gunships turned their attention to the river which ran parallel to the north side of the village.

Within minutes after the sweep had started, enemy gunfire began coming from the edge of the hamlet. The contact was brief—two Viet Cong soldiers were killed almost immediately by return fire, while two others were dispatched as, fleeing from the hamlet, they ran into one of the blocking US platoons.

Search of the hamlet now began in earnest, and the men of the PF platoon were pictures of confidence as they moved through the bamboo thickets within the hamlet, poking and probing the stacks of rice straw, searching bunkers and houses, questioning the somewhat surprised civilians. Suspected members of the Viet Cong movement were collected and sent in groups under guard back to the landing zone where they underwent a more detailed interrogation from Sergeant First Class Charlie Hawk, the battalion's intelligence sergeant, and from two interrogation of prisoner of war (IPW) teams from the Brigade's military intelligence detachment assisted by the two National Policemen.

Those civilians who appeared definitely to be members of the Viet Cong movement were kept under close guard, and as a load was accumulated a request went out for a lift helicopter to carry the prisoners to a holding compound near the battalion's command post. Later, they would be moved by truck to the district headquarters and turned over to the district authorities.

By 1000 the search was completed as the PF platoon linked up with the platoons from Company A. All troops now returned to the landing zone for extraction. By this time, almost 40

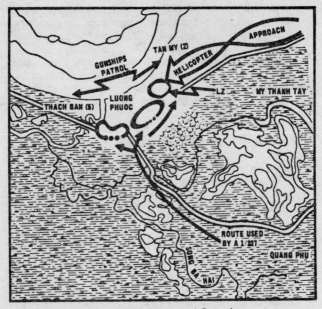

Map 67. Cordon and Search

suspects had been interrogated by Sergeant Hawk, and 14 had been flown back to the holding compound; of the latter group, six would later be identified by the National Police at district headquarters as confirmed Viet Cong members.

Many factors had contributed to the success of this cordon and search operation. Good intelligence had been developed by frequent patrolling through the area. Then, three ingredients had been added:

• A simple plan.

• Cooperation and professionalism on the part of all participating US units.

• The ability of the Americans and the Vietnamese to work together.

Because the necessary resources could be found within the battalion or from among units in direct support of the battalion, the plan could be coordinated and implemented with a minimum of lead time and with less danger of failure because of the sudden withdrawal of a necessary element. And because an effort to establish a good working relationship had been made earlier, a system had been developed whereby smooth and secure joint operations could be arranged on short notice.

anchors aweigh

Imagination and foresight have also been significant in the development of new tactics and techniques to overcome the problems posed by having to fight in the immense delta region of South Vietnam, particularly when the torrential rains come to flood the delta country and to make cross country movement difficult.

The monsoon, or seasonal wind, is ever present in South Vietnam. From November through April it blows from the northeast, carrying the moisture from the South China Sea and depositing that moisture in the mountains of the central and northern provinces. By the time the wind reaches the delta region it is virtually void of moisture, and there is little rain. From May through October, though, the wind reverses its direction and blows from the southwest. Heavily laden with moisture from the Gulf of Thailand, it deposits torrential rain throughout the delta in the form of successive squall lines, then travels on to the mountains clear and dry.

In the past, this condition has brought the movement of friendly forces in the delta almost to a halt. Large troop movements were limited to semi-amphibious operations that required the use of river assault group (RAG) boats, when they were available, or sampans when RAG boats could not be used. Helicopters did much to alleviate the problem, but there were never enough to support every operation.

The enemy took advantage of the monsoon wind to infiltrate supplies and replacements by sampan to their large provincial and mobile forces throughout the delta country. Often they employed large numbers of sampans, organized into sampan companies, to infiltrate supplies and to provide transportation to their maneuvering forces.

To prevent this infiltration, the 5th US Special Forces Group took on the mission of assisting and advising Republic of Vietnam (RVN) forces in establishing and maintaining fortified camps along the poorly defined border between South Vietnam and Cambodia; 12 man teams of highly trained specialists were stationed in these lonely and remote camps as advisors to the

South Vietnamese Special Forces (LLDB) and the Civilian Irregular Defense Groups (CIDG).[5]

From 1963 through 1965 various plans were developed and employed in an attempt to deny the enemy guerrillas their means of supply and maneuverability during the monsoon season. In 1963 and 1964, for example, several CIDG companies, led by the LLDB and advised by members of the US Special Forces, were equipped with 12-man sampans propelled by eleven and one-half horsepower swamp motors, the latter specifically designed to negotiate the inundated delta without entangling the propellers in the thick vegetation that lay not far beneath the surface of the water. While this system did reduce somewhat the effectiveness of the enemy's movements, it was deemed unsatisfactory because of the limited speed of the sampans and the slow reaction time of the forces that manned them.

In 1965, seven styrofoam plastic airboats, each equipped with a 60 horsepower engine, were procured for use in the delta on an experimental basis. They were distributed in groups of twos and threes to selected Special Forces camps; although their employment in this manner reduced their effectiveness against large numbers of enemy sampans, the experiment did show that the larger engines gave sufficient power to let the boats overtake and observe hostile sampans until other friendly forces could be brought into action.

Unfortunately, though, the airboats did not last through one complete flood season. One was destroyed by an enemy water mine, the remainder damaged by improper handling. It was also learned that while the boats would not sink even after being hit by numerous small arms rounds, the holes caused by the bullets were not easily repaired without special equipment.

Early in 1966, Lieutenant Colonel Frank J. Dallas, commanding Company D, 5th Special Forces Group, made a comprehensive study of the problems involved in forming a special airboat unit. With the experience gained during the previous year, he took great care to insure that the earlier mistakes were not repeated, and submitted a request for larger motors and fiberglass boats, the latter to be equipped with their own patching kits, safety devices, and machinegun mounts.

In late September, Dallas, at Can Tho, received the first shipment of 16 boats and immediately requested that permanent

[5]Combat experience submitted by CPT Nelson J. Garcia, USA, and adapted by CPT Arthur P. Littlewood, III, USA.

drivers and gunners be assigned and that those selected for assignment receive a minimum of six weeks training in driving, maintenance, and tactics before being used in an active operation. The drivers and gunners were recruited by the South Vietnamese Army from among members of the IV ARVN Corps' reaction force, which consisted mainly of Nungs. The latter were South Vietnamese of Chinese descent, and were welcomed by the US Special Forces members because of their combat experience, loyalty, and particular willingness to fight.

Dallas' new boats had 90 horsepower engines which gave them a cruising speed of 35 knots, a desirable feature but one which created a rather serious "prop wash" problem: if a boat stopped too quickly or stalled, the wake it had created would catch up with it and it would be either swamped or overturned. During the training period, too, the men learned that the middle of the boat would buckle at high speeds. Both of these problems were eventually overcome through modifications and intensive driver training programs.

By 7 November, the airboats were ready for employment, and the force was organized into two boat platoons, each consisting of one command and control boat and six gun boats; the command and control boat would act both as the communications center and as evacuation boat in the event of an emergency. Each of the gun boats carried five soldiers and a two-man crew.

The plan of employment was to use one platoon of the airboats as frontal and flank security for a company of CIDG troops who would be carried in twelve-man assault boats. When an enemy force had been contacted, the airboats would make the initial attack to soften up the resistance and to provide cover for the slower assault boats.

After all was in readiness, the platoons were airlifted by CH-47 helicopters to their operational areas—one to the camp at Cai Cai, the other to the B Detachment at Moc Hoa.

The first operation began early on the morning of 12 November when the entire force moved out of Moc Hoa along the Vam Co Tay river towards the Cambodian border. The river banks were discernible only by the tops of the trees that could be seen above the waterline; commanded by Sergeant First Class David Boyd, the lead boat preceded the column by about 500 meters.

After a two hour run up river, the force settled down to a systematic check of all high ground—small shrubbed mud flats which rose from six inches to one foot out of the water, and on which the vegetation averaged six feet in height and offered good concealment to enemy sampans.

About 0900, while reconnoitering by fire a patch of high ground, the lead boat received in return enemy automatic weapons fire. Because the piece of ground was fairly large, and since the enemy's fire soon became more intense, Sergeant Boyd estimated that he had made contact with a sizeable enemy force. As the CIDG assault boats stood off approximately 1,500 meters and out of effective small arms range, the airboats began attacking in waves, reminiscent of PT-boat attacks during World War II. *(Map 68)*

Circling in front of the enemy's positions, the airboats swung dangerously close to the enemy fire. On each pass, as the bow machine-gunner poured out his fire, the remainder of the crew fired their carbines and M79 grenade launchers. Three passes were made, and just as it appeared that the enemy force had been overwhelmed, the unexpected happened. The enemy gunners concentrated all of their remaining fire on the last boat as it made its turnaround and so intense and accurate was the fire that the boat's carburetor, manifold, propeller, and part of the steering mechanism were shot away causing it to stall in the water close to shore.

The flank boat, commanded by Specialist-4 Robert Mayo, immediately moved in to cover the disabled boat, and the command and control boat also moved in to tow the damaged craft out of range of the enemy's fire. Although several men were killed and wounded on Mayo's boat, the Nungs on board continued to pour out fire and the extraction went off as planned.

As soon as the dead and wounded could be transferred to one of the assault boats, the attack was resumed. This time, by changing patterns and maintaining high speed, each boat was covered at all times by the fires from another boat. Too, an air strike was called in to cover the assault boats as the latter moved in to attack. So devastating was this combined firepower that a group of ten enemy sampans tried to break from under the foliage and escape; they were quickly overtaken, however, and destroyed.

The assault boats reached the enemy positions without further trouble, disembarked the CIDG company, and the succeeding mopping up operation was conducted against only a few enemy who remained; by 1500, all firing had ceased. A

—IMPORTANT—
PROCESSING DEADLINE

he Accidental Death Plan, for which you are eligible to apply, is
eing made available to a large number of pre-qualified account
olders at this time. Automated processing procedures will be
mployed for efficiency, and to facilitate these procedures it is
equested that all application forms be postmarked prior to:

July 5, 1991

S. The quicker you send in your application the sooner you'll be
rotected!

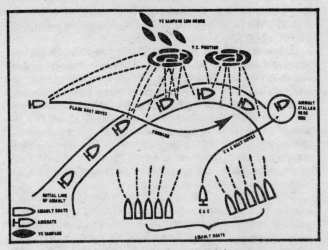

Map 68. Anchors Aweigh

new concept, and intensive training, had been brought to the delta, and the free world forces could now cope with the enemy's activity during the southern monsoon season. Additional operational flexibility had been achieved and the airboat proved a valuable addition to the available arsenal of weapons.

division base camp

At the time the 1st US Cavalry Division deployed to South Vietnam in late 1965, the balance of military power in the northern portion of the II ARVN Corps area was in doubt. Local and main force Viet Cong units and North Vietnamese Army (NVA) forces were believed capable of mounting major offensives of such size as to contest South Vietnamese control in Pleiku and Kontum provinces.

Pleiku was almost totally dependent upon aerial resupply to meet the requirements of the military forces in the area as well as those of the civilian population, and it was not unusual for the supply of aviation gas at Pleiku to drop to a two day level. Highway #19 running from the port of Qui Nhon to Pleiku was used by only scattered civilian traffic, and the operation of supply convoys over this route was rarely undertaken for fear of ambush, particularly at the Deo Mang and Mang Yang passes. *(Map 69)*

Brigadier General John M. Wright, an assistant division commander of the 1st US Cavalry Division, headed a small liaison group that preceded the division's advance party.[6] He had fought for and had gotten approval to establish a single division base camp at An Khe, because from that locality sustained airmobile operations could be conducted to dominate an area within a 60 to 70 kilometer radius. This coverage would also extend far enough to the east toward Qui Nhon to make certain that the division could be resupplied by a ground line of communication, and could dominate Mang Yang pass and Highway #19 west toward Pleiku.

With An Khe as a base, the division would also have the capability of launching airmobile assaults and reaction forces out to at least 150 kilometers by using either existing bases or forward bases secured by the division's ground elements. The area of influence would effectively cover the bulk of the northern part of II ARVN Corps.

Aside from all of these advantages, An Khe was considered highly suitable as a base for the airmobile unit because of the excellent flying conditions that prevailed in the area, as the mountains to the west and east of the Song Ba river valley served to moderate the effects of the seasonal monsoons.

The actual considerations for the selection of Camp Radcliff—as the division base camp was later to be named, in honor of Major Don G. Radcliff—were manyfold.[7] Clear approaches would be needed for a massive division heliport that could handle almost 450 helicopters, and for a tactical airstrip for the US Air Force C130 aircraft that would play a major role in resupplying the division.

Security, too, was involved. The camp had to be far enough from the civilian community not only to lessen security problems, but also to permit the placing of direct and indirect fires forward of the perimeter without creating an unnecessary hazard for the civilian population. While the commanding terrain in the area—such as the nearby Hon Cong mountain—would

---

[6]Combat experience submitted by LTC Ralph S. Dover, LTC Henri G. Mallet, and MAJ DeWayne P. Flanigan.

[7]MAJ Radcliff was the first member of the 1st US Cavalry Division to lose his life in Vietnam.

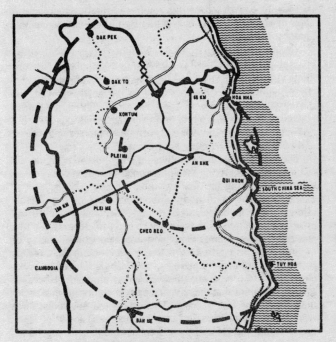

Map 69. Area of Interest

be encompassed within the base camp to deny its use to the enemy, consideration was also given to incorporating other obstacles and natural barriers in the area into the defense of the base. Since the enemy forces did not possess either a tactical air or a nuclear capability, dispersion as a passive defense measure was not a governing factor in the design of the camp.

It was finally decided that the most desirable base would be one that was heavily fortified and of the smallest practicable size, and one that made the greatest possible use of electronic and mechanical surveillance devices; such a base would require only a few of the division's infantry battalions for base defense and would permit the division commander to employ the bulk of his combat power in offensive operations. Operations forward of the base perimeter would make the most important contribution to the effective defense of the base, and all agreed that intensive harassing fires, combat patrols, and sweep and surveillance operations out to at least 82mm mortar range would be employed to the greatest possible degree. *(Map 70)*

When the division's advance party of 1,000 personnel arrived at the An Khe airstrip on 25 August 1965, the 1st Brigade, 101st US Airborne Division was already operating nearby with the mission of providing security to the newly arrived unit during the construction of the base camp. This arrangement permitted the advance party and even the main body, when it arrived, to concentrate their early efforts on preparing the camp and on receiving incoming equipment.

The specific site for the division's heliport, the laying out of unit areas, and fixing the approximate size of the camp were determined during the first two or three days. With the lead elements of the main body—including most of the organic aircraft—due to begin arriving on 13 September, an all out effort was required from the advance party to clear out the tree and brush cover from the heliport area and from as many of the unit areas as possible. Practically everyone in the advance party, from colonels to privates, was fully employed in brush clearing for the next six to seven days, although it became quickly apparent that the advance party's composition was not the best for the task at hand. There were too few tools; there were too many officers and senior noncommissioned officers; and not until the G4 and the G5 could complete arrangements for the hiring of a large number of civilian refugees to assist in the brush clearing effort was real progress made. Because the advance party could not complete all of the necessary clearing, and did not have the time to make a detailed examination of the ground in all of the unit areas, many boundary adjustments had to be made during the several weeks that followed the main body's arrival.

The latter group closed on 21 September, and the development of the base camp continued as a cooperative effort on the part of all of the troop units and the 8th Engineer Battalion, a nondivisional unit borrowed from the 18th US Engineer Brigade. The major and separate divisional units cleared their assigned sectors of the perimeter and constructed fighting positions; they also cleared unit areas and provided drainage; they constructed their semi-permanent facilities—mess halls, showers, command buildings—under the self-help program. The units were given technical assistance and material by the division's engineer battalion so that their construction efforts

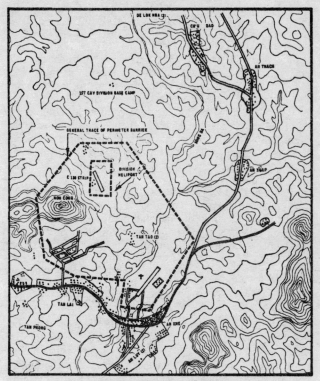

Map 70. The Base Camp

would meet at least the minimum standards that had been established.

At the same time, the division engineer battalion coordinated the base development plan and supervised the perimeter barrier clearing projects. The battalion also improved the division heliport, the service roads within unit areas, constructed a communications facility on Hon Cong mountain, and built the division's command facilities. Because there were recurring problems rising from the great variations in construction standards held by the various units, and by the failure of units to align their obstacle layers properly at unit coordination points, the engineer battalion took over the complete task of installing the perimeter barrier wire. Before it had been completed, this project resulted in the erection of five layers of wire, the laying of numerous mines, and the building of two cattle fences around the entire camp perimeter. *(Map 71)*

The first wire barrier, which was the most distant from the edge of the perimeter, was one of the cattle fences constructed to keep animals and friendly people from straying into the mines which guarded the succeeding layers of wire. The first layer of wire nearest the cattle fence consisted of a double apron barbed wire fence with a double wall of concertina three layers high. Behind this, a ring of claymore mines formed the second layer of defense, while the third layer was a double thickness of concertina wire three thicknesses in height, anchored by long steel pickets.

Between the two cattle fences, the fourth layer of defense was emplaced in depth. Two double apron fences were constructed with three rolls of concertina between the apron fences; then one roll of concertina was secured to the top of each of the double fences to form a truly formidable obstacle. The last barrier, the fifth layer, was separated from the defensive position by a cattle fence which was erected to keep soldiers out of the mine fields that protected the five barriers. The last barrier was a double apron fence guarded on both sides by three rolls of concertina wire.

Reinforced by elements of the 84th US Engineer Battalion, the 70th US Engineer Battalion constructed the access road which linked the base with Highway #19, an inner perimeter road, and several major drainage projects. These units also constructed the tactical C130 airstrip adjacent to the division's storage and maintenance areas and contributed to the unit self-help project by prefabricating rafter sections for mess halls and for troop and command prefabricating.

Civilian labor played a major role in the development of the base camp, although as a security measure the division's policy prohibited the employment of Vietnamese civilians for any purpose within the base camp proper. But the greatest possible use was made of the available civilian laborers for brush clearing operations on and forward of the perimeter barrier; before long the number of civilians employed averaged about 3,000 a day.

After combat operations began in October 1965, the troop units accomplished the needed work in their areas between active operations. The major units still provided one US su-

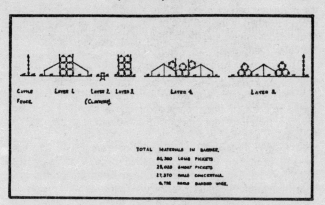

Map 71. Barrier Plan

pervisor for each 20 Vietnamese civilians so that the clearing of the perimeter barrier could continue at full speed, and the barrier and the fighting positions were progressively developed and improved with the single objective of reducing the number of infantry battalions needed for base defense to an absolute minimum.

The base defense mission was usually assigned to one of the division's three brigades, with the number of available infantry battalions depending on the missions that the division had to perform. During long operations, the brigades and battalions rotated between the base and forward areas. If the base defense brigade had two or more infantry battalions, it was also required to conduct operations within the tactical area of responsibility (TAOR) and highway security operations along Route #19. Counter-mortar radars and aircraft flying counter-mortar patrols during the hours of darkness contributed to the defense of the base.

The division's combat support and combat service support units were also required to participate in base security, and these units were levied for augmentation personnel to assist the infantry battalions on the barrier positions at night; they also provided provisional units for executing base security plans. Nondivisional units at An Khe were taken into the defense plans, and their incorporation resulted in more effective security with less effort than if those units had been located in separate compounds scattered throughout the area. At no time was there any evidence that the requirements for base defense participation resulted in any significant interference with the mission of the various division and nondivisional support units.

At first, each brigade charged with the base defense mission drew up its own plan for that purpose. But as the barrier and the fortifications grew stronger and more emphasis and reliance was placed on the augmentation personnel drawn from the support units, it became apparent that a standard plan was needed to reduce the amount of coordination as the brigade rotated in and out.

The division's first year of operation from the An Khe base was proof that the careful and detailed planning of Camp Radcliff had achieved the desired results. From the central base position, airmobile units from the division conducted operations with almost equal frequency in both the western and eastern limits of the II ARVN Corps zone. The success of those operations provided the boost in confidence needed to restore heavy use of Highway #19 for both military and civilian traffic during daylight hours.

In the absence of an enemy air threat, the value of a single, heavily fortified base of the smallest possible size was amply demonstrated. Significant reductions in the number of infantry battalions required for base defense were realized as the strength of the fortifications and the variety of surveillance devices were progressively developed. In more recent times, the base defense forces have usually consisted of one infantry battalion augmented by men drawn from the support units at the base camp.

From their experiences in building Camp Radcliff, the men of the 1st US Cavalry Division learned several valuable lessons. For example, the advance party suffered from a shortage of engineer troops and the necessary tools with which to operate a base camp in an undeveloped area. A report covering this period recommended that the entire division engineer battalion be included in a division advance party if the division again had to move into an area that had not been previously developed.

Other significant lessons learned were:
• Only when it can be properly supervised and supported can the unit self-help program produce good results. Infantry battalions, whose personnel have probably the greatest need for improved facilities, are at a marked disadvantage when compared to the other units, for their combat missions severely

limit the amount of time they can devote to base area development.

• Early development of a model segment of the barrier and fortifications plan is required to prevent the reworking of nonstandard and inadequate construction. Written descriptions and drawings do not suffice.

• The policy of excluding civilians from work within the base camp as a security measure was accepted as necessary by the vast majority of commanders. While this policy undoubtedly slowed the progress of the base camp development, enough suspicious incidents were observed or attributed to civilian personnel working on or beyond the perimeter barrier to point up the value of the policy.

• The concept of developing a small, heavily fortified base to reduce the number of maneuver units required for base defense is a valid one. A great reduction in the number of maneuver units required for base defense can also be attained if electronic, mechanical, and other surveillance devices are used to the fullest extent.

• The commanders and the men of the combat support and combat service support units—both divisional and nondivisional—must be indoctrinated and trained to make essential contributions to the defense of the base camp.

• While the brigade headquarters assigned the responsibility for the defense camp of the base proved capable of controlling a mixture of divisional and nondivisional units, later experience did indicate that the division itself should have published a uniform defense plan long before it actually did to reduce the coordination required when a new brigade assumed the defense mission and to establish a set of standard requirements that all of the participating units could meet with the least difficulty.

• In the final analysis, control of the defense of the base by a divisional tactical operation center (DTOC) proved to be the most efficient system.

The existence and continued improvement of semi-permanent base camps such as Camp Radcliff are vital to extend the effectiveness of the combat soldier; his health and his morale are enhanced because the existence of that camp gives him the mental satisfaction associated with the word "home."

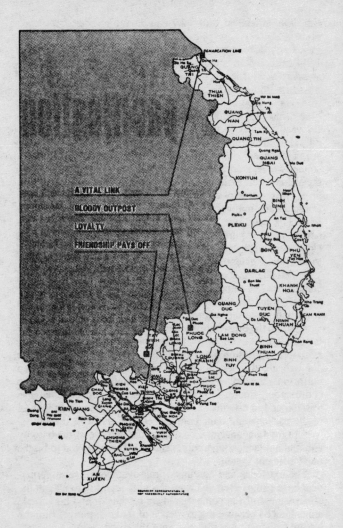

A VITAL LINK

BLOODY OUTPOST

LOYALTY

FRIENDSHIP PAYS OFF

X

Pacification

FROM THE BEGINNING, the conflict in Vietnam has been rife with acts of subterfuge and treachery. As in most wars of this kind, the insurgency in Vietnam has brought with it split loyalties, and it has not been uncommon for the enemy to capitalize upon misfortune in trying to win new subjects. His recruiting policies have often included an inducement to perform a traitorous act, one which tends to bind an individual to the enemy's cause. But those South Vietnamese who are loyal to their government and to their country have been more than willing to forsake personal gain and to risk possible enemy retaliation to support freedom's cause. Military commanders who have coupled this loyalty to their tactical plans have been able to achieve significant victories over their enemies, and have learned that people—not bullets—provide the answer to a final and lasting peace.

loyalty

Nguyen Dong commanded a seven-man Popular Force (PF) outpost at Phu Thuan hamlet near Vinh Long in the heart of the Mekong delta region. On 1 December 1964, the Viet Cong commander of the Chau Thanh district force—about 80 men—approached Dong, ostensibly to barter with the occupants of the outpost for a load of pineapples. It was agreed that future meetings would take place.[1]

---

[1]Combat experience submitted by LTC Donald L. Roberts, USA.

Dong immediately informed the province chief of the contact; the latter, with the agreement of Lieutenant Colonel Donald L. Roberts, the senior US advisor in the area, determined that the contacts between Dong and the Viet Cong commander should continue in an effort to deceive and entrap the Viet Cong unit. Particular care was taken to make certain that no one else was aware of the contacts.

Two weeks later the Viet Cong commander again approached Dong and proposed a plan for the surrender of the outpost during the night of 16–17 December; the choice of date reflected the enemy commander's knowledge that the outpost was due to receive a resupply of ammunition and other items on 16 December. Dong feigned acceptance of the plan, and even accepted some money with which to purchase beer for his men. As outpost commander, he said that he would take the guard duty himself on the evening of the 16th, allowing his men to go to bed to sleep off their drinking. Then, near midnight, he would open the outpost gate, collect his men's weapons, and let the Viet Cong unit into the outpost. After destroying the outpost, the enemy soldiers would withdraw. Dong was assured that he would receive more money for his efforts and would also be given an important position in the Viet Cong's provincial organization.

Again Dong relayed his information to the province chief, who told Dong to follow through with the plan proposed by the Viet Cong commander. But in closing, the province chief told Dong that he would be given additional orders on the 16th. Then, working with Colonel Roberts, the province chief came up with a counterplan to thwart the enemy's ambitions.

The resupply of Dong's outpost would take place as scheduled on 16 December, and Dong would be sent a radio message directing him to send all seven of his men to Ba Cang to pick up the supplies. This was a common policy, since the outpost was not too far from Ba Cang. When the men from the outpost reached Ba Cang, they would be taken to a supply room where they would exchange their clothes with seven of the best regional force (RF) soldiers in the province. These RF soldiers, disguised as the men from the outpost, would then board a sampan with the supplies and return to the outpost, presumably under the observation of the Viet Cong unit. Dong would then sham the drinking party and the men would pretend to go to sleep at about 2000, but ready to occupy their defensive positions as soon as Dong alerted them to the appearance of the Viet Cong troops.

Presumably, the Viet Cong commander would monitor the radio message which would be sent to Dong, so he would be well aware of the fact that the resupply mission was still scheduled.

As soon as he received the agreed on signal from the Viet Cong commander on the night of 16 December, Dong was to radio this information to the Ba Cang Special Zone commander in whose area his outpost was located; the latter would immediately transmit the message to the Vinh Long tactical operations center. Precautions would be taken by everyone to use a radio net other than the one normally used. The Ba Cang commander would also alert his outposts along Route #4 between Vinh Long and Ba Cang to clear the road for a convoy movement, for the military authorities at Vinh Long had agreed to provide the three-company 27th RF Battalion mounted on trucks to move to Ba Cang when the Viet Cong attacked.

Two armed helicopter platoons would also be available and would be on ground alert at the Vinh Long airfield; and a US Air Force AC-47 Puff aircraft would be on air alert in the vicinity waiting for a target.

Late in the afternoon of 16 December, all was in readiness; the planning had been completed, and everything depended now on Dong's call that he had been contacted by the Viet Cong leader.

Just after 2200, the Viet Cong commander, who had positioned his men around the outpost, signalled Dong that he was coming in; the latter immediately notified the Ba Cang commander, who as promptly relayed it to Vinh Long. The operations center received the message at 2227, and the aircraft and the 27th RF Battalion were told to execute their plans. The armed helicopters were over the target area at 2239 firing on suspected Viet Cong positions.

As soon as the helicopters opened fire, the Viet Cong commander, realizing that he had been tricked, ordered his men to attack the outpost. But the helicopters continued to fire near the edges of the outpost and kept the enemy soldiers from overrunning Dong and his few defenders.

The AC-47 aircraft also arrived over the outpost and began to provide illumination for the defenders and for the pilots of the armed helicopters. So crowded was the airspace over the small outpost, though, the AC-47's gatling guns could be used only around the periphery of the target area.

The RF battalion crossed its release point at 2300, and although the plan had called for a vigorous attack from this point, the battalion was hindered by the darkness of the night and the requirement that it cross a number of muddy rice paddies. It was not until midnight that any men from the battalion made contact with the enemy unit.

Eventually the battalion got through to Dong's outpost, but only after suffering a number of casualties which had slowed its progress even more. With the coming of daylight, the remaining Viet Cong soldiers withdrew, leaving behind several dead, and numerous blood trails and blood pools.

Nguyen Dong had proven his loyalty to the cause of freedom.

friendship pays off

Civic action, self-help projects, government aid and assistance, and maintaining good public relations with the individual citizens of South Vietnam are all facets of the pacification program, and can evoke the willing support that can provide the foundation for ultimate and lasting success.

The hamlet of An Thanh, located in the rice lands of Tay Ninh province, was one of the bright spots in the national pacification program.[2] The leaders of the hamlet were men of demonstrated integrity and had gained the confidence and trust of their people. A vigorous civic action program within the district had supplanted the power and influence of the enemy infrastructure. Various US programs had sponsored a number of self-help projects, and these together with South Vietnamese government construction programs flourished and were most evident in a new dispensary and maternity building, a youth center, and in an administration office.

The 3,000 members of this proud community were dependent upon a reinforced popular force (PF) platoon for their protection, the members of which believed firmly in their responsibilities and with high morale discharged their responsibilities in an efficient and willing fashion.

Though life was pleasant in An Thanh, the hamlet was not

[2]Combat experience submitted by MAJ John R. Vilas, USA.

without its problems. For a Viet Cong force, believed to consist of at least two platoons of soldiers, operated on a permanent basis within the district.

On the night of 16 January 1966, a Viet Cong unit built an earthen roadblock across National Highway #1 midway between the hamlet of An Thanh and An Thuan. It was about one meter in height, and was constructed in total darkness and almost complete silence; so silent were the enemy soldiers, in fact, that neither of the friendly security forces heard or saw anything of a suspicious nature.

At the same time, other enemy soldiers rearranged bundles of cut rice straw in the recently harvested fields to camouflage ambush positions north of the paved road, as well as other positions that had been fabricated behind the rough earthen berms that divided the fields.

Daybreak saw Company 2-C-320, a main force Viet Cong unit of about 100 men, well emplaced on a 300 meter front. A few of the company's elements were positioned to the south of the paved road, but were there primarily to create a diversion. The unit had passed through Loi Thuan—a Viet Cong controlled hamlet—the day before where it had been augmented with a number of local force Viet Cong troops. *(Map 72)*

Roadblocks were not infrequent occurrences on this portion of National Highway #1, and the usual procedure followed by a clearing party was to send a security force to screen both sides of a road to a distance of several hundred meters, primarily as protection against snipers but with special interest in trying to find wires which might lead to electrically detonated mines. When a perimeter had been formed at the roadblock, a heavy cargo truck equipped with a massive rice plow that resembled a huge rake would move into position to destroy the obstacle and remove the dirt from the road. To detonate any hand grenades that might have been packed into the dirt obstacle, the rake device would be pulled through the roadblock several times. In most cases, the enemy force which had established the roadblock would not interfere with its removal.

But on this Sunday, 17 January, the Viet Cong unit had no intention of permitting the South Vietnamese forces to peacefully remove the roadblock. Plans for an ambush later taken from the body of a Viet Cong officer sketched in great detail the actions which had been anticipated for that day.

The Viet Cong commander expected that a South Vietnamese popular force (PF) security detail would be clearing the

Map 72. Roadblock at An Thanh

area between An Thanh and An Thuan sometime that morning and would pass in front of the ambush position. When the roadblock was discovered, it was expected that the PF security force would establish a perimeter defense around the obstacle and would bring in workers and equipment to clear the road. At that time—as soon as the workers with the road clearing equipment had moved into the area—the diversionary force located on the south side of the road would open fire; this, the Viet Cong commander thought, would cause the South Vietnamese to take up positions along the north shoulder of the road, firing to the south. Then, as the popular force security platoon drew in from its perimeter to consolidate its fires, the main Viet Cong elements would attack from the north. The action should take no less than five minutes, the Viet Cong commander estimated, and his withdrawal could take place long before South Vietnamese artillery fires could be brought to bear on his unit, assuming that the popular force soldiers had been successful in getting a message through requesting supporting fires.

But the plan so carefully devised did not work out as the Viet Cong commander had anticipated; an observant farmer proved to be the difference.

A few minutes before 0700 a farmer from An Thanh was walking to his fields west of town, but as he neared the camouflaged Viet Cong positions he noted something different about the appearance of the fields. He also saw the roadblock. Rather than continuing on, the farmer turned and started back for the village, not knowing whether the enemy soldiers were aware that he had noted their positions.

The farmer reported directly to the ranking man available in An Thanh, describing what he had seen and suggesting the possible presence of an enemy force. A report was immediately sent off by radio to the district chief, Captain Ngo Thien Phuoc, who made a quick estimate of the situation and directed his military commanders in the area to locate, engage, and fix the Viet Cong unit until additional friendly forces arrived.

He divided the PF platoon stationed in An Thanh into two forces: one would move on each side of the road towards the west to locate and fix the enemy position. The popular force platoon from An Thuan would move along the north side of the highway towards the east, also to locate and fix the enemy position if it could. In addition, two other platoons of popular force soldiers—these from Go Dau Ha hamlet four kilometers

east of An Thanh—were loaded on the available transportation
for commitment in support of the other PF units when the Viet
Cong position had been located. Captain Phuoc also alerted
the commander of the 9th ARVN Infantry Regiment, and notified the fire control facilities of a supporting artillery platoon
that its help would soon be needed.

At about 0730 the popular force platoons from An Thanh
and An Thuan made contact with both flanks and the rear of
the main Viet Cong force, opened fire, and fixed the enemy's
position. *(Map 73)* This information was promptly radioed to
the command post at Go Dau Ha and the two platoons of popular
force soldiers at that place were immediately dispatched to join
the fight. The platoons halted as they neared the fighting area,
dismounted, and then proceeded on foot to augment the force
from An Thanh and to encircle the enemy positions on the
north. *(Map 74)*

Although his unit possessed a 60mm mortar and six automatic weapons, the Viet Cong commander grasped the swiftly
deteriorating situation and began a retreat to the northwest,
through the gap which was now being rapidly closed by one
of the popular force platoons from Go Dau Ha. Artillery fire
was already landing behind the gap, and the Viet Cong unit
had to move as fast as it could if it were not to suffer extensive
casualties.

The fighting ceased shortly after 0800, and with the arrival
of elements of the 9th ARVN Infantry Regiment pursuit of the
Viet Cong unit to the north continued until all contact was lost.

The overall operation had been characterized by good communications, rapid and accurate decisions by the commanders,
and aggressive actions by the popular force soldiers. The ambush had been well planned and could have succeeded if the
local security forces had followed the standard pattern for clearing a roadblock. But a rice farmer on his way to work his paddy
had noticed something amiss and had risked his life to alert the
authorities. His warning had been instrumental in the subsequent defeat of the Viet Cong ambush force.

The necessity for strong and willing popular support was
clearly demonstrated by this action, and the conditions in An
Thanh which had created an atmosphere that prompted an inhabitant to voluntarily divulge the location of a Viet Cong unit
had been the result of an energetic pacification program.

Map 73. Fixing the Enemy's Positions

Map 74. Encirclement

a vital link

Below the demilitarized zone (DMZ) in Vietnam, in the northwest corner of Quang Tri province, lies Huong Hoa district. National Route #9, which connects Dong Ha in South Vietnam with Savannakhet in Laos, bisects the district, the headquarters of which is only 15 kilometers from the Laotian border and which in late 1965 administered to 16,000 Montagnard tribesmen and 800 South Vietnamese civilians. Protection for the population of the district was provided by a South Vietnamese Army (ARVN) battalion at Lang Vie to the west and at the Khe Sanh Special Forces camp to the north. In December 1965 the strength of the latter location consisted of 300 CIDG soldiers, a 105mm howitzer platoon manned by ARVN artillerymen, and a platoon of Nungs, a detachment of South Vietnamese Special Forces soldiers, and Detachment A-101, US Special Forces.[3]

The missions of the troops at the Khe Sanh camp were to protect the local population, interdict enemy supply routes leading to the south, and provide intelligence information on enemy troop movements. Enemy troop crossings had been rare in this area, and most of the enemy movements that had been seen had consisted of supply movements. But this was the period of bad weather—from late November to early May—as the monsoon wind blew in from the coast, and enemy activity could be expected to increase. Aerial resupply of the camp was spotty, aerial reconnaissance almost non-existent, and a thick layer of fog covered the district for weeks at a time. The bad weather required that greater emphasis had to be placed on reconnaissance patrolling, a step up in agent-derived information, and an increased reliance on information given by the local inhabitants.

In November, cross-border reports began to show that North Vietnamese Army (NVA) units were no longer moving south but had halted and were stockpiling large quantities of supplies. These reports continued to come in through December, and all indications were that there was a buildup of rather considerable enemy strength taking place.

On the night of 17 December, a small border village pro-

[3] Combat experience submitted by CPT John D. Waghelstein, USA.

tected by popular force soldiers was overrun, and the weather cleared enough the following day to show that the enemy still occupied the village and had constructed antiaircraft positions in the nearby hills. Fighter aircraft from several US Air Force bases struck the area and reported a number of the antiaircraft emplacements destroyed, but the weather closed in again that night. Apparently the strike had caused some damage, for a Montagnard who had lived in the village said that he had seen many dead enemy soldiers and that the enemy units were moving toward the northeast.

Three nights later, agent reports confirmed the fact that two regiments of NVA soldiers had crossed the border, and a 65-man patrol was sent out from the camp at Khe Sanh to screen the western edge of the district; it was to follow a wide arc from south to north to try to locate the enemy units. By the night of 22 December the patrol was 10 kilometers northwest of the camp and reporting that while it had made no contact with the enemy units many fresh trails had been found that showed signs of heavy traffic. The patrol also reported that the fog had cut daytime visibility to less than 40 meters. *(Map 75)*

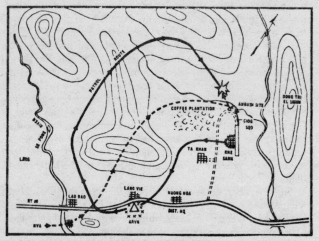

Map 75. A Vital Link

On the morning of the 23d, a local inhabitant came to the camp at Khe Sanh and said that an enemy propaganda team had conducted a meeting at the nearby coffee plantation. An eight man squad was immediately sent to scout the area. Not long after, a half dozen muffled shots were heard, and then the sound of running footsteps. The latter belonged to a Montagnard automatic rifleman from the squad that had been sent on the reconnaissance mission; he reported that enemy soldiers in gray uniforms were at the plantation and had captured the squad without a shot, but when they had grabbed his weapon, he had managed to squeeze off a burst and in the resulting confusion had made good his escape. He estimated that the enemy unit at the plantation was at least the size of a platoon.

All camp personnel were put on full alert, and word went to the reconnaissance patrol to scout the area between its position and the camp to fix the enemy and determine the latter's strength. One of the two remaining full strength companies at the camp was organized as a reaction force, artillery was alerted to be prepared to fire in support of the reconnaissance patrol, and the district headquarters and special forces headquarters at Da Nang notified of the happenings. A wind had come up, and the heavy fog seemed to be moving away.

Just before 1000, the patrol reported that it had found five dead Montagnard soldiers bound with communication wire, but had still not seen any enemy troops. It was told to return to camp as quickly but as cautiously as possible, for the possibility of a head-on encounter with an enemy unit was now great.

Within the next thirty minutes the patrol made contact with an enemy force, and as the solid wall of fog which had blanketed the area began to break, the column began to receive scattered small arms fire. A number of enemy soldiers were killed by the point element, and for the next two hours the patrol was almost continually engaged. The patrol leader kept his troops moving despite the growing volume of enemy fire, and as the weather continued to improve called for friendly artillery fire to hit just behind his rear elements. Every man in the patrol was constantly alert, firing at any suspicious movement in the ghostly atmosphere created by the fog banks; automatic weapons were continually shifted as they were needed to the flanks, to the front, and to the rear to take on targets that materialized suddenly out of the cloying fog.

North Vietnamese Army troops crouched in the patrol's path were overrun and done away with, their rifles and ammunition used as the patrol's ammunition slowly dwindled. It soon became obvious that the enemy force had been taken by surprise and was not reacting effectively to the actions of the South

Vietnamese patrol which had suddenly appeared in their midst.

Two airborne US Air Force forward air controllers, sent out from the province headquarters in Quang Tri, managed to make visual contact with the column and reported that the area to its front was covered with elephant grass that offered little concealment from the air and was full of gray uniformed troops gathered in small groups. One of the controllers began adjusting the artillery fire from Khe Sanh, while the other marked targets for fighter aircraft which had now arrived on station and were orbiting above the column.

As the fog began to move away more rapidly, the enemy fire lost some of its intensity and escape became the chief concern of the enemy soldiers. Then suddenly the skies cleared and the fighters dove to the attack. For the next several hours the attacks continued, and as enemy losses mounted and the enemy troops scattered even more, the reconnaissance patrol moved safely into Khe Sanh, its losses surprisingly light despite the heavy action in which it had just participated.

Prompt reaction to timely intelligence information had been essential to the success that had been won, and the willingness of several local inhabitants to report enemy activity had been directly proportional to the success of the local pacification program that had been in effect for several years. The paramilitary apparatus, by protecting the people and by its civic actions, had won the solid support of a people who otherwise might have developed strong ties with the enemy.

bloody outpost

Pacification—winning the hearts and minds of the people—in a country ravaged by civil strife can only be accomplished if effective control can be extended to the farthest reaches of the contested territory. In Vietnam, this has called for establishing outposts in remote areas to protect and gain the support of people and villages beset with split loyalties and intimidated by terrorist activities.

During the first half of 1965, the overall situation in Vietnam deteriorated rapidly as the insurgents became more active and began receiving more aid from outside the country. They had almost succeeded in cutting South Vietnam in half in the zone of the II ARVN Corps, and were preparing to open a large offensive thrust in the area occupied by the III ARVN Corps.

The South Vietnamese government realized that an immediate need existed to extend its pacification effort to counter the increasing influence of the insurgents in the outer reaches of the domestic domain. At the same time, US Special Forces detachments were being employed in sector advisory roles in the turbulent areas of the border provinces of the III and IV ARVN Corps areas to head off the spreading aggression.

In this atmosphere of deepening crisis, Detachment B-34, 5th US Special Forces Group, was transferred from Kontum in the II ARVN Corps area to Song Be, the capital of Phuoc Long province in the III ARVN Corps zone.[4] This province was astride one of the most critical enemy routes of communication to be found anywhere in South Vietnam, and it interdicted the shortest route between War Zone D and the Cambodian border.

The local force Viet Cong units had begun a campaign of terror in Phuoc Long by overrunning the district capital of Duc Phong in December 1964; simultaneously, they had destroyed many strategic hamlets and brought large sectors of the province under their immediate control.

The 22-man Special Forces detachment arrived in Song Be on 1 May 1965 and was placed under the command of the sector senior advisor with the mission of winning over the people. The small detachment was soon augmented with a five-man Ranger team and several helicopter mechanics, and was located in its own area near the compounds occupied by the 36th ARVN Ranger Battalion. While the Special Forces detachment worked to carve a compound from a commanding hill top, the ARVN Ranger Battalion patrolled the surrounding areas and provided necessary security. *(Map 76)*

The detachment soon began collecting information on large enemy troop movements into the province, movements that indicated enemy units were coming in from three directions; on 9 May, two enemy defectors stated quite firmly that the enemy troops planned to conduct a major attack on Song Be within the next 72 hours.

With what seemed to be confirmed intelligence, the entire troop strength at Song Be was placed on a 50 percent alert and work on the defensive positions went along at a faster pace. Patrolling and outpost activities by the Ranger battalion were also increased, and on the night of 10 May at least one half of

[4]Combat experience submitted by CPT John U. Nix, USA.

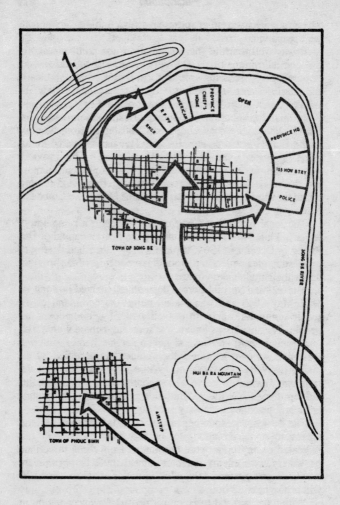

Map 76. Bloody Outpost

the battalion was on either ambush patrol or outpost duty outside the compound.

It was well that the Ranger battalion was so disposed, for early on the morning of 11 May, the enemy attacked behind a heavy barrage of mortar and recoilless rifle fire. The ambushes and outposts that had been set up did manage to slow the attackers and create some confusion among them, at the same time that they alerted the compound defenders to the oncoming attack. Although they succeeded in breaching the protective wire around the US compound, the attackers were finally repulsed with heavy casualties.

Heavy fighting raged throughout the night, particularly after an enemy suicide squad managed to get into the Special Forces compound and capture a mess hall which had been converted into a medical aid station. Weather conditions were on the enemy's side, for low cloud cover prevented the use of friendly air support until 0230. The first aircraft to arrive over the outpost were the armed helicopters, but because of the still limited visibility the defenders on the ground could not direct the helicopter fires on specific targets; although their activities were somewhat curtailed, the pilots of the helicopters placed their fire on the ridge lines around the city, an action which proved most helpful in suppressing the enemy's direct fire weapons.

Fighter aircraft arrived soon after, and concentrated their fires on the enemy's mortar positions. So effective were the fires laid down by both the helicopters and the fighters, in fact, the enemy's momentum seemed to break, and with this, the morale of the defenders took a corresponding leap. Now they had hope that they could last until dawn, for their previous experience led them to believe that the enemy would then withdraw.

With the coming of first light, the remaining enemy soldiers in the captured mess hall tried to fight their way out but were caught up by the few defenders who were still unwounded. The enemy troops outside the compound did retire but only into Song Be itself where they set up a defensive position in the market place, in the heart of the city, and around a large church. Air strikes could not now be employed, and though the Ranger battalion mounted a courageous assault against the enemy positions within the city, it was thrown back after sustaining heavy casualties.

But now airmobile reaction forces which had been held in

readiness throughout the night and during the bad weather period were unleashed to relieve the city: a fresh ARVN Ranger battalion was landed to the west, an ARVN infantry battalion came in from the south, and a CIDG company was committed from Loc Ninh. Aware that the enemy often attacked an isolated outpost to lure sizeable relief forces into ambushes, the three relieving forces approached Song Be cautiously, keeping close lookouts for ambushes along their routes.

This time, though, there were no ambushes, and Song Be was relieved when the three forces converged to drive the enemy out of the city.

Had the enemy units been successful at Song Be, the victory would have constituted a major victory for them. So strongly did the enemy commanders want a victory at Song Be that they committed two regiments of infantry and a heavy weapons battalion against the outpost. But because of a combination of good intelligence information, air power, airmobile relief forces, and determined defenders, the enemy was denied his sought after win, and had to withdraw after suffering almost 300 dead.

The road to pacification is not an easy one to travel, and the first step may always be a bloody outpost, as was Song Be. Yet the baptism of fire might also be the first step in winning the hearts and minds of people who have been filled with stories of the enemy's invincibility. If a seed of doubt can be planted in the minds of the intimidated inhabitants, then a giant stride has been made to insure eventual victory.

XI
Leadership

IN TODAY'S WAR in Vietnam, leadership is as important as it ever has been in our military history. It is important because the tactics being used place great responsibility on small units and on small unit leaders. When battle is joined, success or failure often depends on the actions of a junior officer, or of a noncommissioned officer; if they know their jobs and are willing and ready to accept their responsibilities without hesitation, if they use initiative and act with force and determination, they are leaders who will bring their units through to victory.

In combat, men demand more from their leaders; they demand, and have a right to expect, efficiency and leadership—a leadership that will produce willing, unhesitating obedience and loyalty, and a devotion that will cause them, when the time comes, to follow their leader through hell and back again.

Leadership is a composite of a number of qualities: knowledge, judgment, tact, endurance, initiative, bearing, courage, dependability, justice, and enthusiasm. If a leader possesses all of these qualities in sufficient degree, he will be a self-confident, well-balanced individual, and will inspire the confidence of others. More important than almost anything else, leadership is more than the mere exercise of authority—it is the sum of those qualities that inspire men to positive action in situations when the mere badge of authority will not suffice.

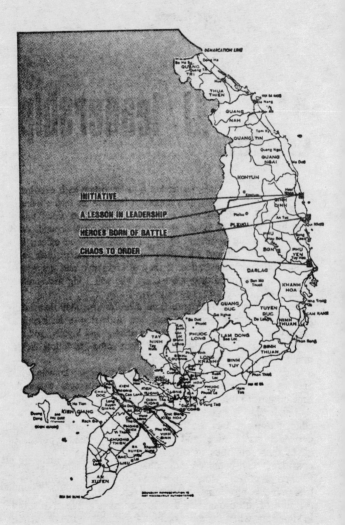

heroes born of battle

Success or failure in battle is often decided by an intangible ingredient that lies dormant in many men until the need is apparent. This intangible but essential ingredient—courage—produced tangible results in unexpected quarters during early October 1966 when the 1st Battalion, 12th US Cavalry, assisted by Companies A and C, 1st Battalion, 5th US Cavalry, met and defeated elements of the 7th and 8th Battalions of the 18th North Vietnamese Army Regiment in the village of Hoa Hoi in the fertile coastal region between the Phu Cat and Min Mieu mountains of central South Vietnam.[1]

Earlier, during Operation THAYER, the 1st Battalion, commanded by Lieutenant Colonel James Root, had met only light, scattered enemy resistance as it had swept toward Hoa Hoi. But now, in the opening phase of Operation IRVING, an enemy battalion had been reported in Hoa Hoi, and as Colonel Root deployed his companies to encircle the village, the feeling persisted that strong enemy resistance would be encountered. *(Map 77)*

Company B, commanded by Captain Frederick Mayer, was the first of Root's units to be air assaulted into the area, landing at 1005, 2 October on an open beach 300 meters east of the village. As Captain Mayer maneuvered his platoons to the southeast of Hoa Hoi, they came under intense enemy small arms and mortar fires, and two of the mortar rounds landed in the immediate vicinity of the company command post, wounding Mayer and four others. Although he bled profusely from fragment wounds in his face and forearm, Mayer continued to direct Company B's drive through a well prepared enemy bunker system that criss-crossed the entire area.

The 2d Platoon, proceeding across an open area, came under particularly heavy fire and was momentarily halted. At this crucial moment, Private First Class Roy Salazer, realizing his platoon's critical situation, stood up and with rifle blazing advanced on the enemy. Although he was mortally wounded during his charge, Salazer succeeded in setting the example for the other members of his squad, who breached the enemy's

---

[1]Combat experience contained in the request for the Presidential Unit Citation submitted by the 1st Battalion, 12th US Cavalry, 1st US Cavalry Division.

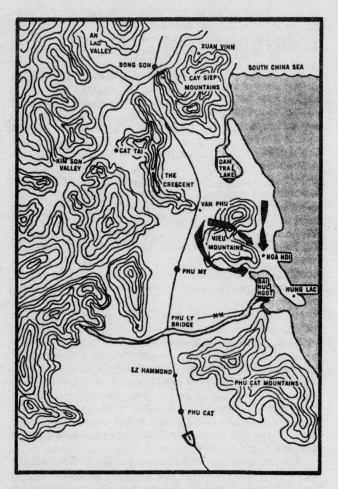

Map 77. Hoa Hoi and Vicinity

booby trapped perimeter and cleared the way for the other squads to break through the enemy's barrier. Within minutes the enemy force in this area was withdrawing into the village.

Private First Class Francis Royal set the example for the 3d Platoon when he carried a wounded comrade across an open field. He had almost reached safety when he, too, was mortally wounded. But despite his wounds, he managed to drag his comrade the last few feet to cover before losing consciousness.

As Company B fought its way into the village from the southeast, Company A landed to the southwest and attacked northeast toward Hoa Hoi. Lieutenant Donald Grigg maneuvered his 3d Platoon toward the village as he and his men came under automatic weapons fire from across an open field. At the same time, though, he noted several elderly men and women, with a few children, walk aimlessly into the line of fire. Grigg threw down his weapon, web gear, and helmet and raced 150 meters through the enemy's fire to the civilians. Picking up two of the small children, he carried them back to the safety of his lines, as the other civilians followed him.

Lieutenant William Prichard's 1st Platoon was the first unit to penetrate the enemy's defenses from the west. When his point squad came under heavy fire as it broke into a rice paddy bordered by enemy entrenchments, Platoon Sergeant John Sinkovitz and two volunteers crawled forward into the trenchworks and shot it out with the North Vietnamese soldiers, position by position. Although Sinkovitz was seriously wounded, he eliminated two machinegun bunkers and drew much of the enemy's fire away from the remainder of the platoon. Sergeant Donald Beltz, realizing that the enemy's fire had slackened, rallied his squad and in a fierce charge ruptured the enemy's lines. With his breakthrough, the platoon advanced toward the village on a three-pronged axis with the three squads on line.

In the meantime, Company C had been committed to the battle at 1250, landing north of the village and moving south under the leadership of Captain Darrell Houston. After clearing out an enemy ambush position along its route of advance, largely the work of Platoon Sergeant Robert Jackson and Private First Class Larry Willis, the company continued a slow but methodical advance on the village.

By this time, Companies A and B had effected a linkup and were beginning to establish positions to keep the enemy from slipping out of the village during the night. Enemy fire again laced Company B, and realizing his unit's exposed situation,

Specialist-4 Norman Jackson crawled forward through booby traps and the enemy fire to a position from which he could employ his machinegun against the enemy. With enemy fire kicking up the dirt around him, Jackson fired his machinegun from this position for more than an hour. When his machinegun jammed, Specialist-4 Richard Schmidt, another machinegunner, voluntarily scurried to Jackson's position and maintained fire on the enemy occupied huts until darkness blanked out his targets.

During the course of the evening, Companies A and C, 1st Battalion, 5th US Cavalry were airlifted into the area to assist in the containment mission, since it was expected that a full scale attack would not be launched against the village until daylight. The latter two companies went into position along the eastern side of the perimeter. *(Map 78)*

On numerous occasions during the night, desperate bands of North Vietnamese soldiers tried to shoot their way out of the encirclement, but every attempt was repulsed. One of the reasons for the successful night containment was the proficiency of the artillery forward observers who called in the fires of the supporting artillery unit—Battery A, 2d Battalion, 19th US Artillery. Captain John Sutton and Lieutenants Stephen Stant and Charles Campanella continually braved enemy fire to get to the best possible locations from which to direct the supporting fires, and during the night, called in almost 900 rounds of artillery fire on the enemy held village. On one occasion, when the battalion command post came under attack and two men nearby were wounded, Captain Sutton remained in his position and simultaneously adjusted artillery fire while directing flareships overhead to illuminate the battlefield.

During one of the enemy attacks, Private First Class James Pender was seriously wounded in a fire fight in Company C's sector, and an immediate helicopter medical evacuation mission was requested by radio. As the helicopter approached to land, though, the pilot could not pinpoint the exact landing zone, so Lieutenant John Rieke, the company's executive officer, grabbed a flashlight and a radio and dashed from his covered position to the LZ. When he began waving the flashlight, the enemy shifted their fires to the new target. But despite the enemy fire, Rieke stood fast and brought in two helicopters, the second with vitally needed ammunition. Rieke then supervised the medical evacuation and the unloading of the ammunition and saw the two helicopters off before he returned to his own area.

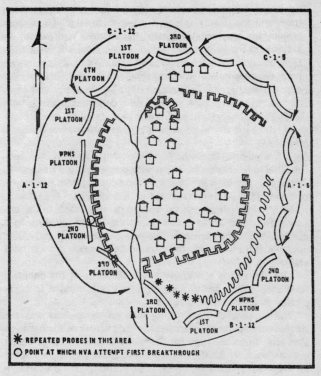

Map 78. Encirclement

Early in the morning, the enemy soldiers almost broke through Company A's sector of the thinly spread perimeter, but when Captain Harold Fields led a counterattack with his headquarters element to plug a gap that had opened in his lines, the enemy charge was stopped in its tracks and eventually thrown back.

When morning came, Company C, 1/12th US Cavalry and Company C, 1/5th US Cavalry attacked south to drive the remaining enemy into Companies A and B, 1/12th US Cavalry which were braced in strong blocking positions to take the attack. Several times Company C, 1/12th Cavalry temporarily slowed its advance because of enemy resistance, but each time the company rallied and by individual combat at almost point blank range drove on through the village.

Lieutenant John Rudd's 3d Platoon took the brunt of the enemy's resistance. Just after jumping off, the platoon was pinned down as it tried to cross a large, open rice paddy. As he lay in the dirt of the rice paddy, Rudd saw Private First Class David Osborne stand up and begin firing his machinegun at the bunkers to his front. Specialist-4 Daniel Shubert, the other machinegunner in the platoon, also stood up, and for a few seconds the two soldiers waged a deadly showdown with the dug-in enemy; then, after killing eleven of the enemy soldiers, they led the platoon in a charge through the enemy's bunkers.

A few minutes later, the platoon was again halted by enemy fire, this time coming from a trench concealed in a hedgerow. Try as they could, none of the soldiers could locate the enemy position. That is, they could not until Specialist-4 Gary Lusk, Rudd's radio operator, stood up, exposing himself to the enemy's fire, and began pointing out the enemy position to a machinegunner on his right. The pair worked well, and as the enemy's fire slackened, the platoon again made a successful charge.

The last action seemingly broke the back of the enemy's resistance effort, and Company C had little trouble in completing its part in the operation.

The courage of the fighting man on the ground was the single most important ingredient in the success of the battle of Hoa Hoi. From the moment Company B landed on the beach outside the well fortified village until Company C completed its final sweep, the men of the 1st Battalion, 12th US Cavalry displayed a gallant determination to win, no matter how grave the risks involved. The combination of quick reaction, sound planning, exemplary leadership, and aggressive teamwork fused the men of the battalion into a fighting unit that would not be stopped as they repeatedly charged through enemy fire to accomplish their mission.

initiative

Earlier in 1966, in February, the 2d Battalion, 5th US Cavalry was participating in Operation WHITE WING near Bong Son in Binh Dinh province. The terrain was rugged with craggy, jungle covered peaks towering to altitudes of 500 meters and more. Gullies and draws common to the area restricted and slowed the movement of the battalion, while the air was warm and moist without any benefit of the ocean breezes.[2]

It was in this environment on 17 February that Company A, commanded by Captain Tom Fincher, took up a mission of providing security for the battalion command post. As the battalion's reserve, the company was also responsible for conducting a local patrol to make certain that the enemy had not slipped into the area without being seen. Company B was 2,500 meters to the northwest on a search and destroy operation, while Company C was on a similar mission 4,200 meters to the north.

Leaving his 3d Platoon and his weapons platoon behind, Captain Fincher left the battalion base with his 1st and 2d Platoons on the local patrol. The day was quiet and peaceful for the first hour of the patrol. But then a jarring note changed the picture: Company B was calling in to report that it was receiving enemy fire from the surrounding hills. Fincher called in his two platoon leaders to tell them of what he had heard on the radio, and continued to patrol the area around the command post.

Fifteen minutes later Fincher monitored another call; this was of a more critical nature, for Company B's commander was now reporting that his artillery forward observer had been killed and his company was suffering numerous casualties. His company could not maneuver against the enemy, he said, because of the heavy volume of fire it was receiving.

Realizing that his unit might be committed to aid Company B, Captain Fincher decided to alert his 3d Platoon and his weapons platoon of what was happening, and told both of those units to be ready to move on a moment's notice to a rendezvous point 1,500 meters north of where they were then located. He also told his weapons platoon to orient its 81mm mortars toward Company B's position, ready to fire in support if needed. He then told the two platoons with him to swing north toward the same rendezvous point.

Fincher's estimate proved to be accurate, for within the next 20 minutes he received word from the battalion commander to go to Company B's assistance. Movement over the rocky terrain was difficult and it was an hour before all of the platoons of Company A could assemble at the point previously selected.

[2]Combat experience related by CPT Tom Fincher, USA, to 1LT Terry H. Reilly, USA.

But fortunately, the rendezvous point was only 1,000 meters
from Company B and more important, it was behind the enemy
force that had been giving Company B such a difficult time.
In effect, the enemy force was trapped. *(Map 79)*

Map 79. Initiative

Fincher deployed Company A with three platoons on line
at the bottom of the hill occupied by the enemy and then gave
the word for the assault. Preceded by the fires from their own
81mm mortars, the men of Company A drove up the hill firing
at any movement from their front. The company clearly had
the initiative, and its assault was so deadly that the enemy force
was totally defeated.

By anticipating the battalion commander's orders, Captain
Fincher had made the necessary preparations to assemble his

company at a rendezvous point within assault range of the enemy's positions and to be there at the right time to assist the hard pressed Company B. Initiative of the kind shown by Fincher is often the ingredient necessary to inspire fighting men in victory, for soldiers unite quickly behind a commander who meets unexpected situations with prompt actions, who sees what has to be done and anticipates a course of action even before orders are issued. In an environment that allows the enemy freedom of movement, the unexpected can be expected to be normal; the side that wins will be the one that can exercise the most flexibility, initiative, and daring.

a lesson in leadership

On occasion, the actions of just one man can influence the tide of battle, and nowhere was this more evident than during the course of Operation BONG SON I, which took place on the coastal plain of South Vietnam in Binh Dinh province in early 1965.[3]

The operational area involved lay north of the town of Bong Son and west of Highway #1, and from the sandy beaches on the South China Sea to the foothills of the central highlands, some 10 kilometers to the west, the terrain was almost completely flat. The only exception was caused by a series of low, flat hills that rose at random out of the rice paddies. Located at the bases of those hills were small mud and thatch hut villages, sheltered by dense concentrations of palm trees which curtailed aerial observation. Under almost continuous cultivation, the rice paddies were divided at intervals of about 100 meters by a series of mud dikes, and the entire area was laced by streams each three to five meters wide with steep banks.

Friendly forces consisted of the 1st, 2d, and 4th Battalions of the 40th ARVN Infantry Regiment, a 105mm and a 155mm howitzer battery, two regional force (RF) companies, and five popular force (PF) platoons. The regional and popular force units were based in Bong Son, while the 40th Regiment and the artillery batteries were stationed at Bong Son airfield, some two kilometers west of the town. Under the command of Lieutenant Colonel Long, the 40th Regiment had been placed in

[3]Combat experience submitted by CPT Richard S. Kent, USA.

operational control of all military forces near Bong Son with the mission of re-establishing control over those areas which had been lost to enemy units.

There was no exact information regarding the enemy's strength or dispositions although the North Vietnamese Army's Yellow Star Regiment was known to be the major enemy headquarters north of Bong Son. This unit's heavy weapons battalion had its 81mm mortars and 57mm recoilless rifles deployed throughout the operational zone, while civilians traveling into Bong Son reported hearing soldiers along Highway #1 speaking in a North Vietnamese dialect.

Colonel Long assigned his 2d Battalion, commanded by Captain Mai, the mission of seizing and searching a series of villages numbered 21, 22, and 23, with the operation to begin at daybreak on 7 January. Mai's troops seemed to be in good spirits and appeared to welcome the operation after the previous period of inactivity. *(Map 80)*

Early on 7 January the battalion moved from its assembly area, going quickly and silently through villages and farms. But the men soon noticed that the only civilians they could see were a few old men and women, or children who would glance furtively at them from doorways and then turn and dart back inside the huts. Barking dogs, who usually greeted the appearance of the soldiers, were also noticeably absent this morning.

As the battalion neared the rice paddies south of the village of De Duc, the terrain opened considerably and Mai adopted a V-formation because all signs pointed to his unit making contact with an enemy force before much more time passed. The 2d and 3d Companies moved through the village without incident, but the atmosphere was openly hostile, and anti-government and anti-United States signs seemed to be on every wall and tree; but the march was completed and the companies moved into assault positions on the north side of the village without contact.

Mai located his command post at the northern edge of the village in the only position where vegetation did not restrict observation of his first objective and the approach to that objective; it was, however, impossible to fire effectively from this position, so the companies took their machineguns with them. The battalion's 57mm recoilless rifle remained near the command post.

At 0915, the 2d and 3d Companies began moving across

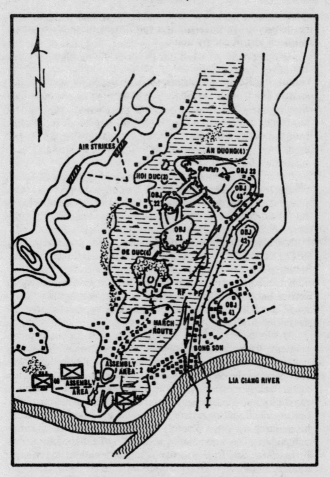

Map 80. Lesson in Leadership

the western half of the rice paddy, each with two platoons on
line and one in reserve. They had moved only about 25 meters
when a 60mm mortar round burst in the 2d Company's reserve
platoon position, seriously wounding one man. At the same
time, extremely heavy and effective enemy small arms fire
erupted from a trench line on the objective, and the assaulting

troops took what cover they could find behind the rice paddy dikes and began returning the fire. The artillery forward observer called back for supporting fires, and one of the first rounds evidently knocked out the enemy's mortar, for it was not heard from again.

But the two companies in the rice paddy remained pinned down, and though the platoon leaders tired to get their units moving their efforts were in vain: the enemy's fire was too heavy and too accurate, and nothing the platoons did seemed to make much difference. Air support was available, but Mai could not call it in because the enemy was located in a population center.

Seeing that the attack was faltering and in danger of failing completely, Mai decided to move his command post to a place where he could better influence the action. A small plot of farm land jutting into the rice paddy seemed adequate for this purpose, and a new command post was quickly established.

Mai also ordered the recoilless rifle section to move forward and to locate enemy positions at which they could fire directly, shooting right over the backs of the troops in the rice paddy. This fire had an immediate effect, as in rapid succession the section knocked out three enemy automatic weapons 600 meters away, each time to the accompaniment of cheers from the assaulting troops.

At this point, Captain Mai saw the need for his personal presence to motivate the two assault companies. His timing could not have been better. As another round from his recoilless rifle burst in the enemy's defenses, Mai stood up in full view of the enemy, seized a portable loudspeaker from an attached psychological warfare squad, and assumed personal control of the assault. Shouting orders through the loudspeaker and using his walking stick as a pointer, Mai began to move the faltering companies. The troops went forward by squads at first, then by platoons, and finally as two companies on line and running the last 300 meters. Overhead the forward air controller could see small groups of enemy soldiers withdrawing, and after receiving permission to attack them, brought in aircraft to complete the enemy's defeat.

Mai had played his hand well. Using the trump card of leadership principles—set the example—he had been able to change the tempo of the battle. His actions had served to weld the battalion into an aggressive fighting team that successfully assaulted and captured this and the other objectives.

In combat, there is no substitute for leadership by example. More often than not, the situation will demand the presence of the leader and will cause him to leave his place of control to move to the front to set the example when the attack falters or the defense is threatened. It is at that time, in the face of the same danger they face, the men will appreciate their leader more than ever and will often rise to superhuman levels to snatch victory from apparent defeat.

chaos to order

Soldiers, of course, must be trained to expect the unexpected. And when they are caught in a situation they do not expect to encounter, they must be able to overcome the initial shock and confusion so that they can effectively engage and defeat the enemy. Good leadership is the deciding factor in a situation of this sort, and plays a most important role in overcoming the first shocks of the surprise attack and turning the unit back into an effective fighting outfit that can overcome the best the enemy has to offer.

On the morning of 9 February 1966, Company A, 2d Battalion, 502d US Infantry, commanded by Captain Hendrik O. Lunde, but minus its 3d Platoon which had been left behind to establish a patrol base at the scene of an earlier battle, moved into a westerly direction to search several valleys 20 kilometers southwest of Tuy Hoa for elements of a reported enemy regiment. At the end of the first valley, the company turned to the south to check another smaller valley.[4]

It was then that the stillness of the jungle was shattered— a single shot from a sniper's rifle found its way into the stomach of a man in the point platoon. Immediately Lunde halted the company's movement and set men to preparing an extraction zone for a medical evacuation helicopter. Because the situation was so uncertain and the enemy apparently nearby, Lunde secured the work site with Lieutenant William Otto's 1st Platoon and the weapons platoon, which consisted of 20 men organized as a small rifle platoon, and sent the 2d Platoon, commanded by Lieutenant Karl Beach, toward the south in the

[4]Combat experience submitted by CPT Phillip W. Mock, USA.

direction from which the sniper's shot had come to try to locate the enemy force and to prevent the enemy unit from surprising the remainder of the company.

Within a short time, the sounds of firing could be heard from the direction in which Beach had taken his 2d Platoon, and soon Beach's voice could be heard on the radio telling Lunde that he had made contact with an estimated enemy squad dug in on the rocky slopes of a hill. Sensing a chance to corral an enemy unit, Lunde took the two platoons at the site and started for the sound of the guns, leaving the company's executive officer, Lieutenant Phillip W. Mock, at the site with an engineer squad, the wounded man and several medical aid men, and a 4.2-inch mortar forward observer team. As soon as the wounded man had been evacuated, Mock was to follow after Lunde.

The evacuation proceeded without difficulty, and Mock collected his heterogeneous group and started walking to the south, from whence the sounds of battle had increased. Then he heard Captain Lunde's voice on the radio calling for medical aid men; instead of an enemy squad, Lunde estimated the company had run into a well-entrenched enemy platoon.

Mock was trying to follow the company's tracks through alternate patches of murky swamp and dense jungle vegetation when he stumbled into the weapons platoon area. After a brief conference with the platoon leader, Mock decided to take that platoon along with his group and moved his men down the fork of a stream bed to a position about 200 meters behind the two engaged rifle platoons. Here he stopped the weapons platoon and the engineer squad while he moved forward with the aid men to find Lunde.

Confusion reigned on the battlefield, for although the two rifle platoons were roughly on line, the high grass made each platoon leader uncertain as to the location of the other platoon. Each was convinced he was receiving fire from the other platoon as well as from the enemy. Matters were further complicated when Captain Lunde was pinned down by machinegun fire and separated from his radio operator. It was virtually impossible to tell friend from foe in the heat of the battle.

Mock finally made radio contact with the two forward platoon leaders, Lieutenants Otto and Beach, and learned that they were preparing to attack the enemy. Eventually, the platoons were successful and gained the enemy's trenches, and as suddenly as it had begun, the action stopped. After some 15 minutes had passed and the enemy had not made a reappearance, Lunde decided that the battle was over and ordered the two platoons down off the hill to consolidate in a relatively clear area at its base; he also told Lieutenant Mock and the weapons platoon leader to join the rest of the company at that location to coordinate medical evacuation and resupply.

At the base of the hill, in a veritable jungle of radio antennae and completely exposed, the leaders of Company A gathered; after ten months of combat in Vietnam they had become accustomed to the enemy disappearing after losing a battle. They relaxed as they talked, and the men around them also relaxed.

Then, without a warning of any kind, enemy weapons again opened fire, this time from very short range. Company A was now engaged with at least one enemy company which had flanked the company's position and had caught it in a crossfire from three sides. The members of the command group reacted instinctively, and without realizing what the others were doing. Lunde, his radio operators, and the artillery forward observer team dashed toward the protective cover offered by a nearby stream bed, while Mock and the weapons platoon leader dropped to the ground and began crawling toward the position occupied by the weapons platoon. One of Mock's radio operators had been shot in the thigh, and Mock and the other operator dragged him with them. *(Map 81)*

But at the weapons platoon, conditions were even worse. The platoon was receiving heavy 60mm mortar fire and an unbelievable number of enemy hand grenades. Men were lying and kneeling huddled together, facing in every direction with stunned expressions on their faces. The weapons platoon leader was killed and numerous other men wounded before many minutes passed.

Finally Mock grabbed the first senior sergeant he could find and ordered him to lead the men of the platoon to the stream bed in an attempt to link up with Lunde's command group. Although they were reluctant to leave the relative security of their positions, the men followed after the sergeant, crawling and keeping as low to the ground as possible. It was 1830 and darkness was coming on, and Mock, still at the weapons platoon position with 15 men, three of whom were wounded, finally learned that the two rifle platoons were intact and were even then consolidating in a tight perimeter at the base of the hill.

Mock had not been able to raise Captain Lunde, but felt he had to keep things moving. He knew that there was an enemy

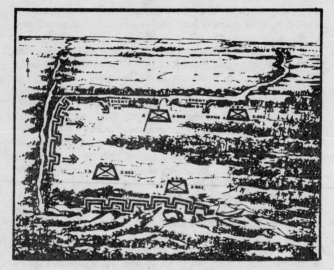

Map 81. Surprise Attack

force between his position and the command group, and he believed there was another group of enemy between his location and the two rifle platoons. He was tempted just to stay put for the rest of the night. But the wounded men needed help, and since he had no aid men in his group, he had to get help somewhere. He also felt that the company would be better off if as many of the men as possible could get together; it would be better to combine their firepower than to have it scattered all over the area.

And so he and his group began a slow movement to join with the two rifle platoons. Eventually, after a tedious and lengthy crawl, the forces joined arms, to be joined by the command group a short while later. The enemy, apparently as confused as Company A, failed to exploit his initial advantage and withdrew to the west with the coming of daylight.

This time Lunde and his men did not relax.